Computer Architectures

Computer Architectures is a collection of multidisciplinary historical works unearthing sites, concepts, and concerns that catalyzed the cross-contamination of computers and architecture in the mid-20th century.

Weaving together intellectual, social, cultural, and material histories, this book paints the landscape that brought computing into the imagination, production, and management of the built environment, whilst foregrounding the impact of architecture in shaping technological development. The book is organized into sections corresponding to the classic von Neumann diagram for computer architecture: program (control unit), storage (memory), input/output and computation (arithmetic/logic unit), each acting as a quasi-material category for parsing debates among architects, engineers, mathematicians, and technologists. Collectively, authors bring forth the striking homologies between a computer program and an architectural program, a wall and an interface, computer memory and storage architectures, structures of mathematics and structures of things. The collection initiates new histories of knowledge and technology production that turn an eye toward disciplinary fusions and their institutional and intellectual drives.

Constructing the common ground between design and computing, this collection addresses audiences working at the nexus of design, technology, and society, including historians and practitioners of design and architecture, science and technology scholars, and media studies scholars.

Theodora Vardouli is Assistant Professor at the Peter Guo-hua Fu School of Architecture, McGill University, Canada.

Olga Touloumi is Assistant Professor of Architectural History at Bard College, USA.

Routledge Research in Design, Technology and Society

Series Editors: Daniel Cardoso Llach (Carnegie Mellon University, USA) and Terry Knight (Massachusetts Institute of Technology, USA)

The Routledge Research in Design, Technology and Society series offers new critical perspectives and creative insights into the roles of technological systems and discourses in the design and production of our built environment. As computation, software, simulations, digital fabrication, robotics, "big data," artificial intelligence and machine learning configure new imaginaries of designing and making across fields, the series approaches these subjects critically from enriched socio-material, technical and historical perspectives — revealing how conceptions of creativity, materiality and labor have shifted and continue to shift in conjunction with technological change.

For a full list of titles, please visit: www.routledge.com/Routledge-Research-in-Design-Technology-and-Society/book-series/RRDTS

Computer Architectures
Constructing the Common Ground
Edited by Theodora Vardouli and Olga Touloumi

Computer Architectures
Constructing the Common Ground

Edited by Theodora Vardouli and
Olga Touloumi

LONDON AND NEW YORK

First published 2020
by Routledge
2 Park Square, Milton Park, Abingdon, Oxon OX14 4RN

and by Routledge
52 Vanderbilt Avenue, New York, NY 10017

Routledge is an imprint of the Taylor & Francis Group, an informa business

© 2020 selection and editorial matter, Theodora Vardouli and Olga Touloumi; individual chapters, the contributors

The right of Theodora Vardouli and Olga Touloumi to be identified as the authors of the editorial material, and of the authors for their individual chapters, has been asserted in accordance with sections 77 and 78 of the Copyright, Designs and Patents Act 1988.

All rights reserved. No part of this book may be reprinted or reproduced or utilised in any form or by any electronic, mechanical, or other means, now known or hereafter invented, including photocopying and recording, or in any information storage or retrieval system, without permission in writing from the publishers.

Trademark notice: Product or corporate names may be trademarks or registered trademarks, and are used only for identification and explanation without intent to infringe.

British Library Cataloguing-in-Publication Data
A catalogue record for this book is available from the British Library

Library of Congress Cataloging-in-Publication Data
Names: Vardouli, Theodora, editor. | Touloumi, Olga, editor.
Title: Computer architectures : constructing the common ground / edited by Theodora Vardouli and Olga Touloumi.
Description: Milton Park, Abingdon, Oxon : New York, NY : Routledge, 2020 |
Series: Routledge research in design, technology | Includes bibliographical references and index.
Identifiers: LCCN 2019024088 (print) | LCCN 2019024089 (ebook) | ISBN 9780815396529 (hardback) | ISBN 9780429264306 (ebook)
Subjects: LCSH: Architectural design–Data processing. | Computer-aided design. | Architecture–Philosophy–History–20th century.
Classification: LCC NA2728 .C664 2020 (print) | LCC NA2728 (ebook) | DDC 720.285–dc23
LC record available at https://lccn.loc.gov/2019024088
LC ebook record available at https://lccn.loc.gov/2019024089

ISBN: 978-0-815-39652-9 (hbk)
ISBN: 978-0-429-26430-6 (ebk)

Typeset in Sabon
by Swales & Willis, Exeter, Devon, UK

Every effort has been made to contact copyright-holders. Please advise the publisher of any errors or omissions, and these will be corrected in subsequent editions.

Printed in the United Kingdom by Henry Ling Limited

Cover Image by Carl Lostritto

One of Carl Lostritto's primary modes of practice involves the creation of drawings with vintage pen plotters. His expressed aim involves addressing contemporary architectural and computational questions by entangling technology and media that would, without aggressive intervention, resist synthesis. This particular drawing is aesthetically inspired by the procedural construction of a stone wall, but the algorithm that structures the drawing process is more a matter of brute force mediated by geometric sleight of hand and a willful instrumentalization of depth cues. More of Lostritto's drawings are at lostritto.com/drawing

Contents

List of figures	ix
List of contributors	xi
Series foreword	xiii
Preface and acknowledgments	xv

1 Introduction: toward a polyglot space	1
OLGA TOULOUMI AND THEODORA VARDOULI	

PART I
Program   **13**

2 Computing environmental design	15
PEDER ANKER	

3 The work of design and the design of work: Olivetti and the political economy of its early computers	35
ANNMARIE BRENNAN	

4 Bewildered, the form-maker stands alone: computer architecture and the quest for design rationality	58
THEODORA VARDOULI	

PART II
Input/output   **77**

5 Augmentation and interface: tracing a spectrum	79
MOLLY WRIGHT STEENSON	

6 The first failure of man-computer symbiosis: the hospital computer project, 1960–1968	94
DAVID THEODORE	

viii   *Contents*

7 The unclean human-machine interface   114
RACHEL PLOTNICK

PART III
Storage   133

8 Architectures of information: a comparison of Wiener's and
Shannon's theories of information   135
BERNARD DIONYSIUS GEOGHEGAN

9 Bureaucracy's playthings   160
SHANNON MATTERN

PART IV
Computation   171

10 Imagining architecture as a form of concrete poetry   173
MATTHEW ALLEN

11 The axiomatic aesthetic   194
ALMA STEINGART

Index   214

Figures

2.1	The problem unstructured	24
2.2	The problem structured	25
3.1	The Olivetti Elea 9003 mainframe computer was invented by an Olivetti team lead by engineer Mario Tchou. The system structure and interface were designed by Ettore Sottsass assisted by Andries Van Onck	36
3.2	The Elea 9003 mainframe computer is a system designed by Sottsass, of modules of standard metal cabinets connected by a series of overhead busways	40
3.3	The central control console with the photoelectric perforated band reading unit on the right	41
3.4	Ettore Sottsass, graphic design for a brochure of the Elea, Olivetti, ergonomic study, n.d. (1957–1960)	42
3.5	Elea 9003 central console	44
3.6	Olivetti Auctor 25A multiplex machine tool center by Rodolfo Bonetto, 1967	47
4.1	Image taken from the *Notes*, showing the "program" and the "realization" tree. The image opened Tuan's review	59
4.2	Sketch of a failure card by Christopher Alexander	67
4.3	A graph drawn in a disordered way transformed into a hierarchical tree	69
6.1	DEC PDP-1 computer at BB&N headquarters in Cambridge, Massachusetts	95
6.2	Cover of The Massachusetts General Hospital, Hospital Computer Project, Status Report, Memorandum Nine (1966c). The cover features a Teletype terminal superimposed on an image of the historic Massachusetts General Hospital ca. 1960. The 1821 Bulfinch pavilion is on the right, featuring its famous pediment and so-called ether dome, the site of early public experiments using ether as an anesthetic for surgery	99
6.3	Diagram of Time-Sharing computer system used at the Massachusetts General Hospital 1966–1968	101

x *Figures*

6.4	Nurses using a soundproofed Teletype machine at the Massachusetts General Hospital. Note the simultaneous use of flip charts	102
6.5	Diagram of the interpretive communication system	103
6.6	Outline of interaction between user programs and patient files	105
9.1	Vertical Files	161
9.2	Spindle, Pigeonhole and Bellows File	162
9.3	McBee Key-Sort	163
9.4	Variadex System	164
9.5	Speed Index	165
9.6	Card Signals	166
9.7	Rotary files	168
10.1	Cover of *Form 8*, 1968	176
10.2	"Three Graces" by Kenelm Cox, photograph by Graham Keen, 1967	180
10.3	Cover of *Form 10*, 1969	181
10.4	Paste-up of *Form*	183
10.5	Reflected Light Compositions of Ludwig Hirschfeld-Mack, reproduced in *Form 2*, 1966	185
10.6	Sketchpad III and Lockheed-Georgia Co. CAD systems in use, reproduced in *Form 1*, 1966	187
10.7	Cover of *Form 2*, 1966	188
11.1	Cover of *Structure in Art and Science*	196
11.2	a. Sketch by the freshman Topology Seminar at the University of Illinois, reproduced in George Francis' *Topological Picturebook* (1987); b. Whitney Umbrella from George Francis' *Topological Picturebook* (1987)	209

Contributors

Peder Anker is Associate Professor at the Gallatin School of Individualized Study, New York University, USA. His research interests lie in the history of science, ecology, environmentalism and design. He is the co-author of *Global Design: Elsewhere Envisioned* (Prestel, 2014) together with Louise Harpman and Mitchell Joachim. He is also the author of *From Bauhaus to Eco-House: A History of Ecological Design* (Louisiana State University Press, 2010), which explores the intersection of architecture and ecological science, and *Imperial Ecology: Environmental Order in the British Empire, 1895–1945* (Harvard University Press, 2001), which investigates how the promising new science of ecology flourished in the British Empire. He received his PhD in history of science from Harvard University, USA, in 1999.

AnnMarie Brennan is Senior Lecturer in Design Theory at Melbourne School of Design, The University of Melbourne, Australia. Her research focuses on history and theory of 20th and 21st-century design with interests in the political economy of design, machine culture and media. She has published in *AA Files*, *Journal of the Society of Architectural Historians*, *Journal of Design History*, and *Design & Culture*, among others.

Theodora Vardouli is Assistant Professor at the Peter Guo-hua Fu School of Architecture, McGill University, Canada. Her research examines histories and cultures of algorithmic techniques for describing, generating, and simulating architectural form and performance. Vardouli has contributed to *Leonardo*, *Design Studies*, *Nexus*, *Perspective*, and several edited collections. She is currently working on a book manuscript that situates the introduction of computers in architecture within postwar architectural and mathematical cultures of structural abstraction.

Molly Wright Steenson is the Senior Associate Dean for Research in the College of Fine Arts and the K&L Gates Associate Professor of Ethics & Computational Technologies at Carnegie Mellon University, USA. She is the author of *Architectural Intelligence: How Designers and Architects Created the Digital Landscape* (MIT Press, 2017).

xii *Contributors*

David Theodore is the Canada Research Chair in Architecture, Computation, and Health at the Peter Guo-Ha Fu School of Architecture and an Associate Member in the Department of Social Studies of Medicine, McGill University, Canada.

Rachel Plotnick is an Assistant Professor in The Media School at Indiana University Bloomington, USA. Her research and teaching focus on historical and STS approaches to information, communication and media technologies. Specifically, Plotnick's research agenda examines human-machine relations, particularly related to tactility, interfaces, and interfacing in everyday life.

Bernard Dionysius Geoghegan is a Senior Lecturer in the History and Theory of Digital Media in the Department of Digital Humanities at King's College London, UK. His research examines cultural and technological change intertwined in fields including the human sciences and visual culture.

Shannon Mattern is Professor of Anthropology at The New School for Social Research, New York, USA. Her writing and teaching focus on media architectures and infrastructures and spatial epistemologies. She has written books about libraries, maps, and the history of urban intelligence, and she writes a column for *Places Journal*. You can find her at wordsinspace.net

Matthew Allen is a Lecturer at the John H. Daniels Faculty of Architecture, Landscape, and Design, University of Toronto, Canada. He holds a PhD in the History and Theory of Architecture from Harvard University. His dissertation describes how concepts and techniques from abstract art and concrete poetry made their way into architecture through computer programming in the 1960s.

Alma Steingart is a Lecturer in the Department of the History of Science at Harvard University, USA. Her research focuses on 20th-century mathematical thought. Steingart is currently completing her first manuscript, *Pure Abstraction: Mathematical Thought and High Modernism*, which tracks the proliferation of midcentury mathematical thought dedicated to abstract and axiomatic ways of reasoning.

Olga Touloumi is Assistant Professor of Architectural History at Bard College, New York, USA. She was guest co-editor for *Sound Modernities: Architecture, Media, and Design*, a special issue of *The Journal of Architecture*. Her writing has appeared in numerous journals and edited volumes, among them the *Journal of the Society of Architectural Historians, Buildings & Landscapes, Harvard Design Magazine* and *Thresholds*, among others. She is co-founder of the Feminist Art and Architectural Collaborative (FAAC).

Series Foreword

Enabled by increasingly multilayered systems comprising software, simulations, algorithms, and other sociotechnical infrastructures, design practices today resist analysis through conventional disciplinary and methodological lenses. Their study — which is essential to address the new formations (of labor, of cities, of artifacts) unfolding in conjunction with technological change — demands new scholarly sensibilities: towards emerging technical conditions and capacities, and towards new sites of historical and sociotechnical inquiry. The *Design, Technology and Society* series nurtures these sensibilities by bringing together innovative scholarship drawing from fields including architecture, design, media, human-computer interaction, software studies, and science and technology studies (STS). Deliberately embracing the conceptual diversity of the word "design," the series outlines the boundaries of a new multidisciplinary field of inquiry focusing on the technological imagination and production of human-made environments.

If scholars have recently called for a radical re-imagining of design as a *political technology* for re-communalizing life,[i] the series' admittedly more modest aim is to make visible the *technological politics* of design, so often hidden by boosterism or mystification. As software, simulations, digital fabrication, robotics, big data, artificial intelligence, and machine learning configure new imaginaries of designing and making across fields, the series creates a space for works that approach these subjects critically from enriched sociotechnical, material, and historical perspectives. With these expanded accounts, it aims to reveal the seams, the uneven distributions, and the messy encounters that dominant narratives of technological prowess tend to obscure. Further, by offering works that situate design in relation to particular sociotechnical histories and substrates, the series seeks to lend specificity to and help chart design's heterogeneous territories.

Works in the series include historical studies examining the roles of university laboratories, government sponsored research, public policies, or technology companies in shaping ideas, systems and practices of design; accounts of specific computational design artifacts, formal languages, algorithms, or software systems which examine their material and cultural

xiv *Series Foreword*

histories, and their role in enabling new design practices and discourses; ethnographic studies exploring how technological ideas or methods have shaped conceptual or practical aspects of design; research projects examining the agencies — both human and non-human — involved in the design, operation of, and interaction with computational design systems; accounts of non-traditional or overlooked design-technological subjects; and studies reporting on speculative or critical technologies addressing questions about the design process, envisioning alternative modes of design participation or engagement with traditions, materials, and the body, or probing innovative theories and practices of design.

Daniel Cardoso Llach and Terry Knight

Editors, *Routledge Research in Design, Technology, and Society* Series

Note

i Escobar, Arturo. "Autonomous Design and the Emergent Transnational Critical Design Studies Field." *Strategic Design Research Journal* 2, no. 11 (August 2018): 139–46.

Preface and Acknowledgments

This book started with one conference and closed with another. In November 2013, fourteen scholars in architectural history, science and technology studies (STS), media studies, and the history of science assembled at the MIT Media Lab top floor for a three day excavation of human-machine systems in design and architecture post-1945. Punctuating their presentations were live interviews with key figures in research efforts to develop such systems. *Futures Past: Design and the Machine*, as we titled the conference, was the outcome of year-long conversations among the two of us and our co-organizer Duks Koschitz. One of our motivations behind that conference was the need to come to terms with the multivalent nature of "the digital" and to challenge the silos that we saw morphing around computational design and digital architecture, both of which seemed to gradually acquire their own histories, set of actors and debates, in relative isolation from one another. Aiming for a productively destabilizing confrontation, we structured the panels as encounters between first-hand accounts and historical scholarship on early touchpoints between architecture and computation.

On the one hand we had key figures who facilitated the introduction of computers and computation in architectural research and practice. On the other hand, we had scholars of architectural history, STS and media studies juxtaposing these first-hand narratives with historical framing of socio-technical networks contemporaneously at work. There was an awareness that somehow these histories were important in unpacking architectural practices around computers, but there was no desire to directly provide one singular genealogy. During the six years that have passed since *Futures Past*, "method" (as historiographic attitude and tactic) has been a sustained topic of debate and conversation between us, especially in developing this book project. Our conversations crystallized with a presentation at the symposium *Other Histories of the Digital* at the Harvard Graduate School of Design in April 2018, where we articulated a methodological intervention and called for a move toward a polyglot space.

xvi *Preface and Acknowledgments*

Projects like ours are social animals that only grow in the presence of others. This book would have never happened if Duks Koschitz had not brought us all together to organize *Futures Past.* Our profuse thanks should go to Terry Knight and George Stiny, who indulged our conference proposal and offered us critical feedback throughout. We also thank Nicholas Negroponte for helping make this ambitious undertaking possible.

For their invaluable first-hand personal accounts, we would like to thank the MIT Architecture Machine Group — Nicholas Negroponte, Steven Gregory, Christopher Herot, Andrew Lippman, Masanori Nagashima, Paul Pangaro, and Guy Weinzapfel — the late Lionel March, Charles (Chuck) Eastman, Alan Kay, Edward Hoskins, Paul Richens, and John Gero. Their stories and retrospections shed new light on the main debates of the first postwar decades, allowing us to peek into the motivations and aspirations that shaped their research and practice.

The historical accounts by scholars were organized in four sessions: *Designing Futures, Systems Thinking, Modeling Information,* and *Mediating Interfaces.* For the vibrant terrain of interpretations, we are grateful to John Blakinger, Larry Busbea, Moa Carlsson, Carlotta Daro, Britt Eversole, Jacob Gaboury, Nikos Katsikis, David Mindell, Gabrielle Schaad, Molly Wright Steenson, Ksenia Tatarchenko, David Theodore, and Alise Upitis.

For expertly chairing and productively framing our panels, we thank the late Edith Ackermann, Arindam Dutta, Peter Galison, John Harwood, Axel Kilian, Daniel Cardoso Llach, Jennifer Light, Yanni Loukissas, João Magalhães Rocha, and Felicity Scott. Our dialogue and conversations with these scholars informed our thinking, and helped us clarify the structure of our edited volume. Interpretations and translations of their input are entirely our own.

A special thank you goes to Masanori Nagashima, whose financial support allowed us to bring together such a unique constellation of actors in Cambridge, MA. We are thankful for his sponsorship that allowed us to issue this book in paperback.

This book project grew and transformed through the years. We are grateful to the authors who adapted conference papers from *Futures Past* for this book and to those who contributed new work. Our editor Grace Harrison, with her patience and diligence, guided us wisely throughout the publication process. We would like to acknowledge George-Étienne Adam for his hard work with organizing the manuscript material.

In closing we are also thankful to Matthew Allen, Phillip Denny, and Christina Shivers, whose provocation to think about "other histories" of the digital from a media perspective arrived at a crucial moment and offered us the opportunity to reflect on our editorial collaboration. Antoine Picon, John May, Andrew Holder, Michael Osman, Sean Keller, Daniel Cardoso Llach, and Andrew Witt indulged our reflections, engaging us in

Preface and Acknowledgments xvii

a conversation over the status of scholarship in architecture, as well as practice(s), while challenging us to envision the future we want to see materialize with this protean, polyphonic field of scholarship on architecture and computing that we put forward.

Our most important interlocutors during this intellectual journey have been Terry Knight and Daniel Cardoso Llach. Our project would be nowhere close to where it is without their continuous support and critical input. Thank you both for making sure our project comes to fruition.

1 Introduction
Toward a polyglot space

Olga Touloumi and Theodora Vardouli

In the decades following the end of World War II, the fields of architecture and computing became conceptually and operationally entangled. Emerging computational concepts and practices inflected design discourse, while design methods and spatial concepts influenced theories and practices of computing. Making sense of this intimate intertwining requires a move away from narratives of unidirectional transfer between computing and architecture, and towards a systematic interrogation of their intellectual and institutional common ground.

The computer's transformative effects upon architecture have often been addressed in recent scholarship. Perspectives on digital cultures or turns in architecture (Picon 2010; Carpo 2017) or lineages of "the digital" (Lynn 2014; Goodhouse 2017) have proliferated in the last decade and a half. These histories, however, have focused mainly upon the production of radically innovative architectural forms, the new digital instruments used to produce them, or the ways in which these instruments changed architectural production. In recent years, scholars have begun to unearth architects' roles as co-producers of the "digital landscape" (Steenson 2017). In such histories, academic, industrial, and military research centers have formed a productive site of scrutiny because they enabled and promoted encounters between architecture, the mathematical sciences, engineering, and computers (Light 2005; Dutta 2013; Cardoso Llach 2015; Keller 2018). Architects were not passive adopters of computational techniques and computer technologies. Instead, they actively engaged in their construction—a construction that unfolded against a backdrop of large discipline-wide debates and within the constraints of specific epistemic and technical contexts.

It is also not possible to think about computers and computation without design and architecture: computing technologies acquired bodies through design choices (Harwood 2011) and presence in the world within specific architectural sites. They also transformed the production of architecture, creating new working protocols and alliances between building industries and designers, and between designers and "users." This is too vast a history to capture in a single account or through a single lens. As

2 Olga Touloumi and Theodora Vardouli

a prelude to, and reflection on, the essays hosted in this volume, we use the first part of this introduction to advance a methodological intervention that reimagines scholarship on computers and architecture in terms of a "polyglot space," a space where a multitude of methods coexist and co-produce. In the essays of *Computer Architectures*, this polyglot space is calibrated against four conditions: the medium, field, obsolescence, and conversation. We call for a historiographic modality that speaks many languages (is multilingual); can only exist as a multitude of voices (is polyphonic), shifts scales of examination (is scalar), and changes form (is protean).

Medium

In a 1984 article in *Scientific American* titled "Computer Software," Alan Kay, the computer scientist often attributed with the invention of object-oriented programming, cast computers as meta-media:

> The protean nature of the computer is such that it can act like a machine or like a language to be shaped and exploited. It is a medium that can dynamically simulate the details of any other medium, including media that cannot exist physically. It is not a tool, although it can act like many tools. It is the first metamedium.
>
> (Kay 1984: 59)

As scholars such as Matthew Fuller and Andrew Goffey (2017) or Casey Alt (2011) have shown among others, this media rhetoric cannot be severed from the particular technical development of object oriented programming, namely the shift from writing programs as procedures, sequences of step-by-step instructions, to building ontologies of abstract entities that exchange data. Built upon Ivan Sutherland's landmark work on SKETCHPAD and systematized in SMALLTALK (developed by Alan Kay, Adele Goldberg, and Dan Ingalls), object orientation transformed programming by centering the design of a program on relations of objects and not on processes. Object orientation made it possible to conceive of, and promote through articles such as "Computer Software," the computer as a medium. The computer, the executor of programs, would turn from a tool for performing a rote process to something that could have an internal life and an architecture: an instrument for creating new and possibly unprecedented ontologies. Speaking about computers in terms of "media" is a historical construct (Manovich 2001; Murray 2003, 2011; Chun 2004; Hagen 2005) that could be approached both analytically and critically. The question we ask here is not whether computers are or are not "media," but what can we learn about "digital architecture" once we consider it from a "media" perspective.

A "medium" is not a stable category with definite characteristics and predilections. A medium can be a tool, but it also can be useless. It can be

Introduction 3

an object, but also an infrastructure. What a media approach does to the study of digital architecture is to provoke a change of focus: it shifts attention from the interpretation of buildings or artifacts made using digital instruments to the study of the technics, instruments, and processes that mediated their making. Or to recall literary theorist Hans Ulrich Gumbrecht, a media focus shifts attention away from "hegemonies of meaning" and interpretation to the "materialities of communication," the channels, infrastructures and protocols that participate in the construction of meanings (Gumbrecht and Pfeiffer, 1994). Paradoxically, although a media focus on digital architecture foregrounds materialities of computing, it can also push the computer itself off-center. In fact, expanding "the digital" "before" and "beyond" computers is the premise animating much of current literature (Goodhouse 2017; Bottazzi 2018). In accounts such as these, "the digital" is a larger category that orbits around technological applications but is seldom about them. In such accounts, the computer, the machine performing computations, often becomes the elephant in the room.

Questions about how the elephant entered the room, where it sat, how big it was, and what color it had, have proved generative for historians such as John Harwood (2011) and, in this book, AnnMarie Brennan, Rachel Plotnick, and David Theodore, who talk about the presence of these massive (or not so massive) instruments in old and new architectural types (factories, clean rooms, offices, houses, hospitals). Seeing the elephant becomes more challenging when talking about the computer as a design medium—a medium for performing the complex web of acts that count as *doing* architecture. Where, when, and how then is the computer: is it the algorithms? Their implications for practice and labor? Their outputs? The cultural, political, economic, discursive effects of these outputs? Does the computer dissolve under a history of cultural techniques (Siegert 2015)? Or can a history of "the digital" not include computers at all?

Field

We see digital architecture as a field of practices, operations, and techniques built around computers, broadly construed (looms and rooms, women calculators, desktops and laptops, programmable materials and synthetic bacteria and the list goes on). Talking about media necessitates consideration of the field they modulate, the infrastructure that supports them, the industries that produce them, the anthropo-technical conduits around them, the older media before them, and the techniques and theories embedded in them.

There may indeed be "eight million stories of the origins of the digital in architecture" (Goodhouse 2017). Yet each of these eight million stories assumes a specific vantage point toward the computer: it either fetishizes it or dissolves it. How about operationalizing this observation to willfully

4   *Olga Touloumi and Theodora Vardouli*

produce an oscillating field: one that ties the digital with the computer, in its socio-technical specificities, but allows the computer to move in and out of focus? What are the implications of a scholar adopting a mobile vantage point toward the computer: tactically centering and decentering it to illuminate negotiations between different modes of agency?

We vouch for histories that are attuned to resonances between wide-lens views of epistemic and cultural phenomena and the micro-operations of making and using technical artifacts. We argue for histories that oscillate between *longue durée* epistemic transformations and situated acts from designers and users. Looking at the embodied and material contingencies beyond the deliberations of auteur architect-technologists and auteur architect-users is our way of venturing to *other* histories of digital architecture.

Obsolescence

It is common for architects involved with digital media to return to early work on computers and design in search of unrealized potential. Common are also stories of anticipation and forecasting, where technologies tangled up in narratives of newness are confronted with their historical echoes. Yet, instead of simply saying "this is not new" one needs to look with some specificity at how these echoes operate, at the conditions by which they persist, and at the kinds of disciplinary and epistemic modes they are reflected on. Cutting against the grain of retro-techno-projections is a critical project that centers on obsolescence: on things discarded and things embedded in every shift and update.

Digital innovation comes with digital obsolescence. One device, one programming language, one software, gives way to another, slowly necessitating updates and new equipment. Obsolescence challenges archival modalities. This is not new for the library and information sciences, which often need to simulate the environments of operating systems and amass obsolete media, from slide scanners to floppy discs. Work on the preservation of digital objects, some of which has sprung out of the *Archaeologies of the Digital* program at the Canadian Centre of Architecture, tackles digital obsolescence: they come to terms with unreadable files, inactive versions of computer programs, and defunct hard drives.

But there is also another form of obsolescence that does not come from a condition of being defunct, but from a condition of being forgotten, sidetracked, and overthrown. It is an obsolescence of meanings, discourses, practices projected upon techniques. History writing as a construction of both memory and obsolescence plays its part here. Despite stated attempts to resist it, stories of digital architecture gravitate towards breaks, shifts, and turns of various kinds. Innovation carries cultural capital and cultural currency; narratives of innovation structure historiographical fields and their cathectic power can produce obsolescence (of makers, old media, and techniques). To grapple with obsolescence, both in history writing and digital production, we need more stories of continuity than of break. We also need to become more attentive to stories of techniques, to reveal processes of naturalization and embeddedness that render them ubiquitous and/or invisible, and to trace these techniques' lives as they traverse intellectual, institutional, cultural, and practical settings. We need more histories of banality and failure. And we need to come to terms with delivering dry histories that do not climax or break ground, but rather shape ground.

Conversation

Can a single, all-inclusive and comprehensive historical narrative describe and explain phenomena as multivalent and complex as those surrounding the concatenation of "digital" and "architecture"? The social construction of epistemic value often demands that a scholar makes with an argument an almost territorial claim toward an entire field. Can we move beyond a competitive, "free-market" logic of argumentation and declare that history writing (as history making) occupies a conversational space?

In our book, we use the idea of a *common ground* as an analytic and as a program of action. The common ground pays tribute to a key-phrase that animated the intellectual landscape in which architecture was imagined as computation and computers were imagined architecturally. The "common ground" was an exciting slogan in postwar intellectual life (Spillers 1974; Galison 1998), tangled up with visions of unification of multiple modes of knowledge and action. The rhetoric of a common ground, be it a common "bedrock," a common "language," or a common communication channel, played a key role in challenging disciplinary boundaries and formations, and in institutionalizing unlikely collaborations.

In a spirit of sustained reflexivity, we also adopt the common ground as a methodological heuristic. Grappling with the variety of technical languages and epistemic cultures that configured relationships between architecture and computers requires active and curious listening for inflections, translations, and transmutations of words and technics. It also entails coming to terms with metaphor, evocation, and imagination as constituents of technological development. It requires a polyglot space of historical inquiry that is:

- *Multilingual*—this space is contingent upon multiple forms of literacy. It requires speaking, with some degree of interactional expertise, architectural, mathematical, programming, and engineering languages. It also crucially requires listening to the languages of multiple epistemic communities: technologists, architects, designers, mathematicians and paying attention to the many valencies and expressions of ideas, practices, and techniques.

6 *Olga Touloumi and Theodora Vardouli*

- *Polyphonic*—it seeks and produces the conditions for a multiplicity of scholarly perspectives and methods. It is generative rather than definitive, expansive rather than convergent. It is reflexive and resonant.
- *Scalar*—actors, practices, discourses, institutions, and objects co-exist in a plane of interrogation and can be centered or decentered in the process of history writing. Thick descriptions and wide-lens readings alternate, and reveal new assemblages at work.
- *Protean*—the field itself changes shape. It is temporal. Yesteryear's "othering" of dominant narratives and approaches to digital architecture provides the conditions for its change.

Architecture of *computer architectures*

These categories are an attitude rather than a framework. Readers may recognize them in the polyphony of methods and approaches reflected in the book, rather than in the structure of the chapters. The chapters are grouped according to four keywords that we gave to the authors, one of which they each tackled with their essays. The keywords came from the classic Von Neumann diagram for a computer architecture. To create resonances and productive dissonances, we grouped our essays according to its main constituents, turning *program* (control unit), *storage* (memory), *input/output*, and *computation* (arithmetic/logic unit) into props for historical inquiry. The authors' essay-responses enacted a diversity of methods and concerns, weaving fortuitous lateral connections. Instead of a methodological proposal, this organizational move acts as a suggestion of what is possible once key-terms move beyond disciplinary definitions. In other words, using Von Neumann's diagram as an organizational tactic provisionally shapes a field of possibility stabilized around four quasi-material objects. Positioned as both technological and cultural constructs, "program," "storage," "input/output," and "computation" provide categories for parsing designers' and technologists' debates around the computer. Collectively, authors bring forth the striking homologies between a computer program and an architectural program, a wall and an interface, computer memory and storage architectures, structures of mathematics and structures of things.

Program

Peder Anker takes on a close examination of environmental design and its history, illuminating one important episode around computers entering architectural culture. He follows the émigré architect Serge Chermayeff from his conservation campaign for the Cape Cod National Seashore Park to the 1964 conference *Architecture and the Computer* at the Boston Architectural Center, and to his later collaboration with Christopher Alexander on the book *Community and Privacy*. In doing so, he traces a modernist desire to manage nature that shaped a new understanding of the environment as a programmable entity. Chermayeff's "environmental design" forged a new field for collaborative work and a deeper integration of the scientific method in design and art. In this sense, Anker's essay shows us that instead of being partners in creating representational complexity, computers entered the architectural imagination with the promise to recover the social project of interwar modern architecture. Anker also warns us that such imaginations carried with them the privileged vantage points of a modernist elite that aspired to protect their summer houses against development. Efforts to preserve privacy and elite status, Anker argues, became abstracted into an ideal of environmental serenity.

Transporting us from Cape Cod bourgeoisie to Italian workerists, and from idyllic serenity to factory floor struggle, AnnMarie Brennan examines new programs of labor that emerged when Olivetti—the Italian manufacturer of typewriters—expanded its operations to include the production of automated computing machinery. From Ettore Sottsass Jr.'s modular design for Elea 9003 in the late 1950s to the critiques of Marxist sociologist Romano Alquati and the *Quaderni Rossi*, Brennan unpacks the new cultural understandings of labor and professional identity that became associated with the design of new computing machinery. She also shows how the design of such machinery motivated exchanges among designers— in the case of the Elea computer between Maldonado and the Hochschule für Gestaltung in Ulm, and Sottsass and the Milan scene of design. Brennan grounds her story in Italy, where the initially favorable disposition toward computing machinery and its capacity to free the worker and "reform capitalism" quickly gave way to resistance against it. In doing so, she reminds us that (computer) programs are malleable to the institutions that run them and that profit-driven techno-social systems can annihilate even the most progressive of social intentions.

If Peder Anker and AnnMarie Brennan investigate "program" as a metaphor through which designers, modernist elites, and workers expressed their aspirations for more freedom and control, Theodora Vardouli shows us its conception as a vehicle for "order" and a "method." Her essay traces the intellectual, institutional, and technical contexts that shaped Alexander's proposition for a logico-mathematical foundation for design. Vardouli focuses on the work that led up to Alexander's landmark publication *Notes on the Synthesis of Form*, which included an application of HIDECS 2: a computer program based on a hierarchical graph theory-based decomposition algorithm aiming to assist "rational" design decision-making. Her essay traces shifting meanings of "rationality," reading not only Alexander's texts but also the mathematical techniques that he mobilized in their cultural and material dimensions. The mathematical object of the graph, Vardouli argues, allowed Alexander to move between structural and procedural understandings of "program," as both representing logical structures and delineating "order" of steps.

Input/output

Molly Wright Steenson tackles one of the most elastic and influential key-words that permeated research around interactive computing in 1960s North America: the interface. Languages and metaphor take on a key structuring and analytical role in Steenson's essay, and are acknowledged as ways of constructing technological imaginations. Spatial metaphors (scale, boundary, and surface) become crucial in conceptualizing the inter-face, and conceptualizing architecture as an interface. Architecture-as-interface both reinforced ergonomic mandates ("cognitive ergonomics") and exploded the architectural object within a relational, dialogic web of actions and reactions. Interface-as-architecture allowed the computer to move beyond the confines of an object and become an environment, to reach ever-expanding scales. Interfaces, Steenson argues, are embodied, but in their embodiment they virtualize the entities that they are installed to connect. Interfaces, she also argues, are successful when they disappear. Disappearance and occlusion then become suggestive openings for critically contemplating ubiquitous computing and interfaces as absorbing the envir-onment, to ultimately become an environment.

If the interface was the vehicle for connecting the "dissimilar" entities of the human and the computer, "symbiosis" was the aim. David Theo-dore rereads computer research patron J.C.R Licklider's influential prop-osition of a "man-computer symbiosis" as an inherently unstable and precarious one. He locates "symbiosis" in architectural space—the hos-pital—showing that there are critical opportunities in seeking out concrete socio-material substrates in which seemingly abstract ideas were devel-oped and tested. His essay foregrounds a history of experimentation through which, or in his essay despite which, rhetoric around the poten-tials of human-computer systems claimed its validity. The failure of the Hospital Computer Project—a human-machine cooperation program set up in the Massachusetts General Hospital (MGH)—was perceived to be one of interface: it appeared that design flaws prevented the coupling of humans and computers to achieve an enhanced "cognitive capacity." Theodore challenges this interpretation and repositions the failure in the cognitive bias of the interface: that it operated based on minds but not bodies. In his essay, automation as including the physical aspects of labor is a more viable imagination of human-machine co-operation than disem-bodied ideas of computerization. Symbiosis's fatal flaw, he suggests, was one of miscasting women's labor as men's cognition.

Continuing Theodore's thread about the persistence of bodies and material traces in histories of interface, Rachel Plotnick examines how ideas of cleanliness and hygiene configured the design of interfaces and the spaces that encompassed them. In her essay, familiar, and less famil-iar, architectural spaces—the computer room, the office, the kitchen—are portrayed as *housing* fragile instruments. Plotnick sees architectural spaces, human behaviors, and technological artifacts, as co-configured under a "clean aesthetic." Initially guardians of this "clean aesthetic" against messy users and contaminating environments, architects and designers were eventually tasked with de-sanitizing computer rooms in offices, with design choices such as color, fabric, and texture. Cleanness became displaced from the room to the machine: to user manuals and to technical decisions. Coming full circle from Steenson's argument about the scalar explosion of the computer through the interface, Plotnick speaks about the consolidation of an architectural aesthetic into the design of the computer.

Storage

Bernard Dionysius Geoghegan moves the conversation away from the computer and into the theoretical frameworks developed around information systems, pointing out that information theory has never been one. Geoghegan concentrates on two central, almost mythical figures in information theory, Norbert Wiener and Claude Shannon. He suggests that their approaches to information embed and enact different cultural and epistemological frameworks. On the one hand, Wiener's theory gravitates toward order and organization, structuring goal-oriented techno-social collectivities that refine their assemblage through constant feedback on their operations. Wiener interpellated his cybernetic model to a variety of fields, reconstructing them *a posteriori* as systems of information and communication. On the other hand, Shannon stayed closer to communications engineering and held coding and mathematical abstraction as the centerpiece of his theory. His theory of information did not reckon with goals or purposes, but rather occupied a "post-organic" universe organized by rules and laws. Geoghegan's essay shows us that the ways in which theories are socialized shape their ontologies, the fields they form, and their disciplinary appropriations.

If Geoghegan's essay considers the theoretical and conceptual frameworks of different information theories upon which ideas about memory, classification, and storage emerged, Shannon Mattern's essay articulates a media archaeological journey within the longer history of filing systems, with personal narrative inflections. With its narrative immediacy, this reprinted piece incorporates memoirs and memories as a mode of thinking about computer storage, in this case as continuous with the material logics of filing systems—cabinets, files, folders—before and beyond computers. Mattern's essay is an example of scalarity—one of the tactics that we discussed above. Her essay is not about computers, yet it becomes a rich device for thinking about the logics and material infrastructures of storage and retrieval. Mattern reminds us that apart from the system of ordering information, "form" also anticipates—and in doing so indicates—types of information management.

Computation

Matthew Allen situates the algorithmic imagination of architecture within histories of structuralist art practice. His essay begins with a strong argument of continuity: that computers became entangled with disciplinary, intellectual agendas that pre-existed their uses. He also highlights the tension between broader disciplinary shifts and local idiosyncrasies. Looking at *Form*—a student-initiated journal at the University of Cambridge—he examines how algorithmic architecture, abstract art, and structuralist theory came together in the context of the British avant-garde. Allen frames concrete poetry as a structuralist art practice and traces its diffusion into architecture. Concrete poetry for Allen suggests a perception machine operating based on the artist's techniques and the machine's effects, with the two being both describable through abstract conceptual structures. Allen follows the shift from specific machines to universal machines (computers), suggesting that algorithmic architecture is, intellectually and historically, a generalization of structuralist activity.

Alma Steingart expands Allen's "structuralist activity," tracing its linkages with twentieth-century mathematical cultures and its broader expressions in postwar scientific humanism. Steingart's essay examines the construction of a common ground between mathematics and the arts, premised upon creativity and aesthetic considerations. She shows how axiomatics, the trademark of modern mathematics, recast the mathematician's activity as a creative and aesthetic one, all the while constructing a new definition of creativity as a process of generating structures as opposed to forms. This definition became pervasive among scientific humanists and, operationalized through techniques from new mathematical fields such as topology, ultimately formed an aesthetic: an axiomatic, structuralist, combinatorial aesthetic. Yet in the building of this aesthetic, Steingart suggests, resided a deep rooted ambivalence toward the senses. For mathematicians, the axiomatic aesthetic was an inward turn toward abstraction, resisting the instrumentalization of mathematics for practical—or specifically, military—purposes. For scientific humanists, including notable architects, artists, and designers, the axiomatic aesthetic mathematized vision and perception, embracing the sensorium and the empirical world.

These ten essays sample possible sites and possible lenses for talking about computers and architecture. These are expeditions in what we envision as an expanded and expandable field of historical inquiry, building worlds of discourse around concepts, objects, and techniques. These essays could be a hundred. And then a few hundred more.

Bibliography

Alt, C. (2011) "Objects of Our Affection: How Object Orientation Made Computers a Medium." In Huhtamo E. and J. Parikka, eds. *Media Archaeology: Approaches, Applications, and Implications*, 278–301. Berkeley, CA: University of California Press.

Bottazzi, R. (2018) *Digital Architecture beyond Computers: Fragments of a Cultural History of Computational Design.* London: Bloomsbury Publishing USA.

Cardoso Llach, D. (2015) *Builders of the Vision: Software and the Imagination of Design.* New York, NY: Routledge.

Carpo, M. ed. (2017) *The Second Digital Turn: Design beyond Intelligence.* Cambridge, MA: MIT Press.

Chun, W. H. K. (2004) "On Software, or the Persistence of Visual Knowledge." *Grey Room* 18: 26–51.

Dutta, A. ed. (2013) *A Second Modernism: MIT, Architecture, and the "Techno-Social" Moment.* Cambridge, MA: MIT Press.

Fuller, M. and A. Goffey (2017) "The Obscure Objects of Object Orientation." In Fuller, M., ed. *How to Be a Geek: Essays on the Culture of Software*, 15–36. Cambridge, UK: Polity.

Galison, P. (1998) "The Americanization of Unity." *Daedalus* 127 (1): 45–71.

Goodhouse, A. ed., publisher's description for (2017) *When Is the Digital in Architecture?* Montreal: Canadian Centre for Architecture/Berlin: Sternberg Press, (2017), https://www.cca.qc.ca/en/events/49967/when-is-the-digital-in-architecture (accessed 29 July 2019).

Gumbrecht, H. U. and K. L. Pfeiffer eds. (1994) *Materialities of Communication.* Stanford, CA: Stanford University Press.

Hagen, W. (2005) "The Style of Source Codes." in Chun W. H. K. and Keenan T (eds.) *New Media, Old Media.* New York: Routledge.

Harwood, J. (2011) *The Interface: IBM and the Transformation of Corporate Design, 1945–1976.* Minneapolis, MN: University of Minnesota Press.

Kay, A. (1984) "Computer Software." *Scientific American* 251 (3): 52–59.

Keller, S. (2018) *Automatic Architecture: Motivating Form after Modernism.* Chicago, IL: University of Chicago Press.

Light, J. S. (2005) *From Warfare to Welfare: Defense Intellectuals and Urban Problems in Cold War America.* Baltimore, MD and London: Johns Hopkins University Press.

Lynn, G. (2014) *Archaeology of the Digital.* Montreal: Sternberg Press.

Manovich, L. (2001). *The Language of New Media.* Cambridge, MA: MIT Press

Murray, J. (2003) "Inventing the Medium." In Wadrip-Fruin N. and Montfort N. (eds.) *The New Media Reader.* Cambridge, MA and London: MIT Press.

Murray, J. (2012) *Inventing the Medium. Principles of Interaction Design as a Cultural Practice.* Cambridge, MA: MIT Press.

Picon, A. (2010) *Digital Culture in Architecture.* Basel: Birkhäuser Architecture.

Siegert, B. (2015) *Cultural Techniques: Grids, Filters, Doors, and Other Articulations of the Real.* Translated by Geoffrey Winthrop-Young. New York, NY: Fordham University Press.

Spillers, W. R. (1974) "Foreword." In Spillers, W. R., ed. *Basic Questions of Design Theory.* Amsterdam and New York: North-Holland Publishing Co.; American Elsevier.

Steenson, M. W. (2017). *Architectural Intelligence: How Designers and Architects Created the Digital Landscape.* Cambridge, MA: The MIT Press.

Part I
Program

2 Computing environmental design

Peder Anker

"[S]urvival of mankind as we know it" is at stake, and the "natural human ecology stands in jeopardy." Serge Chermayeff's 1960 plea for environmental conservation addressed the growing use of cars, as he thought everyone's access to them resulted in a noisy "auto-anarchy" with roads depredating the natural environment (Chermayeff 1960a: 190, 193, 1962a: 4–13). "Personally, I observe these probabilities with profoundest melancholy" in Cape Cod, he noted. The things affected by this predicament ranged from the privacy of his cottage to the ecology of the neighborhood, the social order of the Wellfleet community, and even the planning of the entire peninsula. Only a powerful computer could solve the complexity of the problem, Chermayeff thought.

Through the lens of social history of design, I argue that the early history of computing in design established a managerial view of the natural world benefiting the well-educated, liberal elite. Chermayeff was part of a group of modernist designers with vacation homes on Cape Cod who nurtured political ties to the Kennedy family. Their community was fashioned around using the Wellfleet environment as a place for leisure and vacation, a lifestyle threatened by various local housing and road developments. In response they began promoting a national park to protect the area, and began pondering on finding new tools for proper environmental design that could protect their interests. The computer became their unifying tool for a multilayered approach to environmental planning, which saw nature as rational in character. It offered managerial distance and an imagined socio-political objectivity. As a device the computer emerged out of Chermayeff's comprehensive "Environmental Design" courses at Harvard University, which sought to merge arts, science, and technology in the design process modeled on the Bauhaus legacy.

Environmental conservation at Cape Cod

Since the arrival of former Bauhaus faculty in the United States in the late 1930s the picturesque and beautiful town of Wellfleet, Cape Cod, had been their annual summer residence. Bauhauslers such as László Moholy-

16 *Peder Anker*

Nagy, Walter Gropius, Herbert Bayer, and Marcel Breuer spent their vacations there on an annual basis, along with prominent modernists such as Eero Saarinen, Paul Weidlinger, and Jack Hall. Chermayeff was very much a part of this community, having bought his own property there in 1944. It was 1,500 square feet of playful avant-garde and the only place he would ever feel truly at home. Located at the Slough Pond, close to the beaches, it was in the midst of, what was then, and indeed still is today, beautiful natural scenery. The architectural history of this modernist community has been well documented by Peter McMahon and Christine Cipriani, who tell a story of a tight knit group of friends enjoying a laid-back culture of beaches, woods, art, architecture, and each other (Blum 1986; McMahon, Cipriani 2014).

Hard as it may be to imagine today, back then Wellfleet was a place with no restaurants and only a few tourists. And this was exactly what Chermayeff cherished the most. Though he previously had shown environmental concern, such as in a 1934 lecture about noise prevention in buildings, his turn to nature conservancy began in earnest at Cape Cod (Chermayeff 1934). What raised his concern were numerous new parcels of buildings that were put on the market in the late 1950s, with new developments built for vacationers as well as local residents (Kneedler-Schad, Lacy, Lowenthal 1995: 44–45). The town's modernist designers were less than pleased at seeing their beloved scenery being invaded by people and homes that did not belong to the community of the avant-garde. First among them to express concern about the loss of natural habitat was Gropius, who in his lectures at Harvard tried to convey an environmental ethic to his students that could halt such development:

> ... the greatest responsibility of the planner and architect, I believe, is the protection and development of our habitat. Man has evolved a mutual relationship with nature on earth, but his power to change its surface has grown so tremendously that this may become a curse instead of a blessing. How can we afford to have one beautiful tract of open country after the other bulldozed out of existence, flattened and emptied for the sake of smooth building operations and then filled up by a developer with hundreds of insipid little house units, that will never grow into a community. [...] *Until we love and respect the land almost religiously, its fatal deterioration will go on.*
>
> (Gropius 1955: 184)

Chermayeff was most definitely among those who loved and respected their land almost religiously. His property, his community of designer friends, and the nature scenery that surrounded him were most precious to him, and the arrival of new developments with cars, people, and noise were personally upsetting. As will be apparent, both his writings and teachings addressed this problem head-on, and the computer would surface as an objectifying tool in planning for a more cautious development.

Computing environmental design   17

It was the prospect of creating the Cape Cod National Seashore Park that sparked Chermayeff into action. In the fall of 1959 the Senator of Massachusetts, John F. Kennedy, reached out to Chermayeff and asked him his opinion about a possible park, as he was planning to sponsor a bill in support of it and wanted Chermayeff to testify in its favor. In his enthusiastic reply, Chermayeff said he would gladly testify, and that he could also provide a Harvard study in support of the park (Chermayeff 1959a, 1959b, 1959c; Holborn 1959; Kennedy 1959). He immediately formed the Wellfleet Study Group of Harvard undergraduates, and would, in subsequent months, lobby local and federal politicians about the importance of the park by focusing on the ecological vulnerability of the Cape (Chermayeff 1960b, 1960c; Landstrom 1960). In a show of authority, when contacting people for support, he used the official Harvard letterhead in his personal correspondence (Chermayeff 1960d). In the summer of 1960 Chermayeff invited Directors within the Department of Interior to be shown around the possible park area, which included his own property. And they loved visiting his "delightful summer home" after the tour (Lee 1960). In December the same year he would finally testify at the House of Representatives in favor of the park, arguing that it should be as large as possible. If the Senate voted in favor of a tiny park, he argued, "Conservation would then be just a word. It would not have any serious meaning because the ecology of wildlife cannot jump quarter mile gaps with residents, their pets and cars and so on" (Chermayeff 1961a: 102). What was needed was a larger plan for Cape Cod and Wellfleet that would make sure that neither the town nor the surrounding landscape would be shattered by suburban sprawl. Unless the Senate took action, "the cape as we know it will vanish forever within a decade and be replaced by an endless suburban sprawl, a dormitory for Route 128 industries within 45 minutes commuting time," he argued (Chermayeff 1961a: 105).

Not all his modernist neighbors were equally enthusiastic about the park. His friend and fellow designer, Breuer, for example, was annoyed as he had just subdivided and sold off two properties at Herring Pond and worried the value of his remaining land would dwindle with it being inside a park. Chermayeff tried to convince him about the value of having a cottage within a nature conservation area:

> I am fighting hard for the Park. There is no question that this unique area would be very quickly built over if the Park Service doesn't take over and reverse the process and conserve the natural resources in years to come. [...] However, every house with its traffic and noise and erosion, squeezed into our small pond area, scars the landscape and scares away the wild life which will not be restored in our lifetime.
>
> (Chermayeff 1961b).

18 *Peder Anker*

There was also plenty of local opposition to the park reflecting an ongoing tension between local and summer residents, with the visitors being inclined to support nature conservation. The visitors tended to be wealthier, better educated, or also having a wider social network (Corbett 1955: 214–222). The Kennedys considered themselves to be true Cape Codders, having spent more than forty summers at a place they considered their home. Yet this identification was not recognized by all. Hyannis Port, where their estates were located, was considered a part-time summer colony by most Cape Codders, and John F. Kennedy's self-identification was not taken entirely seriously by true locals. In addition, the average Cape Codders were obviously not up to par with the Kennedy's wealth and social influence. While serving as US Senator for Massachusetts between 1953 and 1960 Kennedy did his best to keep these tensions buried, so as to maintain the political cachet of having a local identity and support base, but despite his attempts, they surfaced in the debate about a possible Cape Cod National Seashore Park. Those living in Cape Cod year-round feared a tax increase with the loss of property tax revenue on the land that was turned into a park, and there was also a fear of a ban on developers in the areas. As a result there was much controversy surrounding Kennedy and his plans for the park in the summer of 1959, even leading to some demonstrations against the project. Francis P. Burling, then Managing Editor of *The Cape Codder* was on Kennedy's side, however, and very much in favor of the park, and he skewed the local newspaper accordingly (Damore 1967; Foster 1985). The managerial culture that later came with the computer planning would magnify the social distance with the machine serving as an objectifying tool controlling such local opposition.

Yet in light of his bid for Democratic nomination for Presidency, Kennedy decided to postpone support of the park so that the local opposition could not be used against him during the election year of 1960. Having been elected President, he finally established the Cape Cod National Seashore Park in August 1961 while he was enjoying his vacation at Hyannis Port. This was his first show of support of environmentalism, and it propelled him to think further about the issue, as he later did in his endorsement of the conclusions of Rachel Carson's *Silent Spring* (Carson 1962). A special edition of Henry David Thoreau's memoirs from Cape Cod was issued on the occasion, with the park being fashioned rhetorically as saving the beaches he had once described (Thoreau 1961; Mulloney 1998). A local historian correctly noted, "[i]t was as much to protect beaches of the lower Cape *for* the people as it was to save them *from* the people" that the park was established (Schneider 2000: 304). The beaches were to be as accessible as possible fostering tourism business, while the green mantle was to be protected. Only homes already built within the park could remain, and one of those belonged to Chermayeff, who was overjoyed about the prospect of "escape into a wilderness" knowing that there would be no new developments in his neighborhood (Chermayeff 1962b: 7).

Gropius was also thrilled. To him, the new park was a vehicle for protecting both the environment and the community of avant-garde that were encroached upon by developments and conventionals' traditional architecture and style. It is telling that he advised the National Park Service that "only fresh and imaginative contemporary design" should be built within the newly established Cape Cod National Seashore Park (Gropius 1963a). Chermayeff agreed. In addition to requiring contemporary architecture, he thought the park authorities should also think using an environmental design aesthetic that included everything from road planning to graphic signage of its displays. True nature conservation, he argued, entailed "a total architecture which must be designed simultaneously with the landscape, the roads and the buildings" (Chermayeff 1963a).

Environmental design

Chermayeff's "total architecture" approach to environmental conservation reflected his adaptation of the Bauhaus legacy. At the Bauhaus school, it is worth recalling, students of the ground course were asked to study biology, along with color studies, history of art, materials, and tools (Moholy-Nagy 1938: 8–21). The curriculum was replicated by the school's former professor Moholy-Nagy at the School of Design in Chicago where students were encouraged to design everything from cities to tea-sets. When Moholy-Nagy learned he had terminal cancer in 1946, he asked Chermayeff to be its new Director, knowing that he endorsed the pedagogy of the Bauhaus program.

Being a Russian émigré from rural Grozny (currently in the Chechen Republic, Russia), Chermayeff had lived most of his life in London, after which he moved to the US in 1940. In London he was known as an architect of modernist buildings, and he, from the mid-1930s on, would hang out with Bauhauslers such as Moholy-Nagy, Gropius, and Breuer, along with scientific socialists and proponents of planning such as Julian Huxley, J.B.S Haldane and J. Desmond Bernal. Following in their footsteps, Chermayeff would, in his capacity as new Director in Chicago from 1946 to 1951, argue that the role of the designer was that of "social therapy" (Chermayeff 1950a: 142). Design should have a "social purpose" and designers should aspire to be like an "artist-scientist-technician" (Chermayeff 1950b: 68). When he used the term "environmental design" for the first time in 1949, it was to promote integration of science and art, but also by bringing together architecture, landscape design, and planning in pedagogy (Powers 2001: 177). Early on, Chermayeff had been skeptical of the word "architecture," a word he thought should be dropped in favor of the more comprehensive word "design," inspired by insights of the natural scientists. In Chicago he envisioned that his students would promote "good housing and schools, well-planned cities, and preserved natural resources" (Chermayeff 1950a: 142). Indeed, the "*social responsibility* and the ethics" of the designer, Chermayeff argued, included an aspiration to

20 *Peder Anker*

protect "*man's physical environment*," a sentiment that was shared by Bauhauslers such as Moholy-Nagy, Herbert Bayer, and Gropius (Chermayeff 1951: 12). They all argued in favor of a comprehensive design that took care of both humans and nature.

In 1951 Chermayeff resigned as Director due to the financial difficulties of the institution and disagreements with the terms of its incorporation into the Illinois Institute of Technology. He subsequently moved to Cambridge where he set up his own office and began a lectureship at MIT, followed by a professorship at Harvard University's Graduate School of Design (GSD) in 1952. Gropius had just retired as Chair of the Department of Architecture, and Chermayeff was hired to reenergize GSD under its new Dean, Josep Lluís Sert.

Under the heading of "Environmental Design," Chermayeff taught Harvard's first year students the environmentally friendly, comprehensive, and interdisciplinary Bauhaus-inspired foundation course that he knew from Illinois, after which the students went on to focus on architecture, urban planning, landscape design, and so forth. He adopted the "total architecture" approach of Gropius, "embracing the entire visible environment from the simplest utensil to the complicated city" (Gropius 1956: 9). In the mid-1950s Chermayeff began advocating moving "Environmental Design" beyond just first year students, as he imagined an Advanced Studies Program with PhD students under the rubric, which, after some dispute, was approved by the school's faculty in 1958 (Chermayeff 1955b). The pushback addressed a real concern: how could a student carry out research and receive a PhD without appropriate specialization? As will be apparent, the computer became an important tool in providing a unifying mathematical language for the comprehensive environmental research design program. Yet the lack of appreciation for his pedagogical program made Chermayeff exclaim in frustration that "most architects have not yet joined the 20th century!" (Chermayeff 1959c: 18).

Indeed, much of the educational program at GSD was badly organized under Sert's leadership. This, at least, was the opinion expressed in a letter to him signed by all the students at GSD in May 1960. They claimed that their hard work only led to "dissatisfaction, confusion, anger, disappointment and finally apathy" (McCagg 1960a). Chermayeff's first year course was the exception, and Sert assumed he was the one firing up the students' anger. At GSD Chermayeff was known as "a tall, elegant, handsome man" and "one of the leading contenders for the title of world's best-dressed professor" (Atticus 1959: 3). Yet despite his striking impression, he was also known to be blunt and lacking in social skills. He kept largely to himself and it is understandable that Sert was suspicious, though the Students Council wrote Sert telling him that Chermayeff did not "instigate" the criticism (McCagg 1960b, 1961). Yet the students' anger refused to fade away, and Chermayeff somehow became associated with the unrest. This may explain why Sert withdrew the funding for Chermayeff's research

Computing environmental design   21

program in 1961, after only two years (Sert 1961a). The fallout was detrimental to Chermayeff's relationship to GSD, as he resigned in protest and accepted a professorship at Yale University where he was allowed to pursue his Environmental Design pedagogy when teaching graduate students (Sert 1961b).

Environmental privacy in a community

His most talented PhD student while at Harvard was Christopher Alexander. Alexander began in 1958 and would feed his adviser with what was worth knowing about computers, as using IBM 704 to model buildings was at the heart of his PhD proposal (Alexander 1958a). The computer could be instrumental, Alexander argued, as a tool for the mass production of house designs so that modernist architecture could be delivered to everyone. He envisioned a "[f]ormulation of mass-produced house design procedure as a cooperative game between architect and society" (Alexander 1958b). Given the urgent need for housing, the computer would enable the architect to be more socially responsible. The computer could also provide a clear mathematical language and thus replace the "abstract phraseology" of architectural theory (Alexander 1958b). In the following years Alexander and Chermayeff would collaborate and merge their thinking. Chermayeff came to embrace the computer while Alexander adapted to the comprehensive program of environmental design. Soon Alexander followed the advice of his mentor in making elaborate notes about the importance of climatic factors and "*bioclimatic discomfort*" in his computer modeling of housing units, while Chermayeff learned from Alexander the possibilities and limits of computers (Alexander 1960).

Addressing environmental problems was at the heart of what they tried to achieve. Chermayeff told his graduate students at Harvard to focus on noise and cars: "The car cuts the countryside to pieces, and it dissolves the city," he would say (Chermayeff 1961c: 50). The task of the environmental designer, as he saw it, was to create architecture of privacy with respect to noise and access to nature, while, at the same time, plan for a social community with minimal use of cars. These were the real issues he knew from Wellfleet which he began to conceptualize into a larger book. "Our humanity is at stake," he told his students. And designers, "in perhaps a dim way, [were] partially responsible for its survival" (Chermayeff 1963c: 8). He decided to bring his student Alexander along on the book project, as Alexander had access to an IBM 704 at the Computation Center at MIT and also intimate knowledge about how to use it. As the historian of architecture Margot Lystra has shown, Alexander was at the time working on innovative methods of computer-inspired highway designs with hand-drawn overlays that included untraditional factors such as noise, pollution, weather, and eyesores (Steinitz, Parker, Jordan 1976: 444–455; Lystra 2017: 157–174).

22   Peder Anker

In the book, Chermayeff and Alexander envisioned to bring forth a novel environmental design approach. The first draft of their manuscript was finished in the summer of 1960 while the debate was raging about the possible Cape Cod National Seashore Park. Entitled *Community and Privacy: Toward a New Architecture of Humanism*, it argued for a humanism that placed environmental concerns at the forefront. They sent it to Athenaeum who rejected it based on a harsh peer-review (Friedlander 1960; Denney 1961), to Chermayeff's old friend Lewis Mumford who was unable to read it as he was away (Mumford 1962), and finally to Peter Blake, the editor of *Architectural Form*, who was "tremendously impressed" but thought it needed better graphic design (Blake 1961). What is remarkable in the first reaction to the manuscript is that none of the recipients noticed what the book became known for, namely the call to protect the environment with the help of computing methodology. In any case, Chermayeff and Alexander brushed up and finished the manuscript at Cape Cod in the summer of 1962. Chermayeff had just resigned his professorship at Harvard and moved to Yale to pursue environmental design there. When the book, which was dedicated to Gropius, appeared in the bookstores in the fall of 1963, it was his first public statement as a professor at Yale.

It was a timely book for designers. Rachel Carson had recently published her *Silent Spring* (1962), and its impact put environmental concerns very much on the public agenda. In his forward to *Community and Privacy*, the poet Kenneth Rexroth pointed to the environmental crisis of the planet caused by radical population growth, and the urgent need to use the science of ecology to inform landscape planning. "Man is so radically altering the ecological situation out of which he emerged as a species and altering it in such an irrational manner, that he is endangering his own future" (Rexroth 1963: 14).

The problem that *Community and Privacy* sought to address was how to find a balance between the town and the individual in the age of environmental destruction. Nature was vanishing and the town was vanishing, resulting in a pseudo-town, a pseudo-nature, and a loss of equilibrium between them. This reflected what they had observed in Cape Cod. What was needed was a new environmental order provided by the architect-planner. Soon "man will have invaded every corner of the earth," with their cars, they pointed out (Chermayeff 1962a: 4–13; Chermayeff, Alexander 1963a: 43). "A New Ecology" in which humans would adapt to the environment was necessary (Chermayeff, Alexander 1963a: 46).

The solution to these problems was to be found in reestablishing the lost equilibrium.

> Either he [the designer] must learn to preserve the existing equilibrium of life or he must introduce a new equilibrium of his own making. If he does neither, his present unplanned conduct may deform human nature beyond all cure, even if it manages to survive the more violent holocaust.
> (Chermayeff, Alexander 1963a: 46)

Computing environmental design 23

This trivialization of Jewish history may illustrate how serious the authors took the issue to be, but also their insensitivity towards the complexity of social processes. In any case, if equilibriums were to be achieved, the designers would have to address head-on the question of how to plan for a world with more people, but fewer cars and less noise.

The computer was to be the tool helping designers to achieve equilibrium by creating a new balanced system for both nature and society, and creative designers should not fear it:

> The problem of this kind cannot be solved without the help of electroniccomputers. [...] The machine is distinctly complementary to and not a substitute for man's creative talent. [...] The computer, while unable to invent, can explore relations very quickly and systematically, according to prescribed rules. It functions as a natural extension of man's analytical ability.
>
> (Chermayeff, Alexander 1963a: 160)

Chermayeff and Alexander used spaceships as their model as they saw the internal environment of these vehicles being in balance thanks to computer technology developed by NASA. The aim was to build a fully functioning framework for ecological equilibrium for the Earth modeled on the order of spaceships. Thus, the computer was to be understood as a useful tool that could enlarge the designer's rational power, but not necessarily their creative ability.

The task of the designer was to make "Art for Ecology's Sake" (Chermayeff, Alexander 1963a: 110). And the computer was to help the artist to design within the complexity of ecological relations, without having to engage too deeply with the social realm. The environmental issues were intricate with many layers of information, they argued: "Problems have outgrown a single individual's capacity to handle them. Society must invent ways and means that, in effect, magnify the designer's limited capacity and make it possible for him to apply himself more completely" (Chermayeff, Alexander 1963a: 109). Both Chermayeff and Alexander saw the computer as the key tool that could bring together the complexity of ecological problems by creating a hierarchy of number systems that would be manageable to the designer. "The IBM 704 computer" at MIT "found the major cleavages for our attachment problem in a few minutes" by framing the questions in terms of number hierarchies, they pointed out (Chermayeff, Alexander 1963a: 161).

Their hopes for computing reflected a deep optimism on behalf of technology and science in the Bauhaus tradition. The unification of art and science to improve culture was at the very heart of modernist architecture. "Designers need to come face to face with the facts of science and technology; their real hope for the restoration of humanism lies in their ability to exploit techniques to its limits," Chermayeff and Alexander argued (Chermayeff, Alexander

24 *Peder Anker*

1963a: 111). The problem was the mass amount of different types of numerical data about the environment the designer had to think through. The computer could help in structuring and ordering this numerical data, thus turning unstructured problems into order by the means of mathematical representation of different aspects of the environment (see Figures 2.1 and 2.2).

"Congratulations on the book! It has been very difficult to obtain a copy in the Harvard Square area. The man in the Mandrake [bookstore]

Figure 2.1 The problem unstructured. Chermayeff S. and C. Alexander, 1963. *Community and Privacy: Toward a New Architecture of Humanism*. Doubleday, p. 152

Computing environmental design 25

Figure 2.2 The problem structured. Chermayeff S. and C. Alexander, 1963. *Community and Privacy: Toward a New Architecture of Humanism*. Doubleday, p. 153

(when I grabbed the last of his third order) told me that each batch has sold out almost immediately," a friend of Chermayeff reported (Floyd 1963). Soon they received letters of praise calling the book "a real contribution to environmental literature" (Temko 1963a; Gropius 1963b, 1963c) and "a smashing success!" (Maass 1963). Indeed, *Community and Privacy* would do well, selling over 2,000 copies in fall of 1963 alone, and

26 *Peder Anker*

over 50,000 copies by 1976 (Riehl 1976). It thus set the agenda for architectural environmental debates for at least a decade.

Yet the immediate response in the form of book reviews was mixed. To one reviewer, it was "a most irritating book" filled with "pompous pseudophilosophy," (Von Eckardt 1964: 620) while another pointed to "a danger in the currently fashionable preoccupation with computer machinery" among designers (Anonymous 1965: 101). The idea that "we should be thinking in terms of the village to which technology has shrunk the globe, our earth," was troubling to one reviewer (Rowntree 1964), while another was excited about the book as "a painstaking demonstration of the computer's role in planning" (Gutheim 1964: 54; Rowntree 1966: 12). For the most part the book was praised for its timely environmental agenda (Rexroth 1964). Typically, *The New York Times* placed it among the growing genre of "environmental literature," arguing for planning with the help of "an electronic computer," and the newspaper placed it on the important "Christmas Guide for Readers" (Temko 1963a: 343; Anonymous 1963b: 86; O'Brian 1964: 116). The most euphoric review came in *The Cape Codder* editorial, which noted that Chermayeff was a "familiar figure" in Wellfleet as one of the backers of the Cape Cod National Seashore and that the book's argument about protecting the environment to secure both privacy and the community was "what Cape Cod is all about" (Anonymous 1964a: 12).

These readers and reviewers saw the computer as central to the book. Apparently, some even thought the authors made a case for replacing human reasoning and imagination with that of a computer, as Chermayeff and Alexander in the preface to the 1964 edition thought it was necessary to answer this concern by emphasizing that "this book does not advocate the substitution of computer techniques for human thought. It simply recognizes the usefulness of this new tool" (Chermayeff, Alexander 1963b: 58–63). Instead, they restated the purpose of the book was to advocate and develop a new "Science of Environmental Design." In a series of articles from the period, Chermayeff would argue that the architectural profession was "obsolete" as it had failed to recognize that humans were responsible for their own environment and that a comprehensive design that included both the natural and social realm was the way forward (Chermayeff 1963d: 301–305, 1964a: 26, 1964b: 880–883, 1964d: 17–23).

The architecture and computer conference

In December 1964 the Boston Architectural Center organized what may have been the first conference on the role of computers in architecture. It became a major event with more than 500 attendees from all parts of the country, including students. This took the organizers by surprise, as they were hoping for 200 (Jaffe 1964: 69). The question at stake was what the relationship should be between designers and machines, and *Community and Privacy* would set the agenda for the conference with Chermayeff as the keynote or "luncheon speaker."

At the podium, in front of people enjoying their white-cloth lunch, Chermayeff embraced the computer as an important tool. It could help the architect in the comprehensive analysis of "Environmental Design" problems. The environmental designer had to deal with "Planning, Construction, Control and Conservation," which meant dealing with "extraordinary quantities, complexity and newness" of environmental information. Only the mastery of sophisticated computers could help the designer in sorting it out, and the design community should consequently embrace the new tool. Indeed, "our survival depends upon our recognition of the pressures upon us and our ability to master new complexities" with the help of the computer, he claimed (Chermayeff 1964e: 22).

There were mixed reactions to this sentiment among these enjoying their lunch. Gropius was enthusiastic and thought computers "might help us to free our creative power" (Gropius 1964: 41). Perhaps computers could bring together the complexity and different fields of environmental design? The computer would, perhaps, make the specialist obsolete while it could empower the comprehensive generalist addressing complex environmental issues, such as planning "a conservation area" for "a nature-starved" city. Yet this approach to nature conservation was not an easy sell to computer geeks and urban planners, as Chermayeff ended his Q&A with the blunt "nobody gives a damn. Thank you" (Millon 1964: 44).

Chermayeff had a point, as much of the conference was focusing on issues such as how computers could aid architects cataloging building products (Sargent 1964: 2–3), how they could help save costs associated with repetitive designs, and how they could solve complex structural analytical problems (LeMessurier 1964: 4–6). These were exciting improvements for the engineers but a bit humdrum for the architects. That computers could use structural thermal data to generate exact load estimations and perhaps cut energy costs of buildings was, of course, a good thing, though there is little evidence suggesting that these papers generated much excitement among designers (Russell 1964: 7–9). The highlight of the conference was, perhaps, a "live" closed-circuit TV installation demonstration of the STRESS software by MIT's new IBM 7094 computer. Could such software help architects in their creative process? Was the machine to be understood as a practical extension of the architect's creativity? There was no shortage of optimism and vision, though few details on the specifics of what this would actually mean. The new instrument was destined to "make a major penetration into our profession," but exactly how was still a bit unclear (Payne 1964: 1; Ceruzzi 1998: 71–74; Vardouli 2015: 137–161).

One paper that stuck out was Howard Fisher's presentation of the technique for processing complex statistical data into meaningful graphic form by using the SYMAP ("synagraphic mapping") program (Fisher 1964: 13–18, 1982; Chrisman 2004). Fisher was a recent professor of city planning at the

28   *Peder Anker*

GSD who, in his study of Boston, used statistical data to generate computer maps visualizing housing density, income levels, and recreational land. What was exciting about his work was not the data, which was well known, but the ways in which his SYMAP program brought together the data through mapping. The SYMAP program was the cornerstone at the Harvard Laboratory for Computer Graphics and Spatial Analysis which Fisher would start the following year. It was exactly this possibility of computers helping designers to master complexities that Chermayeff found so appealing. Fisher argued that computers constituted a critical tool for analyzing and comprehending environmental complexity, allowing for the integration of the built environment into the natural environment.

In the subsequent years the Harvard Laboratory for Computer Graphics and Spatial Analysis would turn the innovative SYMAP program towards environmental issues, thanks to funding from the Conservation Foundation. They were largely responsible for developing what today is known as the Geographical Information System (GIS). The 1964 conference was the very beginning of this endeavor. The laboratory was initially more about urban planning than environmental conservation, though the SYMAP program would train an influential trio of environmental planners. First among them was the soil scientist G. Angus Hill, who designed the Canada Land Inventory in 1968, which was a very early GIS study of landscapes. Second, the landscape architect Philip Lewis, who became a powerful advocate for environmental corridors through his Wisconsin Recreation Study of 1964. And third, Ian McHarg, whose use of transparent overlays of maps in *Design with Nature* (1969) became perhaps the most influential approach to landscape architecture in the 20th century (McHarg 1969; Lewis 1964: 130–142; Hills 1974: 339–371). Their respective work and thinking harkens back not only to the SYMAP program, but also to *Community and Privacy* and Chermayeff's Environmental Design program.

As professor of architecture at UC Berkeley, Alexander would continue to advocate for the use of the computer in dealing with the complexity of environmental design. "Consider the task of designing a complete environment for a million people," he wrote in his PhD thesis (1964). "The ecological balance of human and animal and plant life must be correctly adjusted both internally and to the given exterior physical condition" (Alexander 1964: 2; Grabow 1983: 51–54). This reflected the sentiment that nature and society mirror each other, and that environmental solutions thus in the end would solve social issues. The computer was a useful tool for creating a pattern language "for the whole physical environment" including animals, plants, and humans, as well as their ecological and social lives (Alexander 1966: 1; Steenson 2009: 20–23). The same went for Chermayeff, who, for the rest of his life, continued to enjoy his cabin at Wellfleet, and wrote important books and articles on the value of using computers in environmental design, such as *Shape of Community* (Chermayeff 1964c: 45–50, 1970: 5–13, 1971: 630–637, 1982; Chermayeff, Tzonis 1971).

Computing environmental design   29

In summary, computers were first introduced into the fields of architecture and design in order to reduce the complexity of environmental problems to a manageable mathematical language. They were imagined as useful tools to coordinate the use of architecture, landscape design, and urban planning in comprehensive environmental design. This was a top-down approach to both nature and society, reflecting the liberal elitist culture of modernists. The optimism with respect to what computers and rationalism could do was shared among modernist designers, and it reflected the Bauhaus legacy of trying to unite science and the arts through technology. The computer became a unifying tool, bringing together a diversity of fields in an effort to protect the natural environment and thereby also our humanity. Computers could order both the human and natural environment by using the same mathematical language, thus bringing ecological sciences, landscape, and architectural design together.

Note

Unless otherwise stated, all archive references are to the Serge Ivan Chermayeff Architectural Records and Papers at the Avery Library, Columbia University, New York, USA. I am grateful to Olga Touloumi and Theodora Vardouli for valuable comments.

Bibliography

Alexander, C. (1958a) *Progress Report*, Box 1, Serge Chermayeff Architectural Records and Papers, Avery Library, Columbia University.

Alexander, C. (1958b) *Report on Current Ph. D. Work*, Box 1, Serge Chermayeff Architectural Records and Papers, Avery Library, Columbia University.

Alexander, C. (1960) *Christopher Alexander to Serge Chermayeff*, [Notes] Box 1, Serge Chermayeff Architectural Records and Papers, Avery Library, Columbia University.

Alexander, C. (1964) *Notes on the Synthesis of Form*, Cambridge, MA: Harvard University Press.

Alexander, C. (1966) *The Coordination of the Urban Rule System*, Berkeley, CA: Center for Planning.

Anonymous (1963a) "The City," *Architectural Record*, December, 42.

Anonymous (1963b) "A Christmas Guide for Readers," *New York Times*, December 1, 86.

Anonymous (1964a) "An Important Book," *The Cape Codder*, February 20, 12.

Anonymous (1964b) "Community and Privacy," *AIA Journal*, April, 66.

Anonymous (1965) "Abstracts" *Architecture and Engineering News*, March, 101.

Atticus (1959) "People and Things," *The Sunday Times*, July 19, 3.

Blake, P. (1961) *Peter Blake to Serge Chermayeff, August 21.* [Letter] Box 1, Serge Chermayeff Architectural Records and Papers, Avery Library, Columbia University.

Blum, B.J. (1986) *Oral History of Serge Chermayeff*, Chicago, IL: The Art Institute of Chicago.

30 *Peder Anker*

Carson, R. (1962) *Silent Spring*, Greenwich: Fawcett Crest.

Ceruzzi, P.E. (1998) *A History of Modern Computing*, Cambridge, MA: MIT Press.

Chermayeff, S. (1934) *Noise Prevention*. [Lecture] Box 5, Serge Chermayeff Architectural Records and Papers, Avery Library, Columbia University.

Chermayeff, S. (1950a) "The Social Aspect of Art," in J. Harris (ed.) *The Humanities: An Appraisal*, University of Wisconsin Press, pp. 140–142.

Chermayeff, S. (1950b) "Architecture at the Institute of Design," *L'architecture d'Aujourd'hui* 20, 62–68.

Chermayeff, S. (1951) "Education of Architects", *Perspective*, 2, 16–18.

Chermayeff, S. (1955a) *Environmental Design*. Box 6, Serge Chermayeff Architectural Records and Papers, Avery Library, Columbia University.

Chermayeff, S. (1955b) *Docket for the Faculty Meeting in the Last Week of April*. Box 6, Serge Chermayeff Architectural Records and Papers, Avery Library, Columbia University.

Chermayeff, S. (1959a) *Serge Chermayeff to John F. Kennedy, October 20*. [Letter] Box 1, Serge Chermayeff Architectural Records and Papers, Avery Library, Columbia University.

Chermayeff, S. (1959b) *Serge Chermayeff to Frederick L. Holborn, December 15*. [Letter] Box 1, Serge Chermayeff Architectural Records and Papers, Avery Library, Columbia University.

Chermayeff, S. (1959c) "The Shape of Quality," *Architecture Plus* 2, 18–26.

Chermayeff, S. (1960a) "The New Nomades," *Traffic Quarterly* 14, 189–198.

Chermayeff, S. (1960b) *Serge Chermayeff to Congressman Wayne N. Aspinall, August 5*. [Letter] Box 1, Serge Chermayeff Architectural Records and Papers, Avery Library, Columbia University.

Chermayeff, S. (1960c) *Serge Chermayeff to Congressman Wayne N. Aspinall, November 21*. [Letter] Box 1, Serge Chermayeff Architectural Records and Papers, Avery Library, Columbia University.

Chermayeff, S. (1960d) *Serge Chermayeff to Dear Friend, November 21*. [Letter] Box 1, Serge Chermayeff Architectural Records and Papers, Avery Library, Columbia University.

Chermayeff, S. (1961a) "Statement of Serge Chermayeff, Professor of Architecture, Harvard University" *Cape Cod National Seashore Park: Hearings before the Subcommittee on Public Lands, Dec. 16 and 17, 1960, Serial nr. 28*, Washington: US Government Printing.

Chermayeff, S. (1961b) *Serge Chermayeff to Marcel Breuer, January 12*. [Letter] Box 1, Serge Chermayeff Architectural Records and Papers, Avery Library, Columbia University.

Chermayeff, S. (1961c) "Shape of Privacy," in R. Plunz (ed.) *Design and the Public Good*, Cambridge, MA: MIT Press, pp 47–55.

Chermayeff, S. (1962a) "Mobility and Urban Design," *Program* Spring, 4–13.

Chermayeff, S. (1962b) "The Designer's Dilemma," in E.J. Zagorski (ed.) *A Panel Discussion*, Urbana, IL: Industrial Design Education Association, pp. 1–9.

Chermayeff, S. (1962c) *Chermayeff to President Nathan Marsh Pusey, Harvard, January 24*. [Letter] Box 1, Serge Chermayeff Architectural Records and Papers, Avery Library, Columbia University.

Chermayeff, S. (1963a) *Serge Chermayeff to Josiah Child, January 23*. [Letter] Cape Cod Park files, Department of Interior Archive.

Chermayeff, S. (1963b) *Chermayeff to E. K. Wickham, the Commonwealth Fund, November 5.* [Letter] Box 1, Serge Chermayeff Architectural Records and Papers, Avery Library, Columbia University.

Chermayeff, S. (1963c) "Let Us Not Make Shapes: Let Us Solve Problems," typescript, p. 8.

Chermayeff, S. (1963d) "Search for a New Urbanity," *Ekistics* 16, 301–305.

Chermayeff, S. (1964a) "Random Thoughts on the Architectural Condition," in M. Whiffen (ed.) *The History, Theory and Criticism of Architecture*, Washington, DC: The American Institute of Architects, pp. 23–36.

Chermayeff, S. (1964b) "Private Affluence and Public Squalor," *Punch*, June 17, 880–883.

Chermayeff, S. (1964c) "The Architectural Condition", *Architectural Association Journal*, July/August, 79, 45–50.

Chermayeff, S. (1964d) "From the Other End of the Spectrum," *Image* 2, 17–23.

Chermayeff, S. (1964e) "Luncheon Speaker," in Boston Architectural Center (ed.) *Architecture and the Computer*, Boston, MA: Boston Architectural Center, 21–22.

Chermayeff, S. (1970) "No Simple Answers," *Modulus* 5, 5–13.

Chermayeff, S. (1971) "Design as Catalyst," *Architecture in Australia Special Issue: The Consequences of Today* 59, 630–637.

Chermayeff, S. (1982) "Environmental Design and Change," in R. Plunz (ed.) *Design and the Public Good*, Cambridge, MA: MIT Press, pp. 63–70.

Chermayeff, S. and Alexander, C. (1963a) *Community and Privacy: Toward a New Architecture of Humanism*, Garden City, NY: Doubleday.

Chermayeff, S. and Alexander, C. (1963b) "The Disappearance of Nature," *Current*, October, 58–63.

Chermayeff, S. and Tzonis, A. (1971) *Shape of Community*, Middlesex: Penguin.

Chrisman, N. (2004) *Charting the Unknown: How Computer Mapping at Harvard Became GIS*, Boston, MA: ESRI Press.

Corbett, S. (1955) *Cape Cod's Way*, New York: Crowell Comp.

Damore, L. (1967) *The Cape Cod Years of John Fitzgerald Kennedy*, Englewood Cliffs, NJ: Prentice-Hall.

Denney, R.N. (1961) *Ruth N. Denney, Center of Urban Studies, MIT and Harvard, to Chermayeff, June 22.* [Letter] Box 2, Serge Chermayeff Architectural Records and Papers, Avery Library, Columbia University.

Fisher, H. (1964) "A Technique for Processing Complex Statistical Data into Meaningful Graphic Form," in Boston Architectural Center (ed.) *Architecture and the Computer*, Boston, MA: Boston Architectural Center, 13–18.

Fisher, H. (1982) *Mapping Information: The Graphic Display of Quantitative Information*, Cambridge: ABT Books.

Floyd, P. (1963) *Peter Floyd to Chermayeff, October 24.* [Letter] Box 2, Serge Chermayeff Architectural Records and Papers, Avery Library, Columbia University.

Foster, C.H.W. (1985) *The Cape Cod National Seashore: A Landmark Alliance*, Hanover, NH: University Press of New England.

Friedlander, M. (1960) *Marc Friedlander, Athenaeum Publishers, to Chermayeff, August 19.* [Letter] Box 2, Serge Chermayeff Architectural Records and Papers, Avery Library, Columbia University.

Grabow, S. (1983) *Christopher Alexander: The Search for a New Paradigm in Architecture*, Boston, MA: Oriel Press.

Gropius, W. (1955) *Scope of Total Architecture*, New York: Harper & Brothers.

32 *Peder Anker*

Gropius, W. (1956) "Apollo in the Democracy," in Gropius, W. (ed.) *Apollo in the Democracy*, New York: McGraw.

Gropius, W. (1963a) "On the Desirable Character of Design for the Cape Cod National Seashore" *Letter to the National Park Service, undated*. [Letter] Cape Cod Park files, Department of Interior Archive.

Gropius, W. (1963b) *Walter Gropius to Chermayeff, September 16*. [Letter] Box 2, Serge Chermayeff Architectural Records and Papers, Avery Library, Columbia University.

Gropius, W. (1963c) *Walter Gropius to Chermayeff, November 13*. [Letter] Box 2, Serge Chermayeff Architectural Records and Papers, Avery Library, Columbia University.

Gropius, W. (1964) "Computers for Architectural Design," in Boston Architectural Center (ed.) *Architecture and the Computer*, Boston, MA: Boston Architectural Center, 41.

Gutheim, F. (1964) "Room for All", *The Nation* 198, 54.

Hills, G.A. (1974) "A Philosophical Approach to Landscape Planning," *Landscape Planning* 1, 339–371.

Holborn, F.L. (1959) *Frederick L. Holborn to Serge Chermayeff, December 15*. [Letter] Box 1, Serge Chermayeff Architectural Records and Papers, Avery Library, Columbia University.

Jaffe, N. (1964) "Architects Weigh Computers' Uses," *New York Times*, December 6, 69.

Kennedy, J.F. (1959) *John F. Kennedy to Serge Chermayeff, October 16*. [Letter] Box 1, Serge Chermayeff Architectural Records and Papers, Avery Library, Columbia University.

Kneedler-Schad, L., Lacy, K. and Lowenthal, L. (1995) *Cultural Landscape Report for Fort Hill*, Boston, MA: National Park Service.

Landstrom, K.S. (1960) *Karl S. Landstrom to Serge Chermayeff, November 21*. [Letter] Box 1, Serge Chermayeff Architectural Records and Papers, Avery Library, Columbia University.

Lee, R.F. (1960) *Ronald F. Lee, Regional Director of the United States Department of the Interior to Serge Chermayeff, September 18*. [Letter] Box 1, Serge Chermayeff Architectural Records and Papers, Avery Library, Columbia University.

LeMessurier, W.J. (1964) "Use of the Computer in Typical Building Engineering Situations and Its Future Development," in Boston Architectural Center (ed.) *Architecture and the Computer*, Boston, MA: Boston Architectural Center, 4–6.

Lewis, P.H. (1964) "The Landscape Resources of Wisconsin", in T.H. Rupert (ed.) *Natural Resources of Wisconsin*, Madison, WI: Department of Resource Development, pp. 130–142.

Lystra, M. (2017) "Drawing Natures: US Highway Location, Representational Techniques and the Rise of Ecological Design", *Journal of Design History* 302, 157–174.

Maass, A. (1963) *Arthur Maass to Chermayeff, November 27*. [Letter] Box 2, Serge Chermayeff Architectural Records and Papers, Avery Library, Columbia University.

McCagg, E.K., III (1960a) *Edward K. McCagg III to Jose Luis Sert, May 10*. [Letter] Box 1, Serge Chermayeff Architectural Records and Papers, Avery Library, Columbia University.

Computing environmental design   33

McCagg, E.K., III (1960b) *Edward K. McCagg III to the Fculty GSD, September 14*. [Letter] Box 1, Serge Chermayeff Architectural Records and Papers, Avery Library, Columbia University.

McCagg, E.K., III (1961) *Edward K. McCagg III to Jose Luis Sert, May 15*. [Letter] Box 1, Serge Chermayeff Architectural Records and Papers, Avery Library, Columbia University.

McHarg, I.L. (1969) *Design with Nature*, Garden City, NY: Doubleday.

McMahon, P. and Cipriani, C. (2014) *Cape Cod Modern: Midcentury Architecture and Community on the Outer Cape*, New York: Metropolis Books.

Millon, H. (1964) "Panel Discussion," in Boston Architectural Center (ed.) *Architecture and the Computer*, Boston, MA: Boston Architectural Center, 44.

Moholy-Nagy, L. (1938) "Why Bauhaus Education?," *Shelter* March, 8–21.

Mulloney, S. (1998) *Traces of Thoreau: A Cape Cod Journey*, Boston, MA: Northeastern University Press.

Mumford, L. (1962) *Lewis Mumford to Chermayeff, December 26*. [Letter] Box 2, Serge Chermayeff Architectural Records and Papers, Avery Library, Columbia University.

O'Brian, G. (1964) "Designed for Privacy," *New York Times*, September 13, 116.

Payne, H.M. (1964) "Welcome," in Boston Architectural Center (ed.) *Architecture and the Computer*, Boston, MA: Boston Architectural Center, 1.

Powers, A. (2001) *Serge Chermayeff: Designer Architect Teacher*, London: RIBA Pub.

Pusey, N.M. (1962) *Pusey to Chermayeff, February 20*. [Letter] Box 1, Serge Chermayeff Architectural Records and Papers, Avery Library, Columbia University.

Rexroth, K. (1963) "Forward," in S. Chermayeff and C. Alexander (eds.) *Community and Privacy: Toward a New Architecture of Humanism*, Garden City, NY: Doubleday, pp. 13–17.

Rexroth, K. (1964) "On Fouling up Our Nests," *Book Week*, March 8.

Riehl, C. (1976) *Constance F. Riehl at Doubleday to Chermayeff, March 30*. [Letter] Box 2, Serge Chermayeff Architectural Records and Papers, Avery Library, Columbia University.

Rowntree, D. (1964) "Chermayeff Architect," *The Guardian*, April 29.

Rowntree, D. (1966) "The Place of the Race (review)," *The Guardian*, November 25.

Russell, L.G. (1964) "New Methods of Environmental Analysis," in Boston Architectural Center (ed.) *Architecture and the Computer*, Boston, MA: Boston Architectural Center, 7–9.

Sargent, D.K. (1964) "Introduction," in Boston Architectural Center (ed.) *Architecture and the Computer*, Boston, MA: Boston Architectural Center, 2–3.

Schneider, P. (2000) *The Enduring Shore: A History of Cape Cod, Martha's Vineyard and Nantucket*, New York: Henry Holt.

Sert, J.L. (1961a) *Jose Luis Sert to Chermayeff, June 14*. [Letter] Box 1, Serge Chermayeff Architectural Records and Papers, Avery Library, Columbia University.

Sert, J.L. (1961b) *Jose Luis Sert to Chermayeff, December 8*. [Letter] Box 1, Serge Chermayeff Architectural Records and Papers, Avery Library, Columbia University.

Steenson, M.W. (2009) "Problems before Patterns: A Different Look at Christopher Alexander and Pattern Languages," *Interactions*, 16(2), 20–23.

Steinitz, C., Parker, P. and Jordan, L. (1976) "Hand-Drawn Overlays: Their History and Prospective Uses," *Landscape Architecture Sept*, 66 44–55.

34 *Peder Anker*

Temko, A. (1963a) "Things are Getting Too Crowded, Too Mechanized and Too Noisy (review)," *New York Times Book Review*, October 13, 343.

Temko, A. (1963b) *Allen Temko to Chermayeff, December 24.* [Letter] Box 2, Serge Chermayeff Architectural Records and Papers, Avery Library, Columbia University.

Thoreau, H.D. (1961) *Cape Cod*, New York: Thomas Y. Crowell Company.

Vardouli, T. (2015) "Making Use: Attitudes to Human-Artifact Engagements," *Design Studies* 41, 137–161.

Von Eckardt, W. (1964) "Architecture," *Library Journal*, 89, 620.

3 The work of design and the design of work

Olivetti and the political economy of its early computers

AnnMarie Brennan

In 1962, the Italian periodical *Almanacco Letterario Bompiani* focused on the theme of early computers and their application to the field of literature. The ground-breaking issue made it one of the first publications to introduce the concept of computing and cybernetic thinking and its effect on society and culture. The content of the articles presented the application of computing technology to the arts; with essays from writers discussing the history of binary calculation, to scholars decoding French medieval literature, to artists programming computers to compose musical scores and poetry.[1]

The Italian business machine company Olivetti sponsored the issue as a means to promote the company's entry into computing and publicize the creation of Italy's first commercial mainframe computer, the Elea 9003 (see Figure 3.1).

One of the first pages of the issue featured an Olivetti advertisement publicizing its innovative work in the field of computers. It did not contain an image of the computer, only an abstract design representing its electronics division and the following text:

> In the framework of integral mechanization and automation, Olivetti presents electronic machines of high capacity and flexibility for the calculation and processing of data. From scientific institutes to industrial research centers, from theoretical research to production, administration, and commerce: the range of applications and uses of Olivetti electronic machines are as vast as human labor.
>
> (Olivetti 1961)

At the time, Olivetti was predominately known throughout the world as the Italian manufacturer of stylish typewriters and calculators, yet it began to intuit how its computers would reorganize traditional notions of work. Its operations included the establishment of a factory town in Ivrea, distinguishing itself from other firms by providing its employees with a generous array of amenities and social services uncommon in the rest of Italy, such as employee housing, transportation, medical services, childcare, and educational and

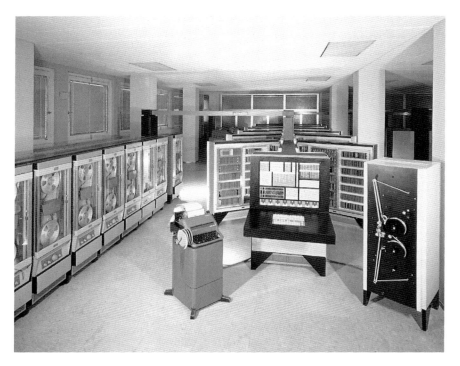

Figure 3.1 The Olivetti Elea 9003 mainframe computer was invented by an Olivetti team lead by engineer Mario Tchou. The system structure and interface were designed by Ettore Sottsass assisted by Andries Van Onck. (Associazione Archivio Storico Olivetti, Ivrea, Italy).

training facilities. This management approach, fostered by a political environment dominated by a Socialist imperative, sought to *reform* capitalism, rather than overthrow these systems of production. This reform occurred through the application of rational scientific principles of management to production processes and assembly lines, with the intention of alleviating the fatigue of manual labor, and elevating the welfare of the factory worker by mitigating the exploitative effects of capitalism. (Wright 2002: 50) The solution to assuaging the drudgery of the factory floor worker was found in the development of programmable machine tool automation.

Olivetti was one of the most successful companies in the postwar era of the Italian economic miracle, with a global distribution network accounting for 30% of global sales of mechanical typewriters and over 30% of adding and accounting machines. This economic success was fostered by the company's goal of making machine production a humanistic endeavor of enlightened cultural and social values coupled with advanced technical knowledge. To assuage the public's fear that Olivetti machines would compromise the traditions of Italian culture with the manufacturing of electronic computers, the company marketed its products as both works of art and as mythical instruments to further the progressive goals of society through the principles of good design.

This essay revisits a chapter in the history of the design and production of early computers in Italy. It looks at the creation of the Olivetti Elea 9003 and the company's manufacturing of numerically-controlled machine tools in order to examine their effect on transforming traditional modes of production. These machines, along with their theorization by writers and artists, brought about a new strategy of design – parametric thinking – to Olivetti designers. With these changes, members of the Workerist movement began to theorize the changing role of the factory worker, and discovered that the design and engineering of Olivetti computers and numerically-controlled (NC) machines generated a new type of worker called "the technician." This essay illustrates the connection between the Olivetti designers and engineers who created these machines and the design of the novel modes of labor these new machines conjured. All of these events and characters converged around one of the major industries in Italy at the time: the Olivetti Company.

Olivetti and computing

To present the history of the Olivetti ELEA 9003 mainframe computer is to not only recite the origin story of the Electronics Division at the company, but to present the early history of computing in Italy.

In 1954, the only computers existing in Italy were imported from overseas. With funds from the Marshall Plan, the Politecnico di Milano purchased a CRC102A mainframe computer designed at MIT costing $115,000. In addition to the university, private companies such as Pirelli would use the computer to study the electricity passing through the cable grid and the Edison company for calculations related to hydroelectric dams (Iannitti 2001: 248). The Institute for Calculation Applications at the Italian Research Council (CNR) in Naples purchased a Ferranti Mark 1 mainframe computer from the University of Manchester in 1955.

At the University of Pisa, the renowned scientist Enrico Fermi suggested that the university invest 150 million lire (about €2 million today) to create its own Italian electronic computer, rather than import a foreign one. This challenge would serve as a crucial instrument for scientific research; its development would increase the necessary technical knowledge in computing and electronics in Italy (Pierotti and Del Furia 2009: 19). Called the *Calcolatrice Elettronica Pisana* (CEP), this initiative required a private co-sponsor and Olivetti volunteered to collaborate, contributing funding and the expertise of a group of highly skilled engineers, physicists, and technicians to work alongside scientists from the University of Pisa. To many it seemed incomprehensible for the successful company to divert its energy and financial

38 *AnnMarie Brennan*

resources toward a totally new endeavor into an unknown field. However, the director of the company, Adriano Olivetti, was convinced that if his company did not develop electronic business machines, it would be left behind and its products deemed obsolete.

In 1954, Adriano Olivetti and his son Roberto, head of the Olivetti Electronics Division, traveled to New York and met the Italo-Chinese electrical engineer Mario Tchou.[2] They invited him to return to Italy to lead the CEP team at the Olivetti Electronic Research Laboratory located in Barbaricina, outside of Pisa.[3] He moved to Italy the next year, and after two years of development, Tchou and his team presented their first computer, Machine Zero (aka Elea 9001) in the spring of 1957. The mainframe computer, composed of knots of cables and wires with large cumbersome cathode tubes and valves systems based on the von Neumann machine, was formed by input/output units, an arithmetic unit, a control unit determining the sequence of operations, and the central memory core, which processes both programs and data (Parolini 2015). The thermionic valves, traditionally used in radio electronics, were the size of eggs and had a very high internal operating temperature thus requiring their own airconditioning system (Tarantini 1960: 47). Despite these setbacks, Machine Zero was the first fully electronic computer, released a few months before IBM's 709 vacuum tube mainframe computer (De Biase and Caravita 2013).

Two significant problems with Machine Zero entailed the need to switch from the signal amplification system of thermionic values to a more efficient system, and the issue of deciding on the best way to construct the memory core. Work on the second computer, Elea 9002, was a hybrid of both valves and transistors, with the transistors used for the management of the perforated tapes (programming). Tchou intuited that the technology of future computing would be based on the transistor, and therefore decided to build the computer entirely on a transistor architecture (Iannitti 2001: 251). The team abandoned the Elea 9002 model and started anew with a third computer model using only diode-transistor logic.[4] This change allowed for a reduction in the size of the machines and eliminated the need for intense cooling.

In addition, the programming capabilities of the Elea 9002 were inadequate. To address the problem, Adriano Olivetti assembled a group of mathematicians to concentrate on the programming and the development of software. For the memory, a magnetic core for data processing was manufactured, consisting of 30,000 circuits of fine copper wires wrapped around tiny rings of magnetized ferrite in the form of a square. The magnetic core allowed the computer to have the significant ability of multiprogramming, which entailed running three programs simultaneously. These innovations would lead to the world's first transistor-based computer, named the Elea 9003 (Pierotti and Del Furia 2009: 19–22; Parolini 2015).

New forms: the Olivetti Elea 9003 mainframe computer

The technical research term for the first Italian computer was the *Elaboratore Elettronico Automatico* (Automatic Electronic Processor), yet once the computer was ready for mass production, Franco Fortini, a noted writer/poet and political intellectual working in the Olivetti Advertising Office, named the Olivetti mainframe computer series after the ancient Greek Eleatic school of philosophy, science, and mathematics located in southern Italy. Known for seeking clarity and truth through mathematics, Fortini thought the name Elea evoked the ideals of the Olivetti Company, which envisioned itself, like the historic school, as the synthesis of the enlightened values of humanistic culture with technological advancement.

Olivetti moved the computer laboratory from Barbaricina closer to the company headquarters in Borgo Lombardo outside of Milan, once Tchou and his team reduced the size and improved the computer's functioning with a transistor architecture. In this way, the engineering and design team could fast-track its development and prepare the Elea 9003 to transition from an experimental machine into a viable computer product for the international market where it sold for about 800 million lire; equivalent to €9.2 million today. With such a high price, the market for the Elea 9003 consisted of institutions such as large companies, universities, and banks. Olivetti eventually sold a total of 40 models of the Elea 9003 within the Italian and international markets. However before it was sold, the mainframe computer required a manageable form and designed interface to make it a marketable product.

This task was assigned to the Italian architect/designer Ettore Sottsass Jr. Hired as the head designer for the Olivetti Electronics Division in 1958, Sottsass considered the project to design the computer as a significant opportunity to provide some identifiable form to an entirely new piece of electronic computing technology for a company that previously only manufactured mechanical machines: "How do you make an entire electronics industry from scratch? How is it done and what does it mean to give shape to a world inhabited by electronic equipment?" (Sottsass 2002: 312).

Together with Tchou and Roberto Olivetti, Sottsass shared a similar utopian vision of creating tools for a renewed bourgeois intellectual class that would work, collaboratively, in an enlightened neo-capitalist society (Sottsass 2002: 313). The challenge of designing one of the first computers entailed having no real precedents and, unlike mechanical machines, the form did not follow the function. "Designing electronic equipment," according to Sottsass, "means giving shape to organisms or parts of organisms that never have a well-designed physiognomy" (Sottsass 1958: 27). The character of the large mainframe computer was more akin to furniture than machines, and that when operating the system, the users were surrounded by the computer, as if "moving around and inside a room" (Sottsass 1961b). The goal of the designer was to create "design complexes of

Figure 3.2 The Elea 9003 mainframe computer is a system designed by Ettore Sottsass comprised of modules of standard metal cabinets connected by a series of overhead busways. (Associazione Archivio Storico Olivetti, Ivrea, Italy).

machines, that is, to create landscapes, or if you want furniture, or if you want architectures, or if you want atmospheres" (Sottsass 1962: 5). Sottsass' final result for the computer featured a modular-based system designed to be like a type of game or kit of parts: flexible within a set of parameters, easily assembled, delivered, and then re-assembled and re-configured within a grid-like configuration in a client's laboratory or office basement (see Figure 3.2).

The modules consisted of a series of light, small-volume cabinets that connected to create a more extensive, but flexible structure that allowed the possibility of adding additional machines. The metal framed cabinets with interchangeable silver anodized aluminum covers accommodated different machines, from the tape readers to the governors, or memory cores. Other covers with a glass panel were available for units requiring visibility, such as the perforated tape band reader machine (see Figure 3.3).

Figure 3.3 The central control console with the photoelectric perforated band reading unit on the right. (Associazione Archivio Storico Olivetti, Ivrea, Italy).

42 *AnnMarie Brennan*

A distinct design feature setting the Elea 9003 apart from its competitor, the IBM 360, was the suspended busways hung above the cabinets to carry the cables and wires for the power supply and signaling lines. Rather than storing these wires in a cavity under the floor, the structural configuration

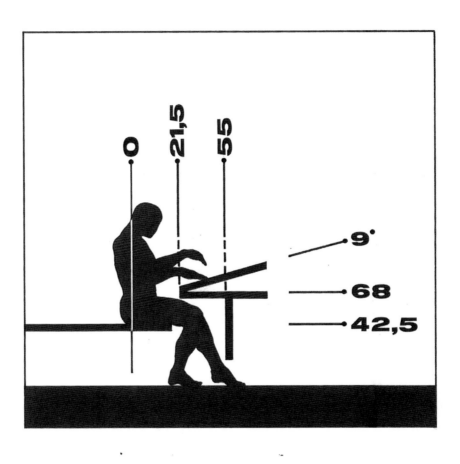

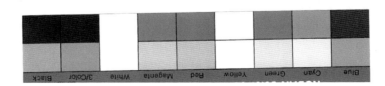

Figure 3.4 Ettore Sottsass, graphic design for a brochure of the Elea, Olivetti, ergonomic study, n.d. (1957–1960). (CSAC, Università di Parma.)

The work of design and the design of work   43

was less expensive and allowed the designers to consider the entire computer complex of machines as a variable unit that accommodates any space (Sottsass 1959). The busways, painted in red and supported on steel rods, provide a grid-like modular structure to the organization of the cabinets.

In a study commissioned by Olivetti, Sottsass researched the ergonomics of the human/machine relationship to re-imagine the workspace (see Figure 3.4). He studied how the body interacts with these new machines, furniture, and other office equipment, in an effort to design according to the choreography of an actor's performance on a stage rather than measure a static, rationalized body adjacent to a machine (Zanella 2018: 27). This design objective was accomplished by concentrating the design into parts which the human operator communicated or interacted with the computer in each of the recurrent Elea iterations: keyboards, supports, and covers that tilt (Sottsass 1958: 28). The cabinet height, kept at a maximum of 150cm, permitted users to look over them, make eye contact, and converse with others in the room. Sottsass's modular design strategy for the Elea 9003 was similar to that of his IBM contemporary Eliot Noyes, where the System/360 consisted of two elements: the wall and the module. Unlike the System/360, the Elea 9003 had the overhead busway instead of a wall, and Noyes based his ergonomic dimensions on the work on anthropometric proportions of Henry Dreyfuss (Harwood 2011: 88–99). Sottsass conducted his own ergonomic studies so it is unlikely that the work of Dreyfuss influenced him in designing the Elea 9003 since the book, *The Measure of Man*, was published in 1959, a year after the Elea 9003 was completed.

Other means of integrating symbolic communications into the Elea design occurred through the strategic use of color in the electronic data processing system, controlled through a color-coded console containing a vertical panel with numerous lights and symbols and a sloping keyboard. This control unit included a tape punch and a tape punch reader for the input/output operations in which the user understood the processes and functioning of the system and inserted commands using the keyboard. Indeed, the computer form challenge consigned to Sottsass was not simply about designing a single object, or atmosphere, but about designing a new form of work, of immaterial labor, arising from the emergence of computers.

New theories: Ulm School of Design

Assisting Sottsass in the development of design drawings for the Elea 9003 were two graduates from the Ulm School of Design (Hochschule für Gestaltung Ulm) in Germany: the Dutch designer Andries Van Onck and Czech designer Hans von Klier.[5] The Ulm School of Design served as

44 AnnMarie Brennan

a postwar reincarnation of the Bauhaus, with some design scholars claiming that Italy played a similar role for graduates and instructors from the Ulm School in the way that the United States operated as the destination for many noted design emigres from the Bauhaus before and during World War II (Anceschi and Tanca 1984: 25). While actual computers did not exist at the Ulm School, it was at the forefront of teaching theories of information and cybernetic thinking. Regarded as the incubus for new concepts of art in the cybernetic era, the school served as an intellectual reference point for the

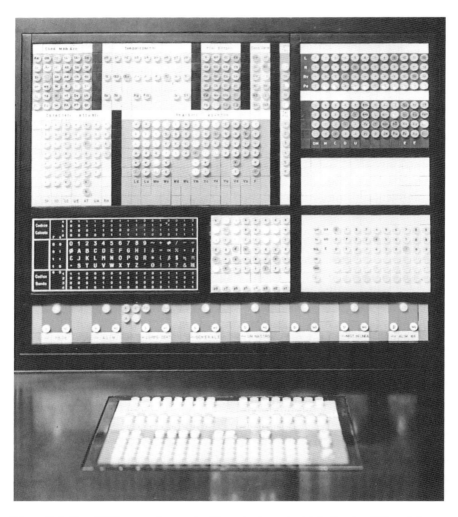

Figure 3.5 Elea 9003 central console. (Associazione Archivio Storico Olivetti, Ivrea, Italy.)

Milanese design scene (Anceschi and Tanca 1984: 25; Riccini 2014). Before the arrival of computers, the Ulm curriculum promoted the synthesis of science and design to advance a new scientific humanism premised on methodology and the issues pertaining to industrial culture (Maldonado and Bonsiepe 1964: 10). The director, artist, and designer Tomás Maldonado assigned students exercises devoted to the fundamentals of design, semiotics, information technology, scientific operationalism, and computational and parametric design thinking, thereby exposing the student cohort to "computational design thinking without the machine" (Neves et al. 2014: 3).

The relationship between the Ulm School of Design and Italy was channeled through the Olivetti Company. Interested in exchanging ideas between Ulm and the Milanese design scene, Sottsass invited Maldonado to work on a project involving a new symbol design for the displays and controls of the Elea 9003 console (Mori 2013; Riccini 2014; Neves et al. 2014: 15–16).

The original console (see Figure 3.5) contained command buttons using words and abbreviations in Italian however this posed a problem as the language-based system was not suitable for international use. To resolve the issue, Maldonado designed a universal symbolic alphabet. His approach entailed analyzing existing sign systems from cartography, meteorology, typography, electrical circuit design, chemistry, and music to create a new symbolic code for electronic data processing machines. Once he assembled an inventory of signs, Maldonado extracted a visual language to create another two classes of signs: basic signs functioning as nouns in grammar, and determinatives, which functioned as adjectives and verbs (Maldonado 1963: 20–24). The project included re-designing the modular system for lights, buttons, symbol carriers, and the structure containing these parts.

While never adopted for the Elea 9003, this new symbolic language project demonstrates how the designers re-examined the human/machines interface and investigated how humans communicate with machines. In 1959, the design for the Elea 9003 was finalized and the computer put into production, winning the prestigious Compasso D'Oro medal for that year.

Metadesign and machine tools

While assisting on the design of the Elea 9003, Van Onck, after graduating from Ulm, worked at the Olivetti Research Centre. It was there, through his research on machines, that he gained early insight into the direct effect of computing machines on the field of design and the advantages of these machines in form-making. He became familiar with NC machine tools (what would become continuous numerically-controlled machines, or CNC). These automated machines were the next step in the evolution of machines; merging the programming power of a computer with the operations of a machine tool.

46 *AnnMarie Brennan*

The pairing of the technology behind the Elea 9003 with the company's machine tool division seemed logical, as Ezio Testore, head of the Olivetti Technical Services Department noted: "Almost simultaneously, with the development of electronic calculators, the idea of applying the numerical control to the machine tool was born, precisely in this sector where the results derived from computing would have been substantial" (Testore 1964: 3). The role of the designer in creating the technologically complex project of the machine tool involves the careful organization of the operator/machine working space and addressing issues such as accident prevention, productivity, and ergonomics (Gregotti 1998: 320). In the case of numerically-controlled machine tools, the design strategy included the electronic side of the project, its power-generating, governing unit, and the actual design of the machine tool.

Two of the most notable Olivetti NC machines were the Auctor and Horizon 3 automatic series, designed by Rodolfo Bonetto, a significant Olivetti designer who taught at the Ulm School of Design. He worked with students on designing the bodywork for a car and on the Olivetti numerically-controlled machine tool Auctor-Multiplex machining center (Bonetto 1963: 42; Burdek 2005).

These sophisticated complexes, called "machining centers," were designed and engineered to configure multiple types of machining operations, combining multiple tools into one; eliminating the need for the skilled laborers. In 1965, the Auctor-Multiplex (see Figure 3.6) contained 12 different tools for manufacturing pieces, and included the Inspector 16–6, a precision measuring device that could measure the accuracy of machined parts.[6] The multiscope machines and machining centers did not only improve productivity but were "a new technological process philosophy [that] has come to change traditional systems of work fundamentally" (Testore 1966: 10). As with the design for the Elea 9003, the scheme for the Olivetti NC machine tools and machining centers involved the designing and the reorganization of labor.

The objective to automate production processes in Italy differed from contemporaneous development of NC machines in the United States. For American engineers, the challenge of machine tool automation primarily addressed the military's need for total control of production in order to monitor quality, allow for flexibility in manufacturing for strategic purposes, and secure the nation's vital technological innovations (Noble 1984: 85). Conversely in Italy, the advancement of NC machines increased productivity, accuracy, and precision, and modernized the country's industry, yet most significant impetus for NC development was to minimize fatigue as part of the socialist political imperative of capitalist reform.

NC machine tools could manufacture complex items such as turbines, other machine tools, and textile and typographic machines which previously required highly skilled workers (Testore 1964: 3). These types of highly skilled workers were becoming more and more difficult to find as that level of skill required years of training and instruction. Testore claimed that such

Figure 3.6 Olivetti Auctor 25A multiplex machine tool center by Rodolfo Bonetto, 1967. (Associazione Archivio Storico Olivetti, Ivrea, Italy.)

a workforce with that type of specialized knowledge and professional training would prefer to work in an office rather than on the workshop floor, stating,

> Between the white coat and the overalls, there is no doubt that, as of now, and more than ever, young workers, after having an intense period of preparation in the professional schools, do not hesitate to choose: they want to carry out office work.... The specialist worker has turned into a programmer.
>
> (Testore 1964: 3)

48   *AnnMarie Brennan*

Moreover, the training for operating the NC machine was reduced from a few years to a few weeks – similar to the time it took to learn the new programming language.

Testore describes the factory of the future as the result of the NC revolution in the mechanical workshop:

> [It will be] composed of machine tools equipped with numerical controlled units, and will require only manual work for the loading of blanks and removing of the finished parts, and possibly for the replacement of tools. Man's [sic] labor is reduced to a minimum. The finished piece does not need more than a careful check.
>
> (Testore 1964: 3)

In order to produce a new model of typewriter or calculator, the Machine and Tool Production Department needed to manufacture several thousand tools and modify and repair existing tools. Eventually, the Olivetti Company would produce "at least five thousand different tools each year" (D'Auria 1962: 10). At Olivetti, these machining centers subsumed the production line to improve productivity and evolved into the workshop itself, requiring "only one or a few workmen to perform the work, which previously required the employment of hundreds of persons"[7] (Testore 1966: 10). Engineer Roberto Graziosi, head of the Olivetti Machine Tool Division Project Office, described the manufacturing process using machine tools, claiming "from the technical point of view, it is possible to perfect automatic machines where the worker merely places the article in position and presses the starter button" (Graziosi 1964: 6).

Van Onck had access to the company's numerically-controlled machine tools and machine tool division, Officina Meccanica Olivetti in Ivrea. With a background in the theory of computational and parametric design at Ulm and his practical experience at Olivetti, Van Onck quickly understood the design advantages that NC machines introduced to the discipline. In 1964, he demonstrated in an article titled "Metadesign" that he was not only one of the first designers to understand the benefits of NC manufacturing, but was perhaps one of the first designers to fully comprehend the parametric rules and mathematics behind this method of production and the possibilities it offered in generating forms in the design process (Van Onck 1964).

In his article, Van Onck challenges the industrial design discipline and its focus on the arbitrary association with style and "good design" by positing an alternative way to assess the success or failure of designed objects formed by rational modes of fabrication, with a "logical procedure of form finding [that] would now be replaced by a precise theory of values which are integral to architecture's project" (Van Onck 1964: 52). Metadesign was not dependent on the motion or force of air or water that formed the most optimized shape of a car, boat, or airplane; instead the kinematics

The work of design and the design of work   49

involved the rotation, smoothing, and rounding operations which could be carried out with NC fabrication machines, defined by Van Onck as a "system composed on moving elements and parameters" (Van Onck 1964: 54–55). The setting of parameters using an algebraic formula became a prerequisite of designing with computers and a necessity for coding NC machines, and therefore the form generated was the result of NC technology programming criteria. As Van Onck claimed, "As the NC tool tracked precise automorphisms (the kinematic patterns related to formal transformations), so would it shift the field's understanding of form" (Van Onck 1964: 57).

In describing this new way of understanding form in a state of becoming and being formed, he was relating a new mode of designing according to parametrics with an emphasis on topology. Van Onck illustrates his argument in the section "Metadesign Instruments" with an experiment he conducted at the Olivetti Central Research Laboratory, where every twelve hours a 20 x 20 x 20 mm quartz cube underwent continuous abrasive action by a special NC machine. The cube was replaced with a new one every 12 hours in order to keep the quality of cubes constant in the machine and to observe the series of curves in successive stages of the constant process. Through processing the cubes in this manner he claimed:

> [We] have revealed a series of curves that resemble the family of curves defined by the formula, where n = 2 represents a circle, and where the more n tends toward (infinity), the more the form tends to represent a square. The last object visible in the photograph, extracted after 290 hours, is almost spherical.
>
> (Van Onck 1964: 55–56)

These automated machine tools, according to Van Onck, add an element of artisanal character that remains with the product throughout the production cycle. He cited a passage from a catalog for the *Olivetti System for Continuous Numerical Control of Machine Tools*, explaining that technological and geometric information of the object to be machined is translated directly into the movement of the machine tool. This process, categorized into three phases: a programming phase, a processing phase, and a phase of execution (Van Onck 1964: 57). The geometric information is transcribed, through the programming language, onto a perforated band and sent for data processing at the Olivetti Calculation Center. Once the magnetic tape was programmed, it was sent to the workshop so that the NC machine tool could execute the program and manufacture the piece.

NC machining, according to Van Onck, is more flexible, more precise, and allows for faster verification of the design (rapid prototyping). In terms of form, the NC machine is conducive to producing profiles of straight lines and arcs of circles with the addition of parabolas and ellipses (Van Onck 1964: 57). The advantages, Van Onck points out, included the

50 *AnnMarie Brennan*

elimination of errors and dead times, highly specialized machines, and, most importantly, highly specialized workers.

"New forces"

These changes in the technological and economic forces of an automated workflow of programmed assembly lines and human/machine configurations of NC machines would not go unnoticed. Indeed, these shifts in the mode of production converged to prepare fertile ground for the growth of a new political movement based on a re-interpretation of Marxism called *Operaismo*, or Workerism. The initial objective of this group was to deal with the growing antagonism between classes and examine the working conditions within Italian industry through a critique of political economy by unearthing the dynamic position of the worker within a technologically-driven mode of production in a system of advanced global capitalism (Alquati 1962). Beginning with the inaugural issue in 1961, the Workerists established the organ *Quaderni Rossi*, a journal premised upon the group's belief that if production was the main driving force behind economic and cultural growth in Italian postwar society, *the worker*, therefore, was the central force behind heightened production within capitalist relations, and ultimately the creation of the Italian Economic Miracle. The leading founders of the group were the Italian Marxists Raniero Panzieri, Antonio Negri, Alberto Asor Rosa, Mario Tronti, and Romano Alquati, among others, who were dissident members of the Italian Communist (PCI) and Socialist (PSI) parties.

Workerism illuminated the paradoxical position of the factory worker as a crucial subject situated within capital while, at the same time, positioned in opposition to it. The group maintained that profit through capitalist development was achieved by a steady rate of growth by means of controlling labor. This occurred through capital re-structuring, such as introducing innovations in technology, followed by the containment of worker antagonism, and more innovation to alleviate further worker antagonism (Alquati 1962: 155). The cycle would continuously perpetuate, and while the worker was acting negatively on the system of production, for instance in calling for strikes and work stoppages, he/she still functioned as a major productive and beneficial component to capital, *as both a productive and antagonistic force*, since workers' antagonism led to technical innovation and economic growth. This theory contradicted the economic model of Keynes, who claimed that capitalism does not want conflict, but equilibrium.

In order to demonstrate and ground many of their theories, the Workerists implemented a novel method of investigation called "worker's inquiry," a way of interviewing workers derived from practices usually applied by mainstream sociologists and deployed by Human Relations departments of large firms. This method of research directed them toward

The work of design and the design of work   51

a critical examination of large Italian industries to understand the conditions of the working class, placing the FIAT and the Olivetti Company as case studies for their investigations (Panzieri 1994).

The first worker's inquiry by Alquati occurred at the FIAT factory, which was one of the first applications of the Olivetti continuous numerical control systems for manufacturing in their aircraft plants (Brescia 1964: 22). The Olivetti NC milling machine replaced a copying machine to cut the contours of the airplane wing and ribs. According to Riccardo Brescia, an engineer from the Olivetti Numerical Control Systems Division, "Labor and equipment can be reduced because they are replaced by the magnetic tape, while the stocking of spare parts can be eliminated," since any piece required for an airplane could be manufactured on-demand (Brescia 1964: 22).

In Alquati's second inquiry, which took place at the Olivetti factory in Ivrea, he researched the subject of machines, technology, and labor. The *Quaderni Rossi* journalists received access to the workers on the Olivetti factory floor because they worked under the guise of CGIL (union) supporters. Before Adriano Olivetti's death in 1961, the company was perceived by its employees and the general public as a benevolent employer offering benefits and wages superior to any other Italian company. However, the Workerist group saw that after the death of the company's main protagonist, the Olivetti Company exemplified the Socialist and Communist parties' mystification of the relation of production and capital with their belief that the development of advanced machines would reform labor.

Alquati noted that the company's introduction, adherence, and promotion of scientific principles of management, and its cybernetic, human/machine assembly line of NC machines obscured the alienating effects of mechanized labor and the dispersal of class organization (Alquati 1961: 99–112). His article for *Quaderni Rossi*, "Composizione organica del capitale e forza-lavoro alla Olivetti" (Organic composition of capital and labor force at Olivetti), was of unique importance in that it stood as one of the most thorough examinations of class composition at that time, serving as the fundamental basis for the Workerist movement.

Alquati was interested in the correlation between machines and workers, where the former acted as an indicator of working and class relations. Olivetti's journal *Tecnica ed Organizzazione* proselytized the benefits of Taylorist and Bedeaux systems of management to industries throughout the country. Despite the endorsement by unions and Socialists parties, machines became a significant means of capital's dominance over labor (Alquati 1961: 206–208).

By the 1950s, the most significant loss of efficiency in Olivetti factories was identified in the transportation of pieces of partially assembled typewriters and calculators from workstation to workstation (Eddone 1971:6). The new management structure, which replaced Adriano Olivetti after his death in 1961, focused on extracting profit from the production process through the updating of the assembly line and the installation of more automated NC machines in order to create a continuous cybernetic protocol of closed feedback loop of worker and machine (Brennan 2015: 236). Technology, according to the Olivetti managers, resolved production problems of antagonistic human labor, as witnessed in the installation of a "feedback loop" to oversee and regulate the speed of its assembly line.

Alquati saw the potential in targeting the automated assembly line and its effects on the attitudes and morale of the Olivetti workers. His inquiry into Olivetti, along with the article by fellow Workerist Raniero Panzieri, "The Capitalist Use of Machinery: Marx versus the 'Objectivists,'" is premised upon Marx's insight into capital development usurping trades, where the worker, skilled at using a specific tool within a mode of production, was forced to adapt to a new scenario in which he/she became a mere appendage of a large automatic machine like the Olivetti machining centers. The consequences of this shift are found in the reduced costs for the factory owner; however, the workers, now dependent on the machine and the factory as a whole, are displaced as the subject of production by the assembly line. At the same time the previous workers' skills, experience, and knowledge are embodied within the design and organization of the factory machinery. Panzieri continued to point out that technological development is not independent from capital, but rather that technological innovation reciprocally contributes to the increased authority of industry leaders. As methods of production are advanced to counter worker antagonism, the need for capital to control more of the production process grows.

The entire Olivetti factory-city in Ivrea was part of the machinic apparatus that contributed to the advancement of capital, with the "development of capitalist planning as something closely related to that of the capitalist use of machines" (Panzieri 1980: 48). Panzieri's claims were quite abstract, yet Alquati grounded his theories with his practical workers' inquiry into Olivetti and its automated assembly line of NC machine tools:

> Every "new" machine, every innovation expresses the general level and quality of the balance of power between the classes at that time. When we say that the assembly line is more or less a function of manufacturing, we refer to the specific way in which the functions [of assembling] were the historical product of revolutionary struggles determined by the intrinsic character of class exploitation that guides the capitalistic division of labor.
>
> (Alquati 1962: 105)

While in retrospect these observations on the connection between workers and machines may seem obvious, at the time Alquati, Panzieri and other members of the *Quaderni Rossi* were witnessing, first-hand through the case of Olivetti, many of Marx's claims regarding machinery as the main instrument in which capital was able to dominate and overcome an antagonistic labor force.

The work of design and the design of work   53

The potentially subversive "technician"

Alquati and other Workerists discovered the potential in a new category of worker – the Olivetti technician – who was the same, white-coat office worker or engineer who operated the NC machines. This class of worker, created alongside the human/machinic assemblage of the Elea 9003 and NC machines, was strategically positioned to foil the authority of management and industry's use of technology over labor. The technicians were unique in that they were still considered a type of factory worker, laboring among the men and women on the factory floor, but they also possessed a level of access to management, high salaries, and specialized knowledge in the innovative technology of computing and cybernetic systems. Alquati explained,

> [I]n these jobs, where the work is, for the most part, about 'conceiving' the type of information entered in the circuit of valorization (design, planning, revising, maintenance, tooling, etc.) [...] these workers officially symbolize in their 'qualified tasks' the global level of the quality of labor of the working class. These young [technicians], in the real conditions in which the work takes place, are the first to arrive at a class consciousness in new terms.
>
> (Alquati, 1962: 142)

The Olivetti technicians were allowed more movement throughout the factory and access to the machinery and the other workers on the factory floor. Along with their technical knowledge, they had a more global vision of the company and understood the reach of its international communication and distribution networks. With this combination of advanced class consciousness, technical knowledge, and access to the workplace, the technicians were in a strategic position to use those very same systems of capital expansion as a means of sabotage (to clog up the gears of production, so to speak), as well as to exploit their access to these networks as vehicles for communication and organization with other Olivetti workers around the world.

What Alquati described is the realization that counter forces can usurp the same networks and distribution networks used in post-Fordist production and "adapt to the new conditions of post-Fordist production, in line with information systems and network structures" (Hardt and Negri 2004: 80–81). Unlike the disciplinary regimes of the Fordist factory and military institutions dependent upon the creation of an ordered and disciplined subject, the new role of the technician and its form of immaterial labor based on post-Fordist networks of information, communication, and cooperation, began to define a new subjectivity founded on the principles of creativity, communication, and self-organized cooperation.

Conclusion

Olivetti's success in the making of computers was short-lived. The company proclaimed another significant victory in the field of computing after it designed and engineered the world's first desktop computer, the Programma 101 in 1965 (Perotto 1995: 53; Brennan 2015: 236). However, following Adriano's death, Mario Tchou, the head of the electronics laboratory, was killed in a car accident in 1961. Without these two critical leaders in the company, the managerial rivalry and conflict between the mechanical and the electronics divisions proved difficult. Moreover, the company was unable to compete internationally as Italy's burgeoning computing sector did not receive any financial support from the government for research and development that was occurring in other countries. As a result of these factors, the company incurred severe financial loses and was forced to sell the electronics division to the US General Electric company (Perotto 1995: 21–33; Iannitti 2001: 255; Parolini 2015).

The inquiry of Olivetti workers by the *Quaderni Rossi* group was a reversal of forces implemented to uncover the underlying logic of capitalist development through first-hand observation of the designed human/machines assemblages that Olivetti sold and used in its factories. At the heart of their observations was a belief shared by Olivetti and other industrialists at the time – that the politics of production, driven by organization, the technological development of machines, and the division of labor, was the fount of capitalism's power over its labor force. For figures such as Alquati and Panzieri, the Olivetti Company and its automated assembly line was the location where they were able to envision how this new cybernetic human/machine technology of computing and NC machines would forever shift the political economy of production.

Ironically, worker antagonism would finally meet a dead-end when Olivetti workers, the same laborers, designers, and engineers whom Adriano Olivetti theorized as contributing to his industrial-based utopian community in Ivrea were, in effect, developing a new means of production by making innovative electronic machine tools through programming, and thereby displacing the human worker as the central figure in the production process. This shift in the mode of production would ultimately eliminate the factory jobs that initially developed and manufactured these machine tools. Automation, through the implementation of programming languages and numerical control, replaced *homo faber*, the worker who made things, with an era of automated manufacturing and "informationalized" production. The organization and distribution of information, in the form of computer programs, converted a method of production reliant on human labor to one centered on a universal computing machine driven by the flow of information.

Notes

1 Olivetti employed another campaign, the organization and sponsorship of the *Arte Programmata* exhibition, to educate and prepare the public for the forthcoming arrival its personal desktop computer, the Programma 101. See (Brennan 2015).
2 Born in Rome, Tchou was the son of a Chinese diplomat to the Vatican. He was raised and educated in Italy until 1947 when he moved to Washington DC to earn a Bachelor of Electrical Engineering at the Catholic University of America. After graduating, he moved to New York where he first studied at the New York Polytechnic in Brooklyn, earning a Master of Science. He then worked as a consultant in the television and electronic components sector and taught in the Department of Electrical Engineering at Columbia University.
3 Other technicians, physicists, mathematicians, and engineers in the Olivetti research group included Giorgio Sacerdoti, one of the first Italian graduates to complete his thesis on the electronic calculator and who worked on the installation of the Ferranti computer in Naples, Remo Galletti, Franco Filippazzi, Piergiorgio Perotto, Martin Friedmann, a Canadian expert on ferrite core memory structures, and the designer and architect Ettore Sottsass Jr. (Iannitti 2001: 250).
4 Most of the *Notizie Olivetti* n. 78 issue of May 1963 is dedicated to describing the benefits and shift to transistor technology.
5 Von Klier would go on to design the first Olivetti corporate identity style manuals called "the Red books" in 1977.
6 These NC machines brought about the need for Olivetti to develop a new programming system termed PAGET (Galeotti 1964: 18). Both the designer of the object to be machined and the NC technician used PAGET language to transmit the control information to the system in a symbolic form.
7 The first Olivetti NC machine tool was the FAC milling machine for the automatic milling of cams. It received instructions from a perforated tape that was prepared by an Olivetti accounting machine, the Audit 623. By 1963, the company developed the Planer Type Milling Machine with Numerical Controls, Series FPCN. The FP 16 machine model provided four different milling heads powered by 32 horsepower motors. It specialized in cutting a continuous profile under numerical control on three axes and it "assured precision machining of intricate parts for the aeronautic industry" (Olivetti Company 1963).

Bibliography

Alquati, R. (1961) 'Documenti sulla lotta di classe alla FIAT,' *Quaderni Rossi*, n. 1, Sept: 198–215.
Alquati, R. (1962) 'Composizione organica del capitale e forza-lavoro alla Olivetti,' *Quaderni Rossi*, n. 2, Sept: 63–98.
Anceschi, G. and Tanca, P. G. (1984) 'Ulm and Italy: Rodolfo Bonetto, Enzo Fratelli, Pio Mazu, Andries Van Onck, Hans von Klier, and Willy Ramstein,' *Rassagna*, 19/3, 4: 9. 25–33.
Bonetto, R. (1963) 'Educational Activities: Interior and Body-Work of a Car,' *Ulm: Journal of the Hochschule für Gestaltung*, 8/9: 42–45.
Brennan, A. (2015) 'Olivetti: A Work of Art in the Age of Immaterial Labour,' *Journal of Design History*, 28, 3: 235–253.
Brescia, R. (1964) 'Il controllo numerico negli stabilimenti aeronautici FIAT,' *Notizie Olivetti*, 12, 81: July. 22–24.
Burdek, B. E. (2005) *Design: History, Theory and Practice of Product Design*, Basel; Boston: Birkhäuser-Publishers for Architecture.

56 AnnMarie Brennan

D'Auria, A. (1962) 'Le attrezzature nella produzione delle machine per scrivere e da calcolo,' *Notizie Olivetti*, 75, July: 10–14.

De Biase, L. and Caravita, G. (2013) 'Elettronica italiana: una storia con un future,' *Il Contributo italiano alla storia del Pensiero – Tecnica*. (www.treccani.it/enciclope dia/elettronica-italiana-una-storia-con-un-futuro_%28Il-Contributo-italiano-alla-storia-del-Pensiero:-Tecnica%29/)

Eco, U. (1961) 'La forma del disordine,' in Sergio Morando (ed.). *Almanacco Letterario Bompiani. Le applicazioni dei calcolatori elettronici alle scienze morali e alla letteratura*, Milan: Bompiani. 175–176, 186–187.

Eco, U. (1962, 1989) *The Open Work*, Anna Cancogni, trans. Cambridge, MA: Harvard University Press. The first edition was published in Italian in 1962.

Eco, U. (1965) *Arte Programmata*, (exhibition catalogue) Milan: Olivetti, n.p.

Eddone, G. F. (1971) '*Le funzione della formazione del personale in relazione della divisione del lavoro all'intero di un grande industria*,' II. 6 (no publisher listed) Biblioteca Civica Ivrea.

Galeotti, M. (1964) 'La programmazione nel controllo numerico,' *Notizie Olivetti*, 12, 81: July. 18–20.

Graziosi, R. (1964) 'La progettazione delle machine utensili a controllo numerico,' *Notizie Olivetti*, 81, 12: July. 6–8.

Gregotti, V. (1998) *Il disegno del prodotto industrial. Italia 1860–1980*, Milan: Electa.

Hardt, M. and Negri, A. (2004) *Multitude. War and Democracy in the Age of Empire*, New York: Penguin Press.

Harwood, J. (2011) *The Interface. IBM and the Transformation of Corporate Design 1945–1976*, Minnesota: University of Minnesota Press.

Iannitti, S. (2001) 'L'ELEA 9003 e l'avventura informatica Italia,' in S. Semplici (ed.). *Un'azienda e un'utopia. Adriano Olivetti 1945–1960*, Bologna: il Mulino, 247–257.

Maldonado, T. (1963) 'Teacher's Design Work: Symbol System for Electronic Data Processing Machines (1960/61),' *Ulm: Journal of the Hochschule für Gestaltung*, 8/9: 20–24.

Maldonado, T. and Bonsiepe, G. (1964) 'Science and Design,' *Ulm: Journal of the Hochschule für Gestaltung*, 10/11: 10–29.

Mori, E. (2013) 'Ettore Sottsass jr. and the Design of the First Computers Olivetti,' *AIS/Design History and Research*, no. 1. Accessed 11 Dec 2015. www.aisdesign. org/aisd/ettore-sottsass-jr-e-il-design-dei-primi-computer-olivetti

Neves, I. C., Rocha, J. and Duarte, J. P. (2014) 'Computational Design Research in Architecture: The Legacy of the Hochschule fur Gestaltung, Ulm,' *International Journal of Architectural Computing*, 12, 1: 1–25.

Noble, D. F. (1984) *Forces of Production. A Social History of Industrial Automation*, New York: Alfred A. Knopf.

Olivetti (1959) Elea 9003 Manuale Base di Programmazione/Programming manual, https://archive.org/details/Olivetti-Elea9003-ManualeBaseDiProgrammazione/ page/n9, (Accessed 1 Oct 2018).

Olivetti (1960a) 'Film 'Elea Classe 9000.'.www.youtube.com/watch?v=znapjNYK7sE

Olivetti (1960b) 'Dal meccanico al elettronica,' *Notizie Olivetti*, 68: 45–46.

Olivetti (1961) 'Olivetti Elettronica' (advertisement), in Sergio Morando (ed.), *Almanacco Letterario Bompiani. Le applicazioni dei calcolatori elettronici alle scienze morali e alla letteratura*, Milan: Bompiani. n. p.

The work of design and the design of work   57

Olivetti (1966) 'Film 'N/C. Il controllo numerico: una svolta nella storia dell'officina'. www.youtube.com/watch?v=SFFhr20H80E

Olivetti (1968) 'Film 'Divisione controllo numerico'.www.youtube.com/watch?v=cWNdrm-TMFI.

Olivetti Company (1963) '*Planer Type Milling Machines with Numerical Control Series FPCN*,' (brochure), Archivio Storico Olivetti, OMO-OCN 1963.

Panzieri, R. (1980) 'The Capitalist Use of Machinery: Marx Versus the 'Objectivists,'' in P. Slater (ed.). *Outlines of a Critique of Technology*, London: Humanities Press. Originally published as (1961) 'Sull'uso capitalistico delle macchine nel capitalismo,' *Quaderni Rossi*, 1. 55–72.

Panzieri, R. (1994) 'Socialist Uses of Workers Inquiry,' trans. Adrianna Bove. http://libcom.org/library/socialist-uses-workers-inquiry. Originally published in the book of collected Panzieri writings (1994) *Spontaneità e organizzazione. Gli anni dei "Quaderni Rossi" 1959–1964*, Pisa: S. Merli/BFS Edizioni.

Parolini, G. (2015) *Mario Tchou. Ricerca e sviluppo per l'elettronica Olivetti*, Milan: EGEA, e-book.

Perotto, P. G. (1995) *Programma 101. L'invenzione del personal computer: una storia appassionante mai raccontata*, Milan: Sperling & Kupfer Editori.

Pierotti, W. and Del Furia, S. (2009) 'ELEA 9003/02 Il primo computer commerciale a transistor è in una scuola Toscana,' *Rassegna dell'istruzione*, 4: 18–23. www.rassegnaistruzione.it/rivista/rassegna_04_08-9/Pierotti_pag18.pdf

Riccini, R. (2014) 'Tomás Maldonado and the Impact of the Hochschule für Gestaltung Ulm in Italy,' in G. Lees-Maffei and K. Fallan (eds.). *Made in Italy: Rethinking a Century of Italian Design*, London: Bloomsbury, e-book.

Sottsass E. Jr. (1958) 'Forme nuove per I calcolatori elettronici,' *Notizie Olivetti*, 56, 4: 27–29. 50.

Sottsass E. Jr. (1959) 'Disegno dei calcolatori elettronici Olivetti,' *Stile Industria*, 22: 5–6.

Sottsass E. Jr. (1961a) "L'Elaboratore elettronico Olivetti Elea classe 9000',' *Stile Industria*, 31: 3–13.

Sottsass E. Jr. (1961b) 'Paesaggio elettronico,' *Domus*, 381: 39–46.

Sottsass E. Jr. (1962) 'Automatizzazione e design,' *Stile Industria*, 37, 4: 5.

Sottsass E. Jr. (2002) 'Esperienza con Olivetti, 1979,' in M. Carboni and B. Radici (eds.). *Scritti 1946 – 2001*, Vicenza: Neri Pozza, 312–321.

Tarantini, D. (1960) 'La scienza diventa tecnica,' *Notizie Olivetti*, 68, 15-23: 46–49.

Testore, E. (1964) 'Le macchine utensili a controllo numerico,' *Notizie Olivetti*, 81, 7: 3–5.

Testore, E. (1966) 'Dal torno da vasaio alle machine a controllo numerico,' *Notizie Olivetti*, 14, 87: 9. 10–13.

Van Onck, A. (1964) 'Metadesign,' *Edilizia Moderna*, 85: 52–57.

Wright, S. (2002) *Storming Heaven. Class Composition and Struggle in Italian Autonomist Marxism*, London: Pluto Press.

Zanella, F. (2018) 'Man-Machine', *Domus*, 1022, 3: 27–31.

Zorzi, R. (1983) '*Design Process Olivetti 1908-1983*, Ivrea: Olivetti.

4 Bewildered, the form-maker stands alone

Computer architecture and the quest for design rationality

Theodora Vardouli

In its winter 1964–1965 issue, the journal *Landscape* featured a two-and-a-half page review article titled "Notes on Computer Architecture." The reviewer was geographer Yi-Fu Tuan, at the time still a junior faculty member at the University of New Mexico. The reviewee was Christopher Alexander, a Cambridge University-trained architect and mathematician, who had just completed five years of doctoral work at Harvard and joined, as a faculty member, the Department of Architecture at the University of California, Berkeley. A play on *Notes on the Synthesis of Form*—the title of Alexander's dissertation-based book released by Harvard University Press in 1964, and the focus of Tuan's review —"Notes on Computer Architecture" was not about digital computers. Or rather, not directly so. Instead, it was about casting aspects of design in logical and mathematical terms: devising step-wise descriptions of design processes amenable to potentially automatable mathematical analysis.

Tuan tied the use of such logico-mathematical formalisms with metaphors of revealing, of making visible what was before hidden. The pivotal implication of using a "logical structure [...] made up of mathematical entities" (1964: 12), Tuan remarked, was the possibility of conducting an "explicit mapping of the [design] problem's structure" (1964: 14). "Problem" here denoted the quantitative and qualitative requirements that physical things (spanning from kettles to urban dwellings) ought to satisfy in a particular situation. In *Notes*, Alexander presented a method for breaking down ("decomposing") these requirements into independent sub-groups by evaluating "conflicts" between them. This analytical method dictated the order ("program") by which a designer ought to respond to the different requirements, by making abstract sketches ("diagrams") that addressed the simpler sub-groups and then combining them in the order indicated by the "program." The visual summary of the method was a mathematical representation called a "tree." "Trees" were special cases of "graphs," mathematical entities that consisted of points representing abstract objects and lines representing their relationships. Alexander used "trees" to represent the hierarchical structure of the design "problem" and also the steps by which the designer was to tackle it.

Bewildered, the form-maker stands alone 59

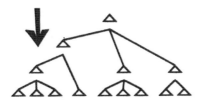
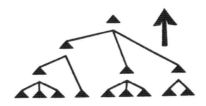

Program, consisting of sets   Realization, consisting of diagrams

Figure 4.1 Image taken from the *Notes*, showing the "program" and the "realization" tree. The image opened Tuan's review. Source: *Notes on the Synthesis of Form* by Christopher Alexander, Cambridge, Mass.: Harvard University Press, Copyright © 1964 by the President and Fellows of Harvard College. Copyright © renewed 1992 by Christopher Alexander.

Although Tuan seemed unconvinced of the practical effectiveness of this method and voiced philosophical critiques on the non-evolving and value-laden nature of "requirements: he endorsed the potential of Alexander's logico-mathematical process to elucidate "without undue arbitrariness" and "in concrete patterns" the "realities of modern life" (1964a: 14). Tuan's remarks against "arbitrariness" moderately echoed Alexander's polemical introduction to the *Notes*, in which he announced a "loss of innocence" (1964b: 8) and urged for the "need for rationality" (1964b: I). "Rationality," Alexander suggested and Tuan repeated, would safeguard designers from resorting to "unexamined preferences" (Tuan 1964: 12), inherited conventions, and the excuse of "intuition" (Alexander 1964b: 2) when faced with ever-changing design "problems" of mind-boggling complexity (Alexander 1964b: 3).

Several scholars have linked early conversations about computers and architecture with debates on the place and form of "rationality" in a modern architectural discipline (for example, Dutta 2013, Halpern 2015). Alexander has also been recognized as one of these debates' key instigators (for example, Broadbent 1988 [1973]: 273; Bruegmann 1989: 141, 146). Alexander put forward a particular mode of calculative rationality consisting of rule-based operations. His method of hierarchically decomposing design "problems" was taken up by several architects and planners in the United Kingdom and North America, who adapted it for pedagogical experiments or developed computer variations of its first digital computer implementation in MIT's Computation Centre IBM 709 machine. With Alexander being among the first architects to engage with the development of a logico-mathematical formalism for design, the *Notes* came to symbolize a pursuit for rigor and a research ethos that burgeoned in Anglo-American architecture schools throughout the 1960s under the

60 *Theodora Vardouli*

broad and interdisciplinary umbrella of "rational theories and methods" of design (Moore 1966: 1). Despite Alexander's disavowal of design methods in the mid-1960s (Alexander 1971: 3), the *Notes* remained, as architect and urbanist Roger Montgomery would later write in *Architectural Forum*, the "first manifesto" of a "worldwide movement" to "modernize design methods and bring scientific rigor into their [the designers'] ancient craft" (1970: 52).

This essay aspires to disentangle and historically contextualize dimensions of Alexander's influential call for "rationality," all the while contributing a productively distinct case in a growing body of scholarship detailing episodes of this hazy slogan's postwar "career" (Erickson et al. 2015). Drawing primarily from progress reports and correspondence found in the archives of Alexander's doctoral advisor, Russian émigré architect Serge Chermayeff, I follow the making of Alexander's design theory from his enrolment at Harvard in 1958 to the launch of the *Notes* in 1964. I pay special attention to the epistemic cultures (Knorr-Cetina 1999) and technical languages that Alexander engaged, and to their relationship with various symbolic meanings and operational embodiments of "rationality" in his work. Specifically, I identify two distinct concerns entangled with his plea for "rationality:" one pertaining to decision-making and one to the organization of empirical data. I discuss how the mathematical device of the "tree" melted and molded both of these concerns into a single structural abstraction of the at once *problem*, *process*, and *outcome (form)* of design. To accounts of import of ideas from cybernetics, linear programming, and decision theory (Upitis 2008; Steenson 2017) into architecture, I juxtapose a story of *translations* of architectural concerns emanating from realities of postwar industrial housing into a mathematical language.

I further argue that the specific mathematics that Alexander used, namely graph theory, enabled him to pursue a reconciliation between rule-based rationality and its perceived opposite, intuition. As Tuan remarked in his *Notes* review: "The logical structure does not prescribe [physical] form; but it does express pattern, order and relations which can then be translated, through processes still largely intuitive, into an orderly complex of forms" (1964: 12). Alexander attacked but did not ostracize intuition. Instead he delegated subjective judgment *on top of* an objective mathematical substrate—a scheme that, I will argue, propelled a specific imagination for the place of computers in design processes. This chapter describes an episode in the construction of common grounds among architecture, mathematics, and computers at the nexus of multiple epistemic communities and technical languages. More than that though, it tells a story of the co-construction of a particular image of "rationality," one inextricably linked with the mathematical technique enlisted to deliver it.

The need for choice

With a psychoanalytic undertone, biographers and scholars of Alexander's work have persistently repeated the anecdote of a dismayed father seeing his mathematical prodigy son choosing the "disreputable" and "idiotic" (Grabow 1983: 299) career path of architecture instead of a properly "scientific" field. They have also repeated Alexander's fast and forceful disillusionment with the uncoordinated, nonsensical, and "absurd" (Grabow 1983: 31) status of architectural education, soon after joining the Architecture Department at the University of Cambridge in 1953. Self-taught in aesthetic theory, with two years of intensive mathematical training at the Trinity College, and carrying strong opinions about the architectural discipline, Alexander contemplated the next step. After rejecting a PhD in aesthetics under the supervision of logical positivist philosopher Alfred Jules Ayer and a post in the London Building Research Station, Alexander joined one of the emerging epicenters of postwar modern architecture: the Harvard Graduate School of Design (GSD).

When Alexander arrived at the Harvard GSD in 1958, the School was still reverberating with echoes of Bauhaus founder Walter Gropius's 15-year chairmanship, and the function-oriented, technology-driven, interdisciplinary, and future-centric architectural ethos that he had installed. Alexander's enrolment at the GSD also occurred in the context of a growing "urban design" agenda, the term denoting a middle ground between large-scale planning and micro-scale residential interventions. This agenda was being promoted by Gropius's successor Josep Lluís Sert, GSD Dean of the school since 1953 and formerly president of the International Congresses of Modern Architecture (CIAM). One of the Bauhaus' and the CIAM's key characteristics was the espousal of "rational" architecture as a key pillar of their modern agenda. Rationality was a central moral ideal in the *longue durée* of Western architectural theory that prioritized functional or material economy over other considerations and sanctioned reason as the basis of design.

Alexander would mold such values of rational architecture with a distinctive chapter of American intellectual history that scholars have labeled "Cold War rationality" (Erickson et al. 2015). This mode of rationality has been historicized as emanating from US government agencies and decision-making organizations, ultimately trickling down to the hallways of academic departments. "Cold War rationality" was mistrusting of human reason and judgment, with a proclivity for rule-based, universalizing, abstract, and possibly mechanizable operations (Erickson et al. 2015: 2). It was the kind of rationality that elevated mechanical rules to an intellectual virtue, enabling the imagination of computers as superior makers of decisions and performers of operations traditionally delegated to human deliberation (Erickson et al. 2015: 4). Arguably, Alexander's *Notes* sits squarely within this intellectual phenomenon, from both a methodological and a rhetorical perspective. His polemic against "intuition" and "arbitrariness," along with his logico-mathematical

62 *Theodora Vardouli*

rendition of design, cast him as one of the many interlocutors of this particular postwar genre of rationality. It may come as a surprise then that Alexander's trajectory toward the *Notes* began with a call different than, and actually resisting, the book's opening motto. In one of his first PhD progress reports, dated September 1958, Alexander advocated for the "need for choice" as a corrective to an over-reliance to "logic and rationality" (Alexander 1958a: 1).

The progress report opened with a telegraphic synopsis of his proposal: "A conceptual model for the design process. Particular problems of prefabrication and technology. The American house" (Alexander 1958a: 1). Following this curt summary was a list of "men at Harvard" (Alexander 1958a: 1) with whom Alexander had established contact upon his arrival at the University. The list featured his soon-to-be doctoral committee members Serge Chermayeff and Jerome Bruner. Bruner was an eminent American cognitive psychologist who would establish, two years later, the Harvard Center for Cognitive Studies and employ Alexander as a research associate (Grabow 1983: 193). It also included gestalt psychologist Hans Wallach and Harvard professor Martin Meyerson, future founder of the MIT-Harvard Joint Center for Urban Studies where Alexander would also find a research home.

The September 1958 report, however, did not dwell on interactions with these figures, who would come to be decisive influences on Alexander's trajectory. Instead, it focused on two under-discussed actors: Vienna-trained art historian Eduard Sekler and applied mathematician and mathematical psychology pioneer R. Duncan Luce. Alexander reported having consulted with Luce on the possibility of using an IBM machine to plot "utility functions for various domains of decision [in a design process]" (Alexander 1958a: 1). "Utility" was a key term in rational choice theory and game theory, measuring the satisfaction of different stakeholders for a given decision in the context of a decision-making process. However, Alexander declared his mistrust of the results of such a computer model, which were contingent on the choice of "premises" (Alexander 1958a: 1)—the starting statements on which logical operations would be applied. The preoccupation with "premises" in the context of logical inference was cultivated in Sekler's Harvard seminar on art criticism, for which Alexander wrote a paper that "deplored the use of abstract phraseology in architectural writing" (Alexander 1958a: 1).

Alexander argued that the *choice* of premises and the *choice* of the conceptual model were unavoidably "arbitrary" (Alexander 1958a: 1) and that logic could only be applied after these arbitrary choices are made. "Logic and rationality cannot help you to avoid fundamental decisions... the choice of premises is up to the architect, not dictated by logic" (Alexander 1958a: 1). This realization, he argued, would impel a fresh re-examination of architectural conventions. The focus, Alexander appeared to argue, would be shifted from reasoning on the basis of logical-sounding statements and pervasive truisms about architecture to explicit, and mathematically examinable, "choices" and "decisions."

As historian Avigail Sachs has highlighted, rejecting conventions in quest for proven knowledge (2009: 54) was a dominant trope in the multivalent phenomenon of postwar "architectural research"—a key phrase broadly standing for any kind of systematic inquiry aspiring to produce generally applicable knowledge. Replacing unquestioned premises with explicit and mathematically modelable "decisions" aligned with a culture of "re-examining fundamentals freshly and fearlessly," as US architectural research spokesperson Walter Taylor had put it in the late 1940s (1947: 18). Alexander's "need for choice" is not to be mistaken for an embrace of arbitrariness as an epistemic virtue. It was instead an argument for redirecting the use of logic from the justification of general truths and values about architectural design, to the *processing* of factual information, whatever these would be. This reflected the realities of postwar architectural research in a significant way.

While still in the UK, Alexander had come into contact with the Building Research Station (BRS). This was one of several research agencies that engaged in a vast and multidisciplinary project of collecting information on the production of buildings and the needs of their inhabitants in the context of British postwar urban reconstruction. In the US, agencies operating under the 1949 Housing Act had similarly initiated wide-ranging research into technical and social aspects of housing. These inquiries brought together different specialties and confronted architects with a kind of information-based collaborative work. Aside from raising questions about architects' professional roles, languages, and tropes, this work also brought about the realization that housing stood in the cross-hairs of an ocean of requirements—conflicting needs, values, and preferences.

In a draft to Chermayeff, Alexander called these requirements "form-determinants." "Form-determinants" included both the public needs collected through extensive empirical work and the designers' aesthetic preferences or other ideals. Alexander framed this polyphony of "form-determinants" as a corrective to the dominance of singular arbitrary ideals such as "beauty," "social status," "structure," "taste," "economics," "function," and "social structure" (Alexander n.d.-c). The Programming of Design Decisions: 1–2). Alexander's first response to the negotiation of the often irreconcilable tension between form-determinants was a *game*.

A cooperative game

In an October 1958 progress report, Alexander described his dissertation as "formulation of [a] mass-produced house design procedure as a cooperative game between architect and society" (Alexander 1958b: 1). This game would help safeguard the architect's role as "reformer," "form giver," and

64   Theodora Vardouli

teacher of "visual sophistication" (Alexander 1958b: 1, 2) against an increasingly wary public. Alexander proposed deploying a game-theoretic formalism, on which the report did not elaborate, as the mathematical core of a new design process consisting of the following steps: first, collection of information about public needs (requirements) through questionnaires or interviews; second, use of this information to design an ideal physical form as seen from the architect's perspective; third, field work to gauge the public's reactions to the architect's ideal form and use of the game-theoretic formalism to negotiate choices; and finally, mutual settlement to "a balanced solution" (Alexander 1958b: 2).

The degree of Luce's influence on Alexander is difficult to assess, but it is productive to contemplate intellectual and technical parallels between the development of Alexander's thinking and Luce's landmark publication *Games and Decisions* (Luce and Raiffa 1957). *Games and Decisions* was a seminal text in game theory, with exceptional appeal for psychologists and social scientists, that brought mathematical models for decision-making and social negotiation into the human sciences. Graph theory was a prominent technique in the book, used to represent a game (the so-called "game tree"), possible moves at each step, and decisions made in the process. A few years earlier, Luce had published in the *American Journal of Mathematics* two theorems for decomposing a group of entities linked by relationships (1952). The mathematical problem of dividing a graph into sub-graphs based on some property of the relationships between its points, could be readily applied in the study of social groups. Graphs and decomposition would come to be key devices in Alexander's future mathematical repertoire.

Applying game theory to design would not only balance conflicting requirements, achieving a happy medium between the architects' and the public's priorities, but would also offer architects a way of staying afloat in an ocean of information. Alexander argued that despite efforts to "educate designers in this total grasp of form-building," the only good architecture was produced by a "few men of genius" able to "to have a grasp of everything that matters" (Alexander n.d.-c. The Programming of Design Decisions: 2). A growing and unwieldy body of "technical information" "handicapped" even these "freaks of genius" and resisted "intuitive" absorption and apprehension (Alexander n.d.-c. The Programming of Design Decisions: 2). The game would enable rational decision-making in a situation that hampered judgment and turned old ways of reasoning defunct. In *Notes* Alexander would paint a similar picture of architects' ominous predicament. "Bewildered," he lamented, "the form-giver stands alone" (Alexander 1964b: 4).

In their working group book on Cold War Rationality, Erickson, Klein, Daston, Lemov, Sturm and Gordin have argued that the calculative rationality of postwar US flourished in the affectively charged context of threats so grave and stakes so great that could overwhelm human psyche and incapacitated reasoning capabilities (2015: 1). In this context, mechanical, mathematical calculations were seen as a refuge from panic-induced errors in judgment. Alexander's invocation of games and mathematical theories of decision-making in the face of inundating amounts of information collected through building research strikes a similar tone. Apart from decision-making errors, unmanageably large bodies of information posed an additional threat: disorder and confusion. Without a classificatory scheme, Alexander worried that the information for various "form-determinants" would "dissolve into chaos" (Alexander n.d.-b. The Design of the Urban House and Ways of Clustering It: 6). Alexander's research would soon be transposed into finding a way of disciplining information into a neat image comprehensible at first sight.

A logical structure

From 1959 and on, Chermayeff's archives include research proposals and research progress reports jointly written with Alexander. These projects culminated with the co-publication of the influential *Community and Privacy: Toward a New Architecture of Humanism* (Chermayeff and Alexander 1962). The book conceptualized urban organization as a hierarchy of components and subcomponents and presented a method, similar to the one Alexander detailed in *Notes*, for designing such components to account for various "pressures" (the rough equivalent of form-determinants). The final step was combining these components to produce urban complexes with well-ordered hierarchies. In a June 1965 letter to Chermayeff, Alexander characterized his role in the collaboration as elucidating Chermayeff's thoughts. "When we worked together in Cambridge," Alexander wrote, "part of the little help I was to you, came from the fact that I tried to re-state, more clearly, your own thoughts as you saw them" (1965a). This "clarifying" work opened a new set of concerns for Alexander, who shifted his focus from game theory to problems of classification and information storage and retrieval.

Alexander and Chermayeff's collaboration capitalized on the financial, intellectual, and technical infrastructure of the Harvard-MIT Joint Center for Urban Studies, a university-affiliated interdisciplinary research center founded by Martin Meyerson and MIT professor Lloyd Rodwin in 1959 with funding from the Ford Foundation. Alexander was employed in the Joint Center from 1959–1960. There, he worked with Chermayeff on a research project called "The Urban House." The project was the offspring of an effort initiated in one of Chermayeff's Harvard seminars in 1952 and revisited in 1956 and 1959, to identify "a vocabulary capable of describing the infinite variety of elements, situations, activities, or events that make up the complex organism 'house'" (Chermayeff and Alexander 1962: 152).

This endeavor was not a first. Chermayeff's efforts aligned with attempts to classify architectural and urban components in different scales, not only as a way to organize empirical information collected by research agencies, but also as a theoretical problem. Broadly, the problem pertained to the

66 *Theodora Vardouli*

fundamental categories for thinking about architecture and the city in the face of industrialization and accelerating technological change. Among the most influential efforts in this direction was Knud Lönberg-Holm and Theodore Larson's *Development Index* (1953), which, in the authors' words, sought to "outline the various series of factors involved in development relationships" (1953: Index Development). "Development" here stood for a continual assessment of technological change and the new human needs these instigated, and its transformation into new "patterns of activity" (Lönberg-Holm and Larson, 1953: Ia. Development Goals).

Alexander had become aware of Lönberg-Holm's classification scheme while thinking about how to organize the "factual data" collected in the empirical research part of his proposed design process, but dismissed them as "a little awry" (Alexander n.d.-b. The Design of the Urban House and Ways of Clustering It: 6). A nagging sense of arbitrariness also permeated Alexander's attempts to develop other systems of classification. It was not long before he identified the source of his discontent. In 1960, he wrote to Chermayeff that his previous explorations in categories of components had, in fact, been irrational. "Though I had been talking a great deal about logic," Alexander admitted, "I had not yet used it, put it to work" (1960b: 1). After perusing questions of information storage and retrieval and conferencing with IBM research team members, he realized that the categories he was looking for lay in the *information itself*. The classification logic was intrinsic to the set of requirements (the design "problem"). Alexander wrote:

> The practical problem immediately confronting us is to isolate groups of 'failures', areas for research, so that within each one of these limited areas the design problem becomes manageable.
>
> What we had been trying to do was to isolate these groups "by eye" so to speak: a priori; and this is what was wrong.
>
> I realized that the groups were actually given by the logic of the relations tying our failures to one another—if one only knew how to look for them. And that if we could set the system up suitably, the logic would allow us to extract the groups of failures we wanted, quite NON-ARBITRARILY.
>
> (1960b: 1)

"Failure" was the precursor of "misfit," a central concept in the *Notes*. It denoted a kind of physical condition that prevented a need from being satisfied (for example, sleep prevented by bioclimatic discomfort). Because of their definition as physical conditions, "failures" not only established relationships between requirements and aspects of physical form, but also established "linkages" (Alexander 1960a: 2) between the requirements themselves that Alexander would call "interactions."

Sometimes failures shared data, other times they were corrected by the same operations, and other times the correction of one failure aggravated

Bewildered, the form-maker stands alone 67

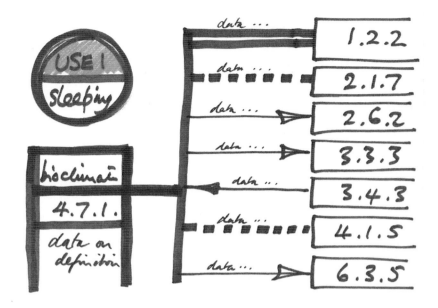

Figure 4.2 Sketch of a failure card by Christopher Alexander. Source: Alexander, C. 1960a. Letter to Chermayeff Re: Failure Cards. [document]. Box 4, Folder "Alexander, Christopher, 1958–1966," Serge Ivan Chermayeff Architectural Records and Papers, 1909–1980. Dept. of Drawings & Archives, Avery Architectural and Fine Arts Library, Columbia University.

the other. Similar relations of overlap, reinforcement, or conflict were then established among the failures' corresponding requirements. By considering "the relations themselves, or links" between failures, it would be possible to achieve Chermayeff and Alexander's main deliverable: "a working programme for design" (Alexander 1959a: 2).

Program, for Alexander, was both structural and procedural: structural, because it represented a logical organization of design requirements and procedural, because it indicated the order by which the designer should address these requirements. The step-wise decision-making rationality cultivated through Alexander's game theoretic interests aligned with the representational ideal of well-ordered, intelligible data developed during his Joint Center appointment. The mathematical device that would enable the collapse of process into structure was, as Alexander first announced in 1961, the "topological 1-complex" or, more simply, the linear graph (Alexander 1962: 117).

68 Theodora Vardouli

The image of rationality

After completing his research appointment at the Joint Center, Alexander requested $166,000 from the US Building Research Institute (BRI) to pursue a three-year experiment on the means and effects of correlating information about building with a specific design "problem." His proposal, titled "Information and an Organized Process of Design," was presented in the Spring 1961 *New Building Research* Conference of the BRI Division of Engineering and Industrial Research. Since 1956, the BRI had been publishing a comprehensive guide listing "sources of information on research and technical developments in the industry" (Building Research Institute 1962: 172) with quarterly supplements and annual indexing. This raised the challenge of documenting building science literature effectively and efficiently, ultimately becoming the theme of the fall 1959 BRI conference. The event featured seminal librarians and information specialists, such as coordinate indexing inventor Mortimer Taube.

The problem posed by the BRI, or at least the way that Alexander interpreted it, had to do with developing a proper organization (structure) on which the abundant knowledge and data about building that were becoming available would be able to hang from. This was a concern that had preoccupied a good portion of his doctoral work. To the arbitrary matching between the organization of building information and the needs of a specific design situation, Alexander counter-proposed "to set up temporary isomorphisms between the library's organization and the cognitive organization of the process" (Alexander 1962: 120). "Isomorphism" etymologically translated as equality of form, was a mathematical term indicating a one-to-one mapping between the elements of two different systems. Achieving Alexander's goal necessitated "some logical or mathematical relation between the two classification systems," the source of which would be "the topological structure of the problem" (Alexander 1962: 120).

In his BRI proposal, Alexander presented one page with five mathematical figures (Figure 4.3). The first figure was an entanglement of straight lines, connecting multiple points (nodes) (Alexander 1962: 118). Alexander explained that the figures were graphs, whose points represented the requirements that compromised the so-called "design problem." The graphs' lines represented "interactions" among requirements. Alexander continued to suggest that the problem's logical structure became *visible* by considering conflicting relationships between its constituent units (the requirements). These conflicts were mathematically translated into relations that bound different requirements together and helped identify the problem's "functional units"—subsystems of strongly connected requirements that could be handled separately from other requirements. The second and third figure showed a transformation of part of the first figure's graph into sub-graphs that revealed the subsystems emerging from the consideration of interactions among tangled and disordered requirements. Alexander annotated the second and third figures with hand-drawn

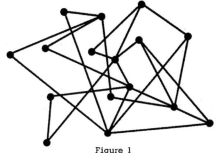
Figure 1

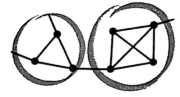
Figure 2

Figure 3

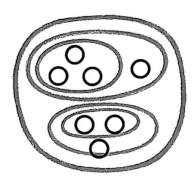
Figure 4

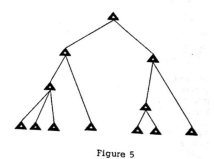
Figure 5

Figure 4.3 A graph drawn in a disordered way transformed into a hierarchical tree. Source: Alexander, C. 1961. Information and an Organized Process of Design: A Research Project Proposal. [document] Center for Environmental Structure Archive.

70 *Theodora Vardouli*

circles, which in the second figure indicated the two independent functional units, and in the third figure, an "arbitrary" functional unit or category that designers traditionally used. The difference between the second and third figures was that the former's subsystems were sanctioned by mathematical analysis while the latter relied on conventions that did not survive mathematical scrutiny.

Pointing to the fourth and fifth figures, Alexander further proposed that the "nested" subsets ("system of systems within systems" (Alexander 1962: 119)) could be redrawn so as to "bring out its hierarchical form more obviously" and that the resulting "picture" "look[ed] like a tree" (Alexander 1962: 119). "This tree," he added, "really *prescribes the process of design* [emphasis mine]. You start at the bottom, solving the simplest systems of requirements, and work your way to the top" (Alexander 1962: 119).

Computer architecture

The mathematical calculations for deriving the design "program" were automatable by a digital computer. While employed in the Joint Center, Alexander had already started taking first steps toward programming an IBM 709 machine to automatically produce design "programs." During a consultancy at the Civil Engineering Systems Laboratory from 1960–1962, Alexander developed the first fully functioning version of such a system in collaboration with civil engineer Marvin L. Manheim. The computer system, called HIerarchical DEcomposition System 2 or HIDECS 2, would gain Alexander the reputation of a computer frontiersman in architecture. Alexander used the computer to perform a rote process: making trial cuts of an initial unordered graph (the set of requirements) into subgraphs, calculating an "INFO" parameter based on the number of links that the partition cut and the number of vertices at each side of the partition, and performing a heuristic optimization method to minimize the parameter. Minimizing INFO would mean minimizing interdependence between the groups partitioned by the system at each step.

In March 1962, Alexander and Manheim circulated a research report documenting how the design "programs" (trees) outputted by HIDECS 2 could be used in the context of an actual design situation: in this case locating a section of the I-91 Interstate Highway System in Western Massachusetts along a 20 x 10 mile area of the Connecticut River valley. This "demonstration project" meant to "to illustrate certain aspects of a new approach to physical design problems" (Alexander and Manheim 1962b: 1). In the context of highway route location, diagrams were simply "lines and areas on a map" (Alexander and Manheim 1962b: 1). Alexander and Manheim identified 26 location requirements and set out to develop diagrams based on calculations of "utility" of various highway positions from the standpoint of each requirement. Unable to calculate the utility of lines, they drew the diagrams using points, with black being the most favorable and white the least favorable. The process resulted in 26 diagrams, or "utility maps" (Alexander and Manheim 1962b: 112), each of which corresponded to one of the "problem's" requirements and was to be combined based on the HIDECS 2-outputted tree.

The synthesis proved exacting. Each map represented potentially incommensurable utility functions. Furthermore, a simple addition of utility per point did not account for the properties of a highway as a whole (Alexander and Manheim 1962b: 91–92). "Even if we combine the 26 diagrams in the order which the tree prescribes," the authors pointed out, "we shall still always hit the same resist if we do no more than add them; we shall *still not overcome the objections to straightforward combinations* [emphasis mine]" (Alexander and Manheim 1962b: 91–92). Although the HIDECS 2 analysis was automatic, the synthesis required seeing and judgment. Alexander and Manheim superimposed the diagrams photographically, projected them on a drawing board, and then sketched over the projection to identify desirable areas in terms of utility, while preserving what they described as the configurational characteristics (a plausible shape) for the highway. HIDECS 2 needed a special supplement that was none other than the designer's eye. Alexander and Manheim wrote:

> While it may be possible in principle to deal with these matters analytically and program them for digital computers, in practice, present digital computer techniques and utility theory are too little advanced to be of much use. [...] Of course people have used their eyes and heads before. But the idea that the human eye is a special purpose computer for solving problems of this type, shows us the process outlined as a framework in which the computer can be used intelligently and efficiently.
>
> (1962b: 117)

It was not the eye-as-computer metaphor that is remarkable here—this was a pervasive metaphor in the cognitive psychology circles that Alexander was part of during his doctoral studies. Rather, it was the idea that humans and digital computers could have complementary roles; that mechanical logico-mathematical rationality did not exclude, but rather called for the intuitions of the human eye. The designer's judgment was never eradicated from Alexander's process: it was instead displaced as the epiphenomenon of a logical structure.

In sketching out his research project, Alexander had written in 1959: "In many kinds of research the findings lead straight to the answer—given the findings, the result is completely determined. In our research this will not be the case. The design [underlined in the original] comes from the designer" (1959b: 1). The HIDECS 2 decomposition method, which made it into Alexander's dissertation and ultimately into *Notes* with minimal modifications, was analytical and largely mechanical. The computer's job

72   Theodora Vardouli

was outputting the "problem's" "logical structure" and a step-wise decision-making process for attacking it.

With the paralyzing data inundation on "requirements" disciplined through rational analysis, with the "bewilderment" cured, designers could exert intuition without risk of errors and slips of judgment. Intuition, preferences and other notorious antonyms to rationality were permissible in the development of the "diagrams" and their hierarchical combination to form "composite diagrams." This combination would be frictionless, as the tree's subgroups' independence would ensure that no "conflicts" among requirements would arise. More crucially though, combining diagrams in the process designated by the tree would establish a one-to-one match between the structure of the design problem and the structure of the physical form. "The hierarchical composition of these diagrams," Alexander wrote in closing to the *Notes*, "will then lead to a physical object whose structural hierarchy is the exact counterpart of the functional hierarchy established during the analysis of the problem" (Alexander 1964b: 131). Analysis and synthesis, decomposition and realization would be isomorphic, with the common skeletal vision of the tree.

The particular mode of "rationality" that Alexander vouched for in the *Notes* introduction cannot be severed from the mathematical object of the tree. A visual shorthand for Alexander's theory, the tree clearly placed geometric shape—visual, aesthetic, intuitive—on top of an abstract structure derived through logico-mathematical operations. This protocol also applied to the roles of humans and digital computers: the former operating within the bounds set by the latter. The I-91 superimposition of "utility maps" was the closest to this protocol being subverted, as the fusion of diagrams by eye and hand blurred their discrete identities and destabilized the categories of analysis. Yet, the use of diagrams in other architectural and urban design examples that Alexander presented remained limited to a building-block model of combination—a telling example being the *Notes*' famous appendix, showing an implementation of HIDECS 2 to derive a master plan for a village of six hundred people in Gujarat, India (Alexander 1962, 1964b).

As I have argued elsewhere, a similar discrete logic and a preoccupation with an invariant structure underlying physical form, or the built environment as a whole, characterized Alexander's post-*Notes* expeditions at the University of California Berkeley (Vardouli 2017). Despite Alexander's correctives to the tree's hierarchical nature, his disavowal of stringent logico-mathematical methods and his professed embrace of intuition and "feeling," his theories never escaped the belief that shape is underpinned by a mathematically knowable abstract structure that precedes and generates it.

Apart from haunting Alexander's trajectory, the scheme of intuition *on top of* logic, shape *on top of* structure, empirical *on top of* abstract, and human *on top of* computer, is productive for critically contemplating the proliferating and ever-bifurcating relationships between computers and architecture. The phantasmagoria of graphics-rich screens and fluidity of computer interfaces evokes a different atmosphere than mathematical formulas and precise calculations. Yet, although these are hidden from view, they are far from absent. In their majority, contemporary computer aided design and drafting applications cast geometric appearance on top of logical operations and mathematical calculations. Computers tame perceptual appearance as the epiphenomenon of logical structures. Recognizing this relationship and its intertwining with historically specific architectural cultures can open alternative imaginations for computer architectures.

Conclusion

Looping back to the start, "Notes on Computer Architecture" was not about the new technological artifact of the digital computer and its promises, or threats, for the architectural profession. Aside from advertising it in the title, Tuan did not mention the word "computer" once in his review. "Computer architecture" appeared to be less about new instruments performing old processes, and more so about conjuring up new theories of process—an argument that Alexander would famously make himself in his influential paper "A Much Asked Question About Computers in Design" (1964a).

In this essay, I took Tuan's decentering of the computer as a methodological heuristic to perform a sketch of a decentered history of computer architecture. Moving the technological artifact of the computer off centre suggests an opening to other histories of computer architecture that speak not of tools but of *translations*—translations of architectural concepts and operations in logico-mathematical terms. This expands the conversation toward the material contexts and knowledge settings of these translations, alongside their cultural commitments, epistemic proclivities, and disciplinary aspirations. My goal in this essay has been to open a seemingly a-contextual and logically complete formalism to historical scrutiny and examine the ways in which it constructs and is constructed by ideas of "rationality."

This essay is not the first to scrutinize the making of Alexander's *Notes*. Alise Upitis has made a strong materialist argument about the determination of the *Notes* method from the practical constraints of programming an IBM computer ca. 1960 (2013). While adopting a similar sensibility that design formalisms are historical artifacts, contingent on the contexts in which they were developed, this essay positions their construction in the middle ground between epistemic cultural tropes and work with particular instruments and techniques. Although the tree's programmability in an IBM machine was plausibly an important force for establishing the tree as the response to Alexander's quest for "rationality," it was not the only one. By following Alexander's pursuit of this misty concept, I shed light on the tree's entanglements with games and decisions, with issues of information organization, and with ideas about architectural and urban hierarchies, all the while

74 *Theodora Vardouli*

relating these conversations to broader anxieties and realities of postwar modern architecture.

Instead of distilling one definition of Alexander's "rationality," this essay has further untwined the term, arguing that the nebula surrounding it was precisely its appeal. I have portrayed a rationality in flux that only temporarily settled into a definition, only to bring into play certain techniques that would shift its shape and meaning. I have also hinted at the critical implications of coupling catchphrases that animated postwar architectural research with their operational definitions, and of developing a discourse at the interface of rhetoric and technique. As logical and mathematical techniques lurk at the backdrop of our computer screens, it is time to tell their stories.

Bibliography

Alexander, C., 1958a. Progress report (September 1958). [document]. Box 4, Folder "Alexander, Christopher, 1958–1966". Serge Ivan Chermayeff Architectural Records and Papers, 1909–1980. Dept. of Drawings & Archives, Avery Architectural and Fine Arts Library, Columbia University.

Alexander, C., 1958b. Report on current Ph.D. work (October 27, 1958). [document]. Box 4, Folder "Alexander, Christopher, 1958–1966". Serge Ivan Chermayeff Architectural Records and Papers, 1909–1980. Dept. of Drawings & Archives, Avery Architectural and Fine Arts Library, Columbia University.

Alexander, C., 1958c. Report on Ph.D. work, current (October 29, 1958). [document]. Box 4, Folder "Alexander, Christopher, 1958–1966". Serge Ivan Chermayeff Architectural Records and Papers, 1909–1980. Dept. of Drawings & Archives, Avery Architectural and Fine Arts Library, Columbia University.

Alexander, C., 1959a. Programme (The Urban House). [document]. Box 4, Folder "Alexander, Christopher, 1958–1966". Serge Ivan Chermayeff Architectural Records and Papers, 1909–1980. Dept. of Drawings & Archives, Avery Architectural and Fine Arts Library, Columbia University.

Alexander, C., 1959b. The Design of an Urban House and Ways of Clustering It. [document]. Box 4, Folder "Alexander, Christopher, 1958–1966". Serge Ivan Chermayeff Architectural Records and Papers, 1909–1980. Dept. of Drawings & Archives, Avery Architectural and Fine Arts Library, Columbia University.

Alexander, C., 1960a. Letter to Chermayeff Re: Failure Cards. [document]. Box 4, Folder "Alexander, Christopher, 1958–1966". Serge Ivan Chermayeff Architectural Records and Papers, 1909–1980. Dept. of Drawings & Archives, Avery Architectural and Fine Arts Library, Columbia University.

Alexander, C., 1960b. Letter to Chermayeff Re: Failures Interlock, IBM Group Extraction. [document]. Box 4, Folder "Alexander, Christopher, 1958–1966". Serge Ivan Chermayeff Architectural Records and Papers, 1909–1980. Dept. of Drawings & Archives, Avery Architectural and Fine Arts Library, Columbia University.

Alexander, C., 1960c. "The Revolution Finished Twenty Years Ago." *Architect's Year Book* 9, 181–185.

Alexander, C., 1962. Information and an Organized Process of Design, in: *New Building Research Spring 1961. Presented at the 1961 Spring Conferences of the*

Building Research Institute, Division of Engineering and Industrial Design, National Academy of Sciences - National Research Council, Washington, D.C, pp. 115–124.

Alexander, C., 1963. The Determination of Components for an Indian Village, in: Jones, J.C., Thornley, D. (Eds.), *Conference on Design Methods: Papers Presented at the Conference on Systematic and Intuitive Methods in Engineering, Industrial Design, Architecture and Communications,* London, September 1962. Pergamon Press, Oxford, pp. 83–114.

Alexander, C., 1964a. "A Much Asked Question About Computers in Design." [document]. Box 4, Folder "Alexander, Christopher, 1958–1966." Serge Ivan Chermayeff Architectural Records and Papers, 1909–1980. Dept. of Drawings & Archives, Avery Architectural and Fine Arts Library, Columbia University, 1.

Alexander, C., 1964b. *Notes on the Synthesis of Form.* Harvard University Press, Cambridge, MA.

Alexander, C., 1965a. Letter to Chermayeff Re: Yale Position Offer. [document] Box 4, Folder "Alexander, Christopher, 1958-1966". Serge Ivan Chermayeff Architectural Records and Papers, 1909-1980. Dept. of Drawings & Archives, Avery Architectural and Fine Arts Library, Columbia University.

Alexander, C., 1967. "The Question of Computers in Design." *Landscape* 14, 6–8.

Alexander, C., 1971. "The State of the Art in Design Methods." *DMG Newsletter* 5, 3–7.

Alexander, C., n.d.-a. (Research) Programme Draft Sent to Chermayeff. [document]. Box 4, Folder "Alexander, Christopher, 1958–1966". Serge Ivan Chermayeff Architectural Records and Papers, 1909–1980. Dept. of Drawings & Archives, Avery Architectural and Fine Arts Library, Columbia University.

Alexander, C., n.d.-b. Research Into the Design of an Urban House and Ways of Clustering It. [document]. Box 4, Folder "Alexander, Christopher, 1958–1966". Serge Ivan Chermayeff Architectural Records and Papers, 1909–1980. Dept. of Drawings & Archives, Avery Architectural and Fine Arts Library, Columbia University.

Alexander, C., n.d.-c. The Programming of Design Decisions. [document]. Box 4, Folder "Alexander, Christopher, 1958–1966". Serge Ivan Chermayeff Architectural Records and Papers, 1909–1980. Dept. of Drawings & Archives, Avery Architectural and Fine Arts Library, Columbia University.

Alexander, C., and Manheim, M.L., 1962a. *HIDECS 2: A Computer Program for the Hierarchical Decomposition of a Set which has an Associated Linear Graph.* Civil Engineering Systems Laboratory Publication 160, MIT, Cambridge, MA.

Alexander, C., and Manheim, M.L., 1962b. *The Use of Diagrams in Highway Route Location: An Experiment.* Civil Engineering Systems Laboratory Publication 161, MIT, Cambridge, MA.

Broadbent, G. 1988 [1973]. *Design in Architecture: Architecture and the Human Sciences.* London: Fulton.

Bruegmann, R., 1989. The Pencil and the Electronic Sketchboard: Architectural Representa-tion and the Computer, in *Architecture and its Image,* in: Blau, E. and Laufman, E. (Eds.), 138–157. MIT Press, Cambridge, MA.

Building Research Institute. 1962. New Building Research 1961. Washington, DC: National Academy of Sciences - National Research Council.

Cetina, K.-K., 1999. *Epistemic Cultures: How the Sciences Make Knowledge.* Harvard University Press, Cambridge, MA.

Chermayeff, S., and Alexander, C., 1963. *Community and Privacy: Toward a New Architecture of Humanism*. Doubleday and Company Inc, Garden City, NY.

Dutta, A., 2013. *A Second Modernism: MIT, Architecture, and the "Techno-Social" Moment*. MIT Press, Cambridge, MA.

Erickson, B.P., 2010. "Mathematical Models, Rational Choice, and the Search for Cold War Culture." *Isis* 101, 386–392.

Erickson, P., Klein, J.L., Daston, L., Lemov, R., Sturm, T., and Gordin, M.D., 2015. *How Reason Almost Lost Its Mind: The Strange Career of Cold War Rationality*, University Chicago Press, Chicago, IL.

Grabow, S., 1983. *Christopher Alexander: The Search for a New Paradigm in Architecture*. Routledge Kegan & Paul, Stocksfield; Boston, MA.

Halpern, O., 2015. *Beautiful Data: A History of Vision and Reason Since 1945*. Duke University Press, North Carolina, NC.

Lönberg-Holm, K., and Larson, T., 1953. *Development Index: A proposed pattern for organizing and facilitating the flow of information needed by man to further in his own development with particular reference to the development of building, communities and other forms of environmental controls*. University of Michigan Press, Ann Arbor, MI.

Luce, R.D., 1952. "Two Decomposition Theorems for a Class of Finite Oriented Graphs." *American Journal of Mathematics* 74, 701–722.

Luce, R.D, and Raiffa, H. 1957. *Games and Decisions*. Wiley, New York, NY.

Mahoney, M. S. 2008. "What Makes the History of Software Hard." *IEEE Annals of the History of Computing* 30 (3), 8–18. Doi:10.1109/MAHC.2008.55.

Montgomery, R. 1970. "Pattern Language - The Contribution of Christopher Alexander's Centre for Environmental Structure to the Science of Design." *Architectural Forum* 132 (1), 52–59.

Moore, G.T., ed. 1966. "What Is the Design Methods Group?" *DMG Newsletter* 1 (1), 1.

Sachs, A., 2009. "The Postwar Legacy of Architectural Research." *Journal of Architectural Education* 62, 53–64.

Steenson, M.W., 2017. *Architectural Intelligence: How Designers and Architects Created the Digital Landscape*. MIT Press, Cambridge, MA.

Taylor, W.A., 1947. "The Architect Looks at Research." *Journal of Architectural Education* 1, 13–24.

Tuan, Y.F., 1964. "Notes on Computer Architecture." *Landscape* 14, 12–14.

Upitis, A. 2008. Nature Normative: The Design Methods Movement, 1944–1967. Thesis, Massachusetts Institute of Technology.

Upitis, A. 2013. Alexander's choice : how architecture avoided computer-aided design c. 1962. in: Dutta, A. (Ed.), *A Second Modernism: MIT, Architecture, and the "Techno-Social" Moment*, 474–506. MIT Press, Cambridge, MA.

Vardouli, T., 2017. *Graphing Theory: New Mathematics, Design, and the Participatory Turn*. Massachusetts Institute of Technology, Cambridge, MA.

Part II
Input/output

5 Augmentation and interface
Tracing a spectrum

Molly Wright Steenson

On December 9, 1968 Douglas Engelbart conducted a legendary demonstration of human-computer interfaces, "A Research Center for Augmenting Human Intellect," during the Fall Joint Computer Conference at the San Francisco Civic Center Auditorium for a crowd of 1,000. But that title isn't the one that most people remember. Instead, they know of it by its colloquial name, "The Mother of All Demos."

The black-and-white video of the event shows Engelbart wearing a lightweight headset and microphone similar to what someone might wear onstage today. He is not standing, but rather sitting at his NLS (oNLine System) console, designed by Herman Miller Research. He was networked to a computer at Stanford Research Laboratory, 30 miles away, itself a rare feat at that time. He acknowledges the unorthodox approach at the beginning of the demo. "I hope you'll go along with this rather unusual setting, and the fact that I remain seated when introduced, and the fact that I'm going to come to you mostly through this medium here"—he nods his head in the direction of a 22-foot by 18-foot screen onstage—

> for the rest of the show. And I should tell you that I'm backed up by quite a staff of people between here and Menlo Park ... And if every one of us does our job well, it will all go interesting.

He looks around, laughs nervously, and forges ahead to introduce the demo. "We're going to do our best to show you, rather than tell you about the program" (Engelbart 1968).

Engelbart's demo presaged word processing, hypertext, and screen navigation. He typed and words immediately appeared, and he could correct them when he made a mistake. He turned those phrases into editable, hierarchical lists that were multiple levels deep; navigated using hypertext links between words and graphics, all using the mouse—his 1964 invention with his colleague Bill English—to move a cursor and select items. He used terms such as "control" and "operate," the language of the quotidian computer operator at work, but also everyday words like "type," "link," and "jump" to accompany his actions and to point out how he corrects a "boo boo"

80   *Molly Wright Steenson*

(Engelbart 1968). He confronted the spatial navigation questions familiar to computer users who work on documents that extend beyond a screen, asking, "Let's see, where was I in this file?" at one point (Engelbart 1968).

The NLS was a vastly different approach to word processing, as compared to, for instance, the IBM MT/ST (developed between 1964 and 1968), which included an IBM Selectric typewriter that sat atop its own cabinet/desk containing a magnetic tape system. The MT/ST stored the user's keystrokes and then typed them out on a clean sheet of paper (Ashenfelder 2019). Engelbart's demo presented a wholly different paradigm from the IBM machine. He believed—correctly, as it would turn out—that in the future, others would work in the same manner as he was demonstrating. As he told his audience, "Better solutions, faster solutions, solutions to more complex problems, better use of human capabilities" (Engelbart 1968). At the end of his demo, he received a standing ovation.

The augmented human

The Mother of All Demos greatly surpassed the expectation for what computers could do and what people could do with computers. It introduced a spectrum of possible uses for computer interfaces that weren't just peripherals and outboard devices to control the computer, but also a way of supporting and extending the reach of human senses: what Engelbart had researched since the early 1960s under the umbrella of "augmenting human intellect." "By augmenting human intellect we mean increasing the capability of man to approach a complex problem situation to gain comprehension to suit his particular needs and to derive solutions to problems" (Engelbart 1962: 1), he wrote in the first sentence of the 1962 *Augmenting Human Intellect: A Conceptual Framework* report for the Air Force Office of Scientific Research. Augmentation referred to a sort of bigger-better-faster-more for human comprehension, an ability to better tackle major societal problems. Part method, part system, part device experimentation, Engelbart's platform for augmentation research included it all. "We refer to way of life in an integrated domain where hunches cut-and-try intangibles and the human feel for situation usefully coexist with powerful concepts streamlined terminology and notation sophisticated methods and high-powered electronic aids" (Engelbart 1962: 1) The 120-page document sketches out the foundation for the ideas that he showed on stage in San Francisco six years later. In the report, he argued that human possibilities for processing information were constrained by the limitations of human senses and that electronic devices would be able to extend the capabilities of human intelligence.

Engelbart began his report with a story of an "augmented architect" who used a new breed of computer-aided design system (published three months before Ivan Sutherland completed his dissertation on the Sketchpad system). "Let us consider an augmented architect at work," Engelbart writes.

Augmentation and interface 81

He sits at a working station that has a visual display screen some three feet on a side; this is his working surface, and is controlled by a computer (his 'clerk') with which he can communicate by means of a small keyboard and various other devices. He is designing a building. He has already dreamed up several basic layouts and structural forms, and is trying them out on the screen.

(Engelbart 1962: 4)

Engelbart's fictional tool brings together tools for design, functional analysis, data flows, and calculations that support the design of a building, its interior, its site, and its structure. The use case of an architect gave Engelbart good means to talk about managing information complexity and multiple functions that computerized tools could offer.

[T]he computer has many other capabilities for manipulating and displaying information that can be of significant benefit to the human in non-mathematical processes of planning, organizing, studying, etc. Every person who does his thinking with symbolized concepts (whether in the form of the English language, pictographs, formal logic, or mathematics) should be able to benefit significantly, he wrote.

(Engelbart 1962: 6)

Engelbart sought to augment human intelligence on four levels of human capability: "artifacts," "language," "methodology," and "training" (Engelbart 1962: 9). Humans already used these four capabilities to extend their senses: Engelbart proposed systematizing them, building an *interface* that would mediate between human and computer and as a mediator of the exchange of "energy." "Where a complex machine represents the principal artifact with which a human being cooperates, the term 'man-machine interface' has been used for some years to represent the boundary across which energy is exchanged between the two domains," Engelbart wrote, which would take place when a human-only process "coupled" to an artifact-only process (Engelbart 1962: 20). While this operation could be computational, it is something core to humans ever since they developed tool use: "the 'man-artifact interface' has existed for centuries, ever since humans began using artifacts and executing composite processes," he wrote (Engelbart 1962: 20–21). Similar capabilities would grow as computers could augment language and writing ability, the structures that people used to organize their information and mental concepts, the executive structures they used for management. He devoted nearly five pages to directly quoting Vannevar Bush's 1945 article, "As We May Think," as an inspiration for information storage mechanisms. The most substantial part of the report is a 42-page scenario, "Hypothetical Description of Computer-Based Augmentation System," all recounted as a dialogue in which a man named "Joe" narrates the way that he manipulates symbols, builds

82 Molly Wright Steenson

words into concepts, and processes with the interfaces that Engelbart envisioned. It set the stage for the eventual 1968 demonstration, a performance of the spectrum of interfaces.

"Whom to augment first?" (Engelbart 1962: 116) asks the *Augmenting Human Intellect* report. Architects and everyday people notwithstanding, Engelbart recommended computer programmers for a variety of practical reasons (they tended to work solo, they were already familiar with computers, their work was easily measurable) as well as ones that had to do with the intellectual problems in programming, and the fact that the results could be folded into the work of programming. Computer programmers were ideal because they had the knowledge and skill to begin to build the interfaces that would institute a ripple effect. The first step in a flow chart that outlined the goals of the project rather grandly stated, "Attacking the critical problems of our society that are discernible by those who can initiate new methods toward their solution" (Engelbart 1962: 126).

In sum, Engelbart had in his sights a long horizon, in which the development of interfaces that could augment human intelligence would ultimately change the possibilities for how humans sensed, understood, and solved problems. The ramifications of these changes would be societal in scale. As he wrote, "man's problem-solving capability represents possibly the most important resources possessed by a society … Any possibility for evolving an art or science that can couple directly and significantly to the continued development of that resource should warrant doubly serious consideration" (Engelbart 1962: 131). The cause of human augmentation, and of a range of interfaces that aided and supported human exchange and knowledge, would change the world.

I've started here with the spectrum of augmentation and interface that Engelbart envisioned. The history of user interfaces, Jonathan Grudin wrote in 1990, is one in which the computer increasingly "reaches out" into the world, moving from hardware, to software, "farther and farther out from the computer itself, deeper into the user and the work environment" (Grudin 1990: 261). The possibilities for this outward expansion are evident in the definitions of the term *interface*. The *Oxford English Dictionary* defines it as a shared spatial or material boundary, a locus of organizational interaction, and as an "apparatus" that connects other "devices" so that they can be "operated jointly" (interface, n. 2018). Essentially, interfaces are bridges, making it possible to connect unlike to unlike. For Engelbart, they could mediate the flow of energy, model a dialogue, or supporting the operation of different devices at both a small, applied scale, and at a large, societal scale so great that it could change human existence. "The computer reaches out," indeed, to borrow from Jonathan Grudin (Grudin 1990: 261).

Engelbart influenced other researchers who supported the expanded notions of augmentation and interface from the computer, to language, to the built environment, to a panoply of computing devices. In the sections that follow, I will trace how the spectrum of computation expands in the research of other individuals who took up Engelbart's questions. I will begin with Warren M. Brodey and Nilo Lindgren, who addressed the issue of dialogue and enhancement from Engelbart, and who influenced discussions about computational technologies, cybernetics, and artificial intelligence in technology journalism and at MIT. Then, I will introduce the work of the MIT Architecture Machine Group and its cofounder Nicholas Negroponte, who took up Engelbart, Brodey and Lindgren's work in the interfaces that the Architecture Machine Group designed between 1967–84. There, interfaces start as devices and peripherals for input and output, and become information surrounds for both entertainment and military purposes. In the early 1990s, the interface and the computer both disappear into the environment: so claimed Mark Weiser at Xerox PARC, the progenitor of ubiquitous computing. In these research projects, people use computer interfaces in novel ways, and bit by bit, the interfaces change the built environment. Ultimately, they realize Engelbart's big ideas and then some, with some startling ramifications.

Enhancement through dialogue

Warren M. Brodey and Nilo Lindgren took human dialogue and situated it as a ground for new possibilities for human-machine interaction. Brodey, a physician and psychiatrist, became involved with cybernetics and consulted at MIT with the Artificial Intelligence Lab, the Architecture Machine Group, and its co-founder Nicholas Negroponte between 1964 and 1968 (Brodey, Westvik 2004). Brodey became increasingly involved with cybernetics and ecology, emigrating to Norway in the 1970s and focusing on new modes of psychotherapy, and developing digital tools for new modes of interaction; now in his 90s, he still lives in Norway. Lindgren, a graduate of MIT, was an electrical engineer and technology editor and writer who helped to develop magazines such as *IEEE Spectrum* (Wisnioski 2019). Their writing in this period supported collaborations on artificial intelligence research through Brodey's collaborations with the MIT AI Laboratory. Brodey was a part of other discussions about architecture and computation, giving an artistic talk at the Yale Computer Graphics Conference in 1968. Nicholas Negroponte, with the MIT Architecture Machine Group, was inspired by Brodey's work to title his second book *Soft Architecture Machines* after Brodey's article "Soft Architecture," which envisioned inhabitable, intelligent environments (Negroponte 1975).

Brodey and Lindgren wrote "Human Enhancement through Evolutionary Technology" and "Human Enhancement: Beyond the Machine Age," a pair of articles in 1967 and 1968 that outlined the possibilities of interacting with burgeoning artificial intelligence. Enhancement does not differ greatly from augmentation, as Engelbart approached it, but rather expands upon the notion of dialogue. Brodey and Lindgren postulated the potential for what they called "'interfacing in depth' between men and machines"—what they envisioned as a dialogue between humans and computers (Brodey, Lindgren 1967: 90). They examined the role of artificial intelligence in achieving evolutionary systems that capitalize upon the distributed intelligence of time sharing systems—and the processes and interfaces that would support this notion of dialogue. In "Human Enhancement: Beyond the Machine Age," they wrote,

> The augmentation research ... looks at the chief design factors, the information characteristics of the messages, the signal forms and the information encoding at the interface, and the computer decoding process—which must be compatible with human ability to learn and perform.
>
> (Brodey, Lindgren 1968: 83)

What was notable about Engelbart's framework, they argued, was that it focused on humans and computers both, and not on one or the other. The interface is the locus of information encoding, but it is also an artifact that serves to support the sensemaking and decoding processes of intellect augmentation through computing.

Dialogue, for Brodey and Lindgren, referred to several things: a means of modeling mutuality of understanding, tracking in conversation, and learning, applied to human-machine interaction that could enhance human capabilities. A dialogue draws good friends out, as each party brings new information to the conversation, testing and pushing the boundaries in a friendly manner, they wrote. Patterns emerge. There are ways to correct errors where they occur. Both people observe, participate, shape the dialogue: it is not a passive endeavor. "We require large systems with which we can engage in humanlike dialogue, of the rich kind that occurs between people," they wrote.

> Our entire machine environment needs to be given a self-organizing capability that is similar to the self-organizing capability of men, so that both kinds of systems can evolve and survive over the long run. Coexistence is better than the slavery to the stupid machines that is accepted now.
>
> (Brodey, Lindgren 1968: 94).

Computers were limited in what they could do, subsequently limiting what we could imagine of them. What if instead of accepting these limitations, we interacted with machines as we do with each other? What if the nuances of interface were humane? "[C]an sensitive capabilities be given to machines? Will it be possible to create a more intelligent and more responsive environment? Or are these merely fanciful and empty wishes?" they asked. It wasn't a fantasy. In fact, "work is already beginning," Brodey and Lindgren wrote (Brodey, Lindgren 1968: 94).

Brodey and Lindgren outlined the state-of-the-art of the AI and neuroscience advances of their time, taking media interfaces into account. "What we have been emphasizing here, largely because of their novelty, are physical applications of new languages growing out of new media," Brodey and Lindgren wrote in their conclusion to their 1968 article, likening the work of AI and cybernetics researchers to work on film in the early 1900s. "[T]his new medium, the movie, could arouse feelings, sensations, and insights that could not be aroused by single photos. The movie was a new language medium, and so too is the computer" (Brodey, Lindgren 1968: 92).

Architecture machines

Nicholas Negroponte and the Architecture Machine Group also adopted this notion of the possibilities for emotional connection through media. In his 1970 book *The Architecture Machine*, Nicholas Negroponte proposed a theory of interfaces for artificial intelligence—"architecture machines." The book, coyly dedicated "To the first machine that can appreciate the gesture," took inspiration from numerous AI and cybernetics researchers. It described projects and collaborations by the MIT Architecture Machine Group that Negroponte and his cofounder and colleague Leon Groisser led in the School of Architecture and the group's work with the MIT AI Lab led by Marvin Minsky. The Architecture Machine Group was in existence from 1967–84, when it rolled into the MIT Media Lab that Negroponte founded—the moniker "media" chosen because it ran counter to the way that people talked about technology at that time: "media was ripe to be claimed and wouldn't be taken on elsewhere at MIT" (Steenson 2017).

What was an architecture machine?

> Given that the physical environment is not in perfect harmony with every man's life style, given that architecture is not the faultless response to human needs, given that the architect is not the consummate manager of physical environments, I shall consider the physical environment as an evolving organism as opposed to a designed artefact. In particular, I shall consider an evolution aided by a specific class of machines. Warren McCulloch calls them ethical robots; in the context of architecture I shall call them architecture machines.
>
> (Negroponte 1970: Preface)

In addition, baked into this definition of architecture machines were elements of sociality and scale. McCulloch considered "ethical robots" to exhibit a tendency toward social interaction—akin to Brodey and Lindgren's notion of dialogue—meaning that architecture machines were social, seeking out connections to one another. Negroponte in 1969 published his own article that alluded to McCulloch's title: McCulloch wrote "Toward

Some Circuitry of Ethical Robots," while Negroponte published "Toward a Theory of Architecture Machines."

Architecture machines, as Negroponte envisioned them, would be symbiotic, a reference to J.C.R. Licklider's 1960 article "Man-Computer Symbiosis," in which Licklider projected human-computer interactions more powerful than what either would encompass alone, in what became the operative vision for interactivity for decades. In applying Licklider's notion of symbiosis to architecture machines, Negroponte envisioned "the intimate association of two dissimilar species (man and machine), two dissimilar processes (design and computation), and two intelligent systems (the architect and the architecture machine)" (Architecture Machine Group 1971: Preface). This characterization also brings to mind Engelbart's *Augmented Human Intellect: A Conceptual Framework*, in which artifacts, methodology, and interfaces work in conjunction with each other. Such systems would be self-organizing, able to learn and develop a personalized view of the user with whom they interacted.

Negroponte still found himself continually frustrated with the limitations of interfaces, of input and output devices. What about the possibilities of fingers—what he called "the insatiable desire to get things immediately" (Negroponte 1978: 1407)?

> Often, the finger is viewed as a 1/2 inch diameter stylus, and thus a low resolution input device. In fact, the finger is a very high resolution, sensitive, and direct means of input with two very important and distinguishing features: one, you do not have to pick it up, and two, you have ten of them.
>
> (Negroponte 1978: 1407)

The Architecture Machine Group began working with touch screens in the 1970s that used pens and fingers as the mode of interaction, and in the late 1970s experimented with a handheld window not unlike a very early version of today's iPad (Architecture Machine Group 1977). It was something that audiences didn't always understand when they were demonstrated: why would you want to touch a screen (Negroponte and Steenson, 2013)? Historian Daniel Cardoso Llach has pointed out that the finger plays an especially lyrical role in everyday life but that computers are still slow on the uptake, demonstrated in the beautiful *Finger Film* by Rachel Strickland that shows the myriad things that fingers do: gesticulate in conversation, dial telephones, and pick things up (Cardoso Llach, 2017). The end of the film shows Architecture Machine Group members James Rubin and Paul Pangaro trying to write with a fingertip on a touch-sensitive display, as the system attempts to render their finger strokes and partly fails on the word END (the D doesn't quite appear). "All my films have hokey endings. Well, what are you gonna do?" Pangaro quips (Strickland 1976).

Negroponte also had a nagging sense that questions of interfaces for AI were also questions of embodiment. In multiple passages in his books and papers, he examines the role of the body in imaginations of AI. He wrote, "It is so obvious that our interfaces, that is, our bodies, are intimately related to learning and to how we learn, that one point of departure in artificial intelligence is to concentrate specifically on the interfaces" (Negroponte 1975: 48). As such, designers and architects should make sensory inputs and outputs the stuff of design. "It seems natural that architecture machines would be superb clients for sophisticated sensors. Architecture itself demands a sensory involvement," Negroponte wrote. "Designers need an involvement with the sensory aspects of our physical environments, and it is not difficult to imagine that their machine partners need a similar involvement" (Negroponte 1970: 111). What might this mean for the machine and its own conception of knowledge? How might it come to know the depth of human experience? "For a computer to acquire intelligence will it have to look like me, be about six feet tall, have two arms, two eyes, and an array of humanlike apparatus?" Negroponte asked (Negroponte 1975: 49). Although he warranted that the question might be ridiculous, he thought it was vital. How else might interfaces be developed that allowed for "witnessing" and "manipulating" the world, understanding its metaphors.

> Does a machine have to possess a body like my own and be able to experience behaviors like my own in order to share in what we call intelligent behavior? While it may seem absurd, I believe the answer is yes.
>
> (Negroponte 1975: 49)

But by 1977, the Architecture Machine Group was focusing less on the concept of the body and embodiment and more on computing environments, what Negroponte called "being in the interface" and what Stewart Brand later referred to as a "personal computer with the person inside" (Brand 1987: 152). The locus of these explorations was the Media Room. Rather than a loud computer installed in the room, it was placed outside the walls, providing the room's user with a quieter experience of being in a computational environment. It was a soundproofed, carpet-walled room, 18 x 11 x 11 ½ feet, that featured an enormous, six-foot by eight-foot rear-projected television screen and an octophonic stereo system. In the center of the room was an Eames lounge chair outfitted with joystick pads in its armrests that could be used to navigate information environments. To the left and right of the chair were two touch-sensitive displays in the user's reach and a ten-inch square data tablet that the user could hold in their lap and operate with a stylus (Donelson 1978).

The Architecture Machine Group projects that took place in the Media Room allowed for navigation of "a sense of place" within an information environment (Negroponte, Bolt 1978: 2). In the Aspen Movie Map, for

88   *Molly Wright Steenson*

example, the user zoomed down the streets of Aspen, Colorado while sitting in the Eames lounge chair and navigating with the joystick pads in the arms. The large screen showed the street scene in Aspen (delivered from images stored on videodisc); the smaller touchscreens showed maps to help the user navigate. The Movie Map supported multiple modes of perception in one experience. As Bob Mohl wrote in his dissertation, it supported "a novel form of spatial representation can be created which substitutes for the actual experience … for pre-experiencing an unfamiliar locale that allows the acquisition of spatial knowledge to take place in a meaningful, natural, and accurate way" (Mohl 1982: 2).

The Media Room also supported novel modes of interaction that involved bodily interfaces. "Put That There" used voice, gesture, and comprehension of abstract commands to support ship fleet navigation in a project that the Office of Naval Research sponsored. In a video, Chris Schmandt of the Architecture Machine Group, and later the MIT Media Lab, demonstrates how the system works. He sits in the Eames lounge chair and wears a small cube attached to his wrist. He makes clear statements and gestures to command the system. The statement "put that there" refers to the abstraction that the system endeavored to comprehend through reading voice and gesture (and was the reason that Stewart Brand referred to the room as a whole as the "Put That There" room in his book *The Media Lab*) (Brand 1987: 152).

Chris Schmandt:	Pay attention. Create a red oil tanker.
System:	Where?
Schmandt:	There. (Points north of the Dominican Republic.) Put a blue cruise ship—
System:	Where?
Schmandt:	East of the Bahamas. Make a yellow sailboat.
System:	Where?
Schmandt:	North of that. (Points at Havana.) Create a green freighter.
System:	Where?
Schmandt:	East of the sailboat … Put That There. (Points to the yellow sailboat and then points to the eastern edge of the screen)

(Schmandt 1979)

The Department of Defense funded much of the Architecture Machine Group's work, in particular the Defense Advanced Research Projects Agency (DARPA) Information Processing Techniques Office and later Cybernetics Technology Office, and the Office of Naval Research. Like other labs at MIT whose work was funded by the DoD, the work needed to be applied to battlefield concerns because defense funding could not be applied to basic, open-ended scientific research. The Architecture Machine Group followed the lead of MIT AI Lab Director Patrick Winston, who said in a 1996 published interview,

I was seeking to find intersections between what the laboratory was doing and what DARPA was either interested in or could be persuaded to be interested in. So in some cases, it was a matter of pointing out the potential application of a piece of work.

(Norberg, O'Neill, Freedman 1996: 37–38)

Negroponte and his Architecture Machine Group colleague understood the stakes of what they were trying to do. On one hand, they sought defense funding to keep the lab going; doing so required tactical, applied military applications of the interfaces the group explored. On the other hand, the lab was a group of self-described tinkerers, interested in playing at the edges of media and entertainment, just at the time that Hollywood released blockbusters like Star Wars, and that movie theaters like the IMAX introduced new, immersive, sci-fi experiences. As a result, while projects like Aspen Movie Map explored place-centered experience and storytelling, and Put That There investigated gestural interaction, voice recognition, and of course the computing technology required to enable the projects, the funded purpose was investigations of command and control interfaces, military simulation, and remote sensing and navigation. The agendas are evident in proposals that Negroponte wrote, and had a direct and explicit connection to the interfaces that the Architecture Machine Group wanted to design.

A particularly vibrant passage is in a 1978 proposal for a project called Data Space. "The immediate goal of this research is to so enrich and to so quicken the Man/Computer interface that the human becomes more than simply a dimensionless point," it began (Negroponte, Bolt 1978: 1).

The inherent paradox of this paper has been that we are proposing to develop human-computer interfaces, on the one hand as sophisticated in conception as a cockpit, on the other hand as operationally simple as a TV. From either perspective, the objective is the same: supreme usability,...We look upon this objective as one which requires intimacy, redundancy, and parallelism of immersive modes and media of inter-action. the image of a user perched in front of a monochromatic display with a keyboard, is obscured by the vision of a Toscanininiesque, self-made surround with the effervescence of Star Wars.

(Negroponte, Bolt 1978: 3)

A few years before Negroponte and Bolt proposed supreme usability and interfaces equally at home in the living room or the battlefield, Negroponte described what he called his "view of the distant future of architecture machines: they won't help us design; instead, we will live in them" (Negroponte 1975: 5). In the future, there would be no boundary between computers and people: the interface would become the surround, would become the world in which we live. There would be no end to the interface because we would inhabit it.

"The fabric of everyday life"

Negroponte's architecture machine is not unlike Mark Weiser's concepts in his influential *Scientific American* article, "The Computer for the 21st Century" more than 15 years later. As Weiser wrote, "The most profound technologies are those that disappear. They weave themselves into the fabric of everyday life until they are indistinguishable from it" (Weiser 1991: 94). Weiser, chief scientist and chief technology officer at Xerox PARC, introduced the concept of "ubiquitous computing." Ubiquitous computing encompassed several ideas: that everyday people would be so accustomed to computing, they wouldn't need to think about how they interfaced with it, and that computing would be absorbed into the world around us, changing the way that we think. He wrote: "only when things disappear in this way are we freed to use them without thinking and so to focus beyond them on new goals" (Weiser 1991: 94)—not unlike Engelbart's claims in the 1960s. Ubiquitous computing also referred to the technical aspects of a disappearing interface—the "tabs, pads, and boards" that Weiser and his Xerox PARC colleagues designed: disposable screens at small sizes (tabs: like "active Post-it notes"), at-hand tablets (pads), and large scale video screens (boards), and the network and security that would be required to link the devices locally and globally (Weiser 1991: 98). This ubiquitous network would support collaboration, communication, office work, and even shopping, Weiser suggested.

Funny how that doesn't look like a disappearing interface at all: it instead seems like a great many interfaces everywhere, each supporting a different kind of information. It was the opposite of a virtual reality. Weiser called it "embodied virtuality ... the process of drawing computers out of their electronic shells" (Weiser 1991: 98). It provided an enmeshing of information and interface, of what Katherine Hayles reminds us:

> ... for information to exist, it must always be instantiated in a medium, whether that medium is the page from the Bell Laboratories Journal on which Shannon's equations are printed, the computer-generated topological maps used by the Human Genome Project, or the cathode ray tube on which virtual worlds are imaged.
>
> (Hayles 1999: 13).

But maybe the status of the disappearing interface is more precarious than we might have thought. "The Computer for the 21st Century" presents a possible scenario of a ubiquitous computing future that goes like this:

> A blank tab on Sal's desk beeps and displays the word "Joe" on it. She picks it up and gestures with it toward her live board. Joe wants to discuss a document with her, and now it shows up on the wall as she hears Joe's voice:

'I've been wrestling with this third paragraph all morning, and it still has the wrong tone. Would you mind reading it?'.

Sitting back and reading the paragraph, Sal wants to point to a word. She gestures again with the 'Joe' tab onto a nearby pad and then uses the stylus to circle the word she wants:

'I think it's this term 'ubiquitous.' It's just not in common enough use and makes the whole passage sound a little formal. Can we rephrase the sentence to get rid of it?'

'I'll try that'.

(Weiser 1991: 98)

Conclusions

Computer interfaces engender the thinking about systems and intelligence of their moment. For Douglas Engelbart, that moment in the 1960s was a spectrum of the augmentation of humans through computational aids. Just as an interface bridges parts of systems, in Engelbart's view, computers would extend the purview of the human senses, allowing for people to solve problems of greater complexity. Ultimately, what humans could accomplish on the world scale would change, thanks to the appropriation of computation on society. He concluded his 1962 report *Augmenting Human Intellect: A Conceptual Framework* with the high stakes of his vision.

After all we spend great sums for disciplines aimed at understanding and harnessing nuclear power. Why not consider developing a discipline aimed at understanding and harnessing 'neural power?' In the long run the power of the human intellect is really much the more important of the two.

(Engelbart 1962: 132)

As Jonathan Grudin writes, the "computer reaches out" into the world around us (1990: 261). In this chapter, we traced that reach: the forces of language and dialogue enabling self-organized system intelligence, as Warren Brodey and Nilo Lindgren proposed, in Nicholas Negroponte's architecture machine that we live within, or Mark Weiser's ubiquitous computing where interfaces are a part of our lives. In numerous ways, we have seen these visions come to pass. The scenarios of Joe's world in 1962 in Engelbart's report, and Sal's world in "The Computer for the 21st Century" in 1991 did come to be, and then some. While our ubiquitous information interfaces have changed the way we work and think, many argue that it doesn't serve to augment our intelligence—they now do the opposite by taxing our "attentional control" as it competes with other thought processes (Ward et al. 2017). While Engelbart postulated that interfaces would ultimately augment the human senses, they also indicate the limits of our capabilities.

92 Molly Wright Steenson

Moreover, writing this from the perspective of 2019, there is much societal critique of whether these augmentations of human intellect are actually good for us on the world scale. To that end, further work could continue to probe the spectrum of interfaces and Engelbart's notion of human augmentation of intellect, including using interface theories on politics or digital materiality as a point of departure, the stack, the cloud, writings by Keller Easterling, Benjamin Bratton, Paul Dourish, Christian Ulrik Andersen and Søren Bro Pold, or Alexander Galloway, to name a few. "The interfaces are back, or perhaps they never left," writes Galloway in *The Interface Effect* (Galloway 2013: 25).

In closing, let us return to Engelbart's stage in San Francisco. The audience has gone home, and now the interfaces operate upon us to augment our being. The interfaces that enable dialogue and learning, that facilitate our interactions with people and machines each and both, that provide a means of operation. The interfaces that bridge the abstract and the concrete, the symbolic and the literal, the human and the computer. The interfaces moved from the peripherals to the peripheries to envelope their users. Interfaces became cinematic, then more than cinematic, then bombastic. Ease of use became usability, usability became tactical military operation. And then the interfaces seeped into the world around us. We can't tell where we stop and where they begin. The stage goes dark.

Bibliography

Architecture Machine Group (1971) *Computer Aids to Participatory Architecture*, Cambridge, MA: MIT Press.

Architecture Machine Group (1977) *Mapping by Yourself*, Cambridge, MA: MIT Press.

Ashenfelder, M. (2019) *The Maryland Institute for Technology in the Humanities | The Signal* [online] Blogs.loc.gov. Available at: https://blogs.loc.gov/thesignal/2014/05/the-maryland-institute-for-technology-in-the-humanities/ [Accessed 2 January 2019].

Brand, S. (1987) *The Media Lab: Inventing the Future at MIT*, New York: Viking.

Brodey, W. and Lindgren, N. (1967) "Human Enhancement through Evolutionary Technology," *IEEE Spectrum* 4, 87–97.

Brodey, W. and Lindgren, N. (1968) "Human Enhancement: Beyond the Machine Age," *IEEE Spectrum* 5, 79–97.

Brodey, W. and Westvik, R. (2004) *US: Portrait of a Pioneer. A Dialogue between Warren Brodey and Rita Westvik*, Oslo: Allkopi.

Cardoso Llach, D. (2017) *Designing the Computational Image, Imagining Computational Design*, Pittsburgh, PA: Miller Gallery, Carnegie Mellon University, 22 September–12 November 2017.

Donelson, W. C. (1978) "Spatial Management of Information," *ACM SIGGRAPH Computer Graphics* 12, 203–209.

Engelbart, D. (1962) *Augmenting Human Intellect: A Conceptual Framework*, Washington, DC: Air Force Office of Scientific Research.

Augmentation and interface   93

Engelbart, D. (1968) *Mother of All Demos* [Online Video]. 8 December 1968. Available at: www.dougengelbart.org/content/view/374/464/ [Accessed 2 January 2019].

Galloway, A. (2013) *The Interface Effect*, New York: John Wiley & Sons.

Grudin, J. (1990) "The Computer Reaches Out: The Historical Continuity of Interface Design," In *Proceedings of the SIGCHI Conference on Human Factors in Computing Systems. CHI '90* ACM, New York, 261–268.

Hayles, N. K. (1999) *How We Became Posthuman: Virtual Bodies in Cybernetics, Literature, and Informatics*, Chicago: University of Chicago Press.

'interface, n.' (2018). *In: OED Online* [online]. Available at: www.oed.com [Accessed 2 January 2019].

Mohl, R. (1982) "Cognitive Space in the Interactive Movie Map: An Investigation of Spatial Learning in Virtual Environments," unpublished Ph.D. dissertation, MIT.

Negroponte, N. (1970) *The Architecture Machine*, Cambridge, MA: MIT Press.

Negroponte, N. (1975) *Soft Architecture Machines*, Cambridge, MA: MIT Press.

Negroponte, N. (August 29, 1976) "PLACE," *Architecture Machinations* 2, no. 35, 2, Box 1, Folder 3, Institute Archives and Special Collections, MIT Libraries, Cambridge, MA.

Negroponte, N. (1978) "New Qualities of Computer Interactions," *Proceedings of the IEEE International Conference on Cybernetics and Society*.

Negroponte, N. and Bolt, R. A. (1978) *Data Space Proposal to the Cybernetics Technology Office*, Defense Advanced Research Projects Agency, Cambridge, MA: MIT Press.

Negroponte, N. and Steenson, M. W. (2013) We Were Bricoleurs: An Interview with Nicholas Negroponte." In *A Second Modernism: MIT and Architecture and the 'Techno-Social' Moment*, Arindam Dutta (ed.), 794–809, Cambridge, MA: MIT Press.

Norberg, A., O'Neill, J. and Freedman, K. (1996) *Transforming Computer Technology: Information Processing for the Pentagon, 1962–1986*, Baltimore, MD: Johns Hopkins University Press.

Schmandt, C. (1979) *Put That There* [online video]. Available at: www.youtube.com/watch?v=0Pr2KIPQOKE [Accessed 14 August 2018].

Steenson, M. W. (2017) *Architectural Intelligence: How Architects and Designers Created the Digital Landscape*, Cambridge, MA: MIT Press.

Strickland, R. (1976) *Finger Film* [Online Video]. 2011. Available at: https://vimeo.com/27354629 [Accessed 2 January 2019].

Ward, A., Duke, K., Gneezy, A. and Bos, M. (2017) "Brain Drain: The Mere Presence of One's Own Smartphone Reduces Available Cognitive Capacity," *Journal of the Association for Consumer Research* 2, 2, 140–154.

Weiser, M. (1991) "The Computer for the 21st Century," *Scientific American* 265, 94–104.

Wisnioski, M. (2019)" Innovation Magazine and the Birth of a Buzzword," *IEEE Spectrum*, [Online]. Available at: https://spectrum.ieee.org/tech-history/silicon-revolution/innovation-magazine-and-the-birth-of-a-buzzword [Accessed 2 January 2019].

6 The first failure of man-computer symbiosis
The hospital computer project, 1960–1968

David Theodore

In 1960, Cambridge, Massachusetts-based research consultants Bolt, Beranek and Newman Inc. (BB&N) began to set up a project based on tightly coupled interactions between human beings and digital, electronic, stored-program computers. BB&N collaborated with the National Institutes of Health, the Massachusetts General Hospital, and the American Hospital Association on an ambitious "total information system," which became known as the Hospital Computer Project (Massachusetts General Hospital Laboratory of Computer Science 1966d).[1]

BB&N conceived the hospital project as a first chance to instantiate J. C. R. Licklider's influential program for man-computer symbiosis (Licklider 1960: 4–11). Licklider is a central figure in the history of electronic computing, a key node in the social networks concerned with all things digital (Edwards 1996: 262–271). He was trained in psychoacoustics, but became known for his work in the Lincoln Laboratory at the Massachusetts Institute of Technology. Notably, he experimented with the Whirlwind computer, helping to set up SAGE (Semi-Automatic Ground Environment), the American military's computer-based anti-missile defense system (Hughes 1998).[2] He started as a consultant at BB&N in 1957, and left in 1962 when he went on to the US Department of Defense. There he directed the new Information Processing Techniques Office (IPTO) of the Advanced Research Projects Agency (ARPA). His mandate was to stimulate computer research across the US.

Licklider was especially eager to find new fields for technological experimentation. He argued that computers should move out of their confined niche in the military-industrial-academic complex. For instance, he thought that library information handling would inevitably be transformed from paper card systems to national and even international digital storage and retrieval systems (Licklider 1965). When he was hired at BB&N, he convinced the firm to purchase a prototype PDP-1 Digital Equipment Corporation computer (see Figure 6.1), and then went looking for ways to use it.

Hospitals were a key target (McCarthy 1983).[3] One of BB&N's founding partners, Jordan J. Baruch, brokered a grant from the National Institutes of Health, an organization with a similar desire to advance the use of

Figure 6.1 DEC PDP-1 computer at BB&N headquarters in Cambridge, Massachusetts. The Massachusetts General Hospital, Hospital Computer Project, Status Report, Memorandum Nine (1966c), p. 9.

computers in biomedicine (November 2012; Walden and Nickerson 2011: 57–58). This turned out to be BB&N's most lucrative consulting job in the early years of the firm. They had 20–30 staff members involved at any one time, who worked in parallel with about the same number of staff at the hospital (Castleman 2006: 6–16).[4]

The Hospital Computer Project was envisioned as a temporary configuration of humans and machines forming a novel kind of thinking thing. Initially Baruch led the project, elaborating Licklider's idea. The man-machine symbiosis article was published in March 1960; Baruch's own article entitled "Doctor-Machine Symbiosis" was published in October of that same year (Baruch 1960: 290–293). The BB&N research team proposed an *interpretive* communication system, dependent on *both* its human users and machine algorithms for editing and routing messages. The system was intended to take over all forms of information processing in the hospital, including machine-aided diagnosis, medication delivery, research activities, and administration. For Licklider and Baruch, the computerized hospital was the hospital of the future.

96 *David Theodore*

Importantly, Licklider did not see the computer as an extension of man's reasoning powers; the technological capabilities of computers were distinct from the rational capabilities of men.[5] He was not seeking to create machine-level artificial intelligence, but rather focused on a new cognitive capacity that he argued would come about through "cooperative inter-action between men and electronic computers": man-computer symbiosis (Licklider 1960: 4). This new cognitive capacity was to be born in the hospital.

And yet, there is a discrepancy. In the history of computing, symbiosis has long been considered influential, visionary and foundational. But looked at from the history of hospitals, symbiosis looks fatally flawed— not at all the best or even a good way to conceptualize man and machine together, and certainly not the best way to see man, woman, machine and architecture together. The Hospital Computer Project shows that in hospitals, computerization had to include *physical* (i.e. architectural) and social (i.e. gendered) as well as cognitive relationships, and it had to proceed inside a medical culture in which there were machines more valuable and more prized than digital computers (McKellar 2018).[6] More unsettling, however, was the possibility that the inability to get symbiosis to work at the hospital revealed conceptual problems. It might just be that at the hospital, BB&N and the computer encountered not a temporary setback, but rather deeper problems that manifest why symbiosis is always doomed to fail. Perhaps "the first failure" is one that *every* interface designer encounters: not just an historical event in BB&N's corporate timeline, but rather an ineluctable impediment to any attempt to couple "man" and "computer."

The postwar research hospital

When BB&N began their experiments with computerized information systems, the hospital was being reformed. The modern hospital had been invented around 1900. While hospitals and hospital care have a long history in the West, scholars have identified a new so-called modern institution that emerged after the American Civil War dedicated to the scientific care of disease. It relied on aseptic surgery, trained nurses, and a switch from volunteer to public funding (Vogel 1980; R. Stevens 1989; Henderson, Horden and Pastore 2007).[7] After reforms to medical education such as the Flexner report in 1910, university hospitals became the accredited home of medical training (Barzansky 2010: 19–25). Hospitals became centers of medical research and experimentation, especially identified with progressivist science and technology, from X-ray machines and modern business methods to team-based surgery (Howell 1995; Adams 2008; Schlich 2010: 71–92).

After World War II, planners struggled to reform hospital design. A common fear was obsolescence. The problem had two main parts. First, hospital stock was aging. Reformers thought that old buildings, simply

First failure of man-computer symbiosis 97

because they were old, were ill-suited to the practice of modern medicine. As hospital consultant Gordon A. Friesen opined, "We're practicing 20th-century medicine in 19th-century buildings" (DeMicheal 1969). New medicine needed new buildings. Reformers also identified a second, more subtle problem, namely, that new hospitals might be built based on outdated ideas. If this was true, then even brand new hospitals could be out of date on opening day. By 1960, this obsession with obsolescence had driven planners to look to technological rather than architectural models (Abramson 2016). There would be no more postcards, no more hospitals as beautiful civic landmarks (Hook 2005: 386–393).[8] Reformers no longer thought of hospitals as beloved cultural institutions but rather as imperfectly designed machines (Hughes 1997: 266–288, 2000a: 21–56, 2000b: 90–103).[9]

Inspired by medical progress, hospital reformers throughout the West looked to rationalize the healthcare delivery system, transforming the hospital from its origins in 19th-century urban philanthropy into basic infrastructure. US reformers, including the American Hospital Association, looked to the computer to help coordinate hospitals into a robust network of independent but interconnected institutions. A committee set up by the American Hospital Association argued that because the main access to the healthcare system was through hospital services, the size and placement of medical facilities should be part of urban planning decisions (American Hospital Association 1970). Hospital size and placement in this new era were to be determined by surveying regions and specifying quantities of hospital beds per 1,000 population.

Hospitals, however, were organized autonomously. Historian Charles Rosenberg calls this characteristic "inward vision," a tendency for each hospital to look inward to its own systems, successes, and failures, rather than outward to its role in a broader healthcare delivery system (Rosenberg 1979: 346–391). Inward vision was reinforced by hospital funding schemes, physician remuneration, medical education, and very emphatically by the architecture itself (Adams 2008). Each hospital thought of its distinctive architecture as an expression of local traditions, local philanthropy, and local civic pride. After World War II, however, architects sought to develop standardized plans ("best practices"). A good plan for a surgery in London, it was thought, would also be good in Boston (Nuffield Provincial Hospitals Trust 1955). British architect and educator Richard Llewelyn Davies produced a guide for the World Health Organization that both described current practices and prescribed new ones: "the similarities between hospital designs all over the world," he wrote, "are more striking than the dissimilarities" (Llewelyn-Davies 1966: 1675).

Computation and hospital life came together quickly (Bennett, Stroebel and Glueck 1969: 709).[10] The same knot of ideas underneath computation also underlay attempts to reform hospital design, namely algorithmic thinking, operations research, and cybernetics (Bailey 1957: 149–157; Thompson and Goldin 1975).[11] One significant and early attempt to engage the

98   *David Theodore*

computer directly in hospital design was Northwick Park Hospital in London (Theodore 2013a: 73–77). In 1962 or early 1963, architect John Weeks teamed up with engineers led by Peter Dunican at Ove Arup & Partners to use computer programming to design the hospital façades parametrically, a quarter of a century before digital parametric design entered everyday architectural practice (Weeks 1965: 203). This was also a decade before other notable proposals for computer-aided hospital design such as OXSYS and the Harness Hospital System (Francis, Glanville, Noble and Scher 1999: 33–36). Computer-oriented algorithms determined the placement of the load-bearing structural concrete mullions, according to the load they carried. The architect boasted that in this early instance of computer-oriented façade composition, the designers of the building simply accepted the computer output from the engineers as the design of the façade (Weeks 1964: 83–106). The future, it seemed, would include such computer-*designed* hospitals.

Licklider also thought computers could help design hospital planning and construction, but he really wanted to use them to manage hospital activities. Licklider in fact saw hospitals as the ideal test case for the development of complex, computer-based technological systems. In 1962, he co-wrote a paper entitled "Online Man-Computer Communication," for the Joint Computer Conference held in San Francisco. The authors wrote that: "Hospitals pose very interesting and difficult—and we believe to a large extent typical—system problems" (Licklider and Clark 1962: 117). They illustrated the article with an oscilloscope image that showed "an outline planning sketch of one floor in a hypothetical hospital" (another early experiment with computer-aided design), and others that mapped "interdepartmental commerce" (i.e. any kind of back-and-forth between different areas of the hospitals, including both transportation of materials and patients and communication). The Hospital Computer Project would (to its detriment) leave out the problems associated with hospital design, and instead concentrate on the issue of interdepartmental commerce.

Four partners

One of the first problems for BB&N was that of pouring new wine into old bottles. Unlike Northwick Park Hospital, which was built from scratch on a greenfield site, the Massachusetts General Hospital in downtown Boston was an old, urban institution with a well-established architecture (see Figure 6.2) (Eaton 1950: 8–11; Faxon 1959).

Charles Bulfinch, architect of the Massachusetts State House, designed the original buildings, which were completed in 1821 (Kirker 1998). In 1846, the first public demonstrations of ether as an aesthetic took place under the dome of the Bulfinch pavilion. Harvard Medical School stood close by the hospital until 1883. By 1960, the MGH was an agglomeration of diverse buildings hemmed in between the Charles River and Beacon Hill.

The Massachusetts General Hospital

Hospital Computer Project

Status Report

1966

MEMORANDUM NINE

Figure 6.2 Cover of The Massachusetts General Hospital, Hospital Computer Project, Status Report, Memorandum Nine (1966c). The cover features a Teletype terminal superimposed on an image of the historic Massachusetts General Hospital ca. 1960. The 1821 Bulfinch pavilion is on the right, featuring its famous pediment and so-called ether dome, the site of early public experiments using ether as an anesthetic for surgery.

100   *David Theodore*

In fact, the MGH was not BB&N's or the American Hospital Association's first choice. It was a research hospital, closely affiliated with Harvard Medical School (Brown 1961).[12] BB&N had wanted to capture data from a typical community hospital, which has a different profile of patients: different illnesses, different treatments, and different social backgrounds. Notes from a meeting in July 1961 with representatives of the MGH, the AHA, the NIH, and BB&N show that the researchers targeted a wide range of facilities. The memo directed the AHA to "name six different kinds of hospitals," and delegated responsibility to William Brines of the Newton-Wellesley Hospital to hold a meeting with representatives of nine Boston-area hospitals (Typescript, "Computer Project File"). But eventually only the MGH came onboard. The characteristics that made the MGH atypical also made it suitable for the project. Through its connection with Harvard Medical School, the MGH maintained a commitment to research and innovation; the staff was willing to participate in an experiment, even knowing the interruptions research could cause (Massachusetts General Hospital Laboratory of Computer Science 1966b, 1967).

The involvement of a prestigious research hospital also helped convince the National Institutes of Health to fund the project. Administrators at the NIH had been looking for ways to advance biomedical computing, since it was clear the biomedical community believed that automated data processing techniques could help researchers deal with the complexity of biological phenomena (November 2011: 9–23). By 1964 the NIH had over $40 million committed to biomedical computing research (Lusted 1966: 365–372).

The third partner, the American Hospital Association, had long been seeking to change the healthcare delivery system. As mentioned earlier, the AHA wanted to overcome the "inward vision" of American hospitals. The 1961 memo notes that, "It must be such that these hospitals can eventually do these things for themselves ... The A.H.A. has an educational responsibility for other hospitals" (Typescript, "Computer Project File"). The AHA saw the research as a pilot project that could later be voluntarily installed in all the hospitals of a regional network, using the computer to link physical locations and data. For the AHA, then, the MGH was a suitable test site partly because the architecture was old: computer systems would have to be retrofitted into existing hospital stock, so it was appropriate that the test hospital was one of the country's oldest.

Technological development of man-computer symbiosis

It is worth noting a couple of technological ideas that are now commonplace, but which BB&N struggled to make work at the hospital: time-sharing and distance computing. They are the key pieces needed to understand the interaction of human and computer envisioned in the Hospital Computer Project.

First, time-sharing. Remember that in this early period of computing, it took some time for the phenomenology of human-computer interaction to

First failure of man-computer symbiosis 101

become an object of reflection. When users began to interact with computers, the programmers remarked that the time it took the machine to "think" was a fraction of the time it took the man to "think"—and to read and type. This time difference meant that one computer could interact with several users simultaneously (*IEEE Annals of the History of Computing*

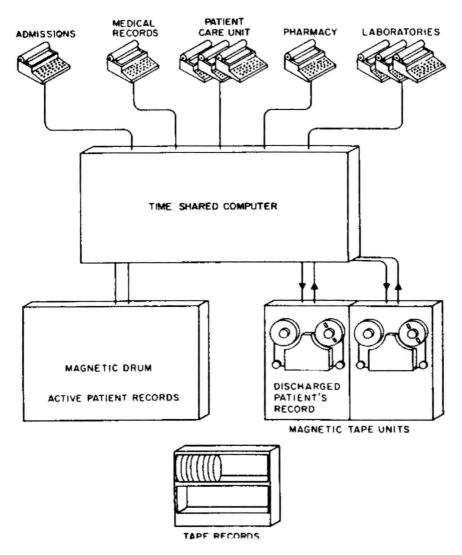

Figure 6.3 Diagram of Time-Sharing computer system used at the Massachusetts General Hospital 1966–1968 Bertoni Castleman, preprint, p. 6.

102 David Theodore

1992). Licklider had worked on time-sharing with John McCarthy at MIT, and, in turn, McCarthy worked with BB&N to create a working version using the PDP-1 computer (see Figure 6.3). It was in operation by October 1962 (McCarthy, Boilen, Fredkin and Licklider 1963: 51–57; Baruch and Barnett 1966: 377–386; Castleman 1969: 707–713).

Second was the novel idea that the computer user did not have to be *physically* close to the machine (Kennedy 1971: 728–752; Land 2000: 16–26; Wenzlhuemer 2013).[13] At first time-sharing meant simply a couple of terminals in the same room as the CPU, but for the hospital, the machine was seven miles away at BB&N's headquarters in Cambridge. It was linked to the hospital using modified Teletype terminals. Baruch wrote in 1960:

> it is expected that within the next decade there will be a single centralized computer at the National Institutes of Health which will be time-shared by many of the laboratories throughout the reservation in such a fashion that it can work in real time.
>
> (Baruch 1960:292).

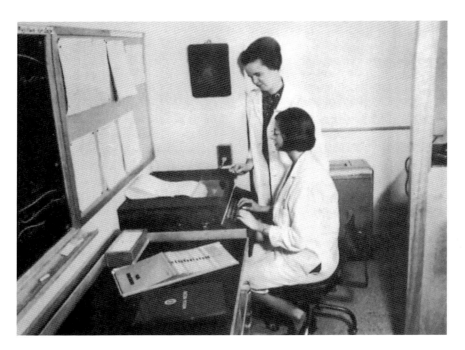

Figure 6.4 Nurses using a soundproofed Teletype machine at the Massachusetts General Hospital. Note the simultaneous use of flip charts. The Massachusetts General Hospital, Hospital Computer Project, Status Report, Memorandum Nine (1966c), p. 9.

First failure of man-computer symbiosis   103

This part of the project, too, was trumpeted as a success. BB&N was able to demonstrate the system over telegraph lines from the AHA's headquarters in Chicago in 1964 (Massachusetts General Hospital Laboratory of Computer Science 1966a).[14] BB&N set up courses for educating hospital staff both about general goals and the nuts and bolts of how to use a computer. The challenge was as much spatial and material as psychological and technical. Staff had to move from a material culture of flip charts to one of keyboards (see Figure 6.4).

BB&N used these two technological concepts in the implementation of their total information, communication, and management system. The main conceptual elements are a basic message, a user, a program, and an action (usually storage). The question was, how should the system interpret and understand communication? The system could do it, BB&N argued, because interpretation, understanding, and communication would occur in a symbiosis between man and computer. Many messages could be "understood" by the machine alone. If a message came in about blood tests or patient room assignments, the machine could process the communication, send the message to the appropriate end user, and store and index it. The

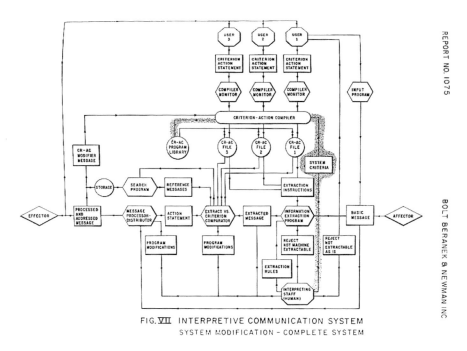

Figure 6.5 Diagram of the interpretive communication system, The Massachusetts General Hospital, Hospital Computer Project, Memorandum Five (1963), p. 39. Note the role for "Human" at the bottom of the diagram.

104   *David Theodore*

system, however, was to grow and change. It would increase in scale because of additional users, but it would also change in kind because new users would instigate new uses. The machine interpretation program, therefore, with its algorithmic decision-making process, would soon enough receive messages that it would not—*could* not—understand. In that case, the messages would be passed to the "Interpreting staff (Human)" (see Figure 6.5). The man is part of a symbiotic system with the computer. The complete system maintained a crucial role for the human interpreter *within* the black box, not just at the input or output stage.

The prototypes worked. The researchers at BB&N introduced a number of programming ideas that "automated" hospital activities: a census of the MGH's 38 hospital care units; a computerized system of worksheets in the chemistry laboratory; computer-based medical history taking; an automated scheduling system for outpatient care; therapeutic aids, such as a computer-assisted therapy plan for burn victims; and computerized X-ray interpretation (Massachusetts General Hospital Laboratory of Computer Science 1967; Barnett and Hoffman 1968: 51–57). A summer project in 1964 using neurological case records established a feasible data processing system; in 1965, Teletypes were placed on a ten-bed care unit on the fourth floor of the Bulfinch building, which the research team had up and running for three to six hours a day (Massachusetts General Hospital Laboratory of Computer Science 1966b: 15–16).

But that was all. The system never met the basic threshold of operability.

The failure of man-computer symbiosis

In 1964, the Massachusetts General Hospital hired G. Octo Barnett to work with the research team implementing computer resources throughout the hospital. In 1968 Barnett wrote a scathing review of the attempt to computerize hospital life, in which he was particularly critical of BB&N's work at the MGH. He wanted to examine the problem of medical computing from the viewpoint of medical practice rather than from the viewpoint of "commercial computer firms." He thought it was a mistake to focus on the technology, such as time-shared computing, and instead focused on the physician's work routine, highlighting seven "functional areas of medical practice" including medical diagnosis, clinical practice, and screening (Barnett 1968: 1321). In short, he argued that BB&N's scheme was conceptually unfeasible. He claimed the project failed due to "overenthusiasm, naïveté, and unrealistic expectations" (Barnett 1968: 1321). Barnett and his Laboratory of Computer Science took over computer research at the MGH after BB&N left.

Barnett identified three key places BB&N failed. He named them "interface" problems: a gap between the user and the terminals; a difference of orientation between the programmer and the system; and an abyss between hospital life and the hospital system mapped by the computer (Barnett and

First failure of man-computer symbiosis 105

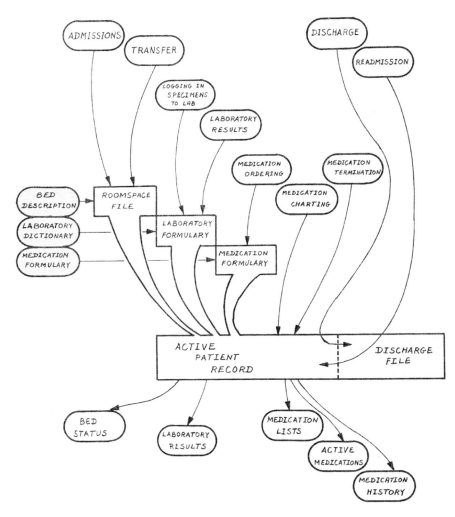

Figure 6.6 Outline of interaction between user programs and patient files, The Massachusetts General Hospital, Hospital Computer Project, Status Report, Memorandum Nine (1966c), p. 61.

Greenes 1969: 756–757). The last was the biggest problem. BB&N's machine-aided administration system was based around the patient's electronic file (see Figure 6.6).

Yet the goal of a *total* information system was too vast. "There is now a keen appreciation of the wide gap separating a demonstration project," he wrote, "and an operational system in daily use" (Barnett 1968: 1326). One issue was that BB&N ignored the importance of information stored in the

106 *David Theodore*

interaction between human and architecture. The combination of man + machine in symbiosis was less efficient than the nurse working alone. For instance, the machine was incapable of effective patient monitoring. Nurses had little difficulty distinguishing between a bed, its physical location, and a patient; they could readily determine if a patient was in a room but not in the bed, or on the ward but not in the room, and so on. Replicating that human skill in a computer program proved was beyond BB&N's capabilities. So instead of a cognitive interaction between nurse and computer, the nurses ended up needing to do their work *plus* providing input to the computer system.

Barnett's second point of failure, the interface gap between machine and user, was quickly noted but difficult to correct. He was not thoroughly pessimistic, but it was clear that the failure was more than technological: "the interface between man and machine," he wrote, "and the computer's ability to respond rapidly and appropriately are of great importance" (Barnett 1968: 1324; Collen and Ball 2015: 201).[15] More broadly, Barnett noted that the requirements for symbiosis placed high demands on a whole range of input and output procedures and devices. BB&N specified Teletype 33 terminals. They were cumbersome and inscrutable, and hospital staff just didn't like them (Orr 1998: 439–455; Castleman 2006: 14).[16] Doctors, especially, didn't like the idea of becoming typists. An article Barnett co-wrote in 1968 with another researcher from the MGH Laboratory of Computer Science asked readers to sympathize with the busy physician. The authors hoped for a future in which "data entry and retrieval could be accomplished by clerical staff and did not require additional effort on the part of over-burdened professional personnel" (Barnett and Hoffman 1968: 52). Moreover, the Teletype terminals made the physical operation of patient care more difficult. The typing added noise to the ward, and so the terminals had to be placed in (modestly) soundproofed rooms (see Figure 6.4). The lack of an appropriate interface between professional staff and computer equipment made it more difficult to integrate the system into routine hospital activity. Overall, Barnett's "interface gap" was more troublesome than even he suggested: there were physical, material, and spatial gaps between human and machine working against the cognitive symbiosis Licklider first projected.

Finally the unreliability of the machines brought the experiment to an end. The hospital had established methods of ensuring 24-hour care; there were no equivalent protocols for ensuring 24-hour operation of the machines—or, especially in this case, *a* machine: the lone PDP-1 back at BB&N headquarters. If it broke, if it went "off-line" in the new jargon, the whole system broke. Therefore, the old routines of management and communication had to be maintained in parallel operation alongside the new electronic prototypes. It also meant that work could not be done by anyone not trained in the new routines. As a result, the staff complained that the computer effectively doubled their work. "Stringent

First failure of man-computer symbiosis   107

reliability requirements and the difficulties attendant when nontechnical personnel (with a high turn-over rate) use a computer system on a round-the-clock basis," Barnet complained. He added, "Computer applications in patient care have been far more dreams than reality" (Barnett 1968: 1326).

Epilogue

The Hospital Computer Project began in 1960. By 1968, it was clear that neither machines nor humans were yet ready for human-machine symbiosis in the hospital. Why not? There are several traditional reasons for the failure, similar to issues common in discussions of technological change, such as experimental programming, unreliable hardware, and the intransigent hospital staff (Dos 1982: 147–162). Barnett's criticisms can be seen as a simple resistance to change, and the staff's commitment to the power of "inward vision," the routines and skills in which traditional medical practices and hospital life were enmeshed. And of course in a hospital, the perceived risks of computer system unreliability or failure were very high: patients' conditions might worsen, or patients might die (Walden and Nickerson 2011: 59);[17] physicians and surgeons would lose reputation; medical researchers would lose grants; and hospitals might lose profit. Taken together, the simplest explanation for the failure of the Hospital Computer Project is thus inchoate technology. The PDP-1 and the newly written programs were simply not ready for hospital use, and the hospital administration and staff, while wiling to experiment with an emerging technological system, were not willing to rely on it.

But it is also possible that BB&N was on completely the wrong track. Computers were not the only new machines entering hospitals. In 1969 heart transplant surgeon Donald Longmore published *Machines in Medicine*, a survey of the myriad biomedical devices under development at around the time of BBN's experiments (Longmore 1969).[18] Longmore included a glossary of 125 different machines then in use in the hospital, in addition to the computer. Hospitals had come to house an array of mechanical equipment, from laundry machines and food supply systems to sterilizing equipment, operating room lights, and a host of analogue electronic diagnostic and therapeutic devices. For many of these pieces of equipment, the issue was automation, not computerization, and the model was the Fordist assembly line and not the MIT computer laboratory. As Canadian hospital consultant Gordon A. Friesen asked, why couldn't healthcare be delivered with the same efficiencies as modern assembly line built products (Weeks 1965: 197–203)?[19]

This difference between automation and computerization identifies a register that the symbiosis concept missed. Licklider thought that the brain was like a computer. Symbiosis could thus be a relationship between two thinking things; brain and computer were not similar in that

108 *David Theodore*

they were both physical, but that in that they were both cognitive. Automation instead relied on a similarity between two physical entities, the working human body and the working machine. The assembly line, that is, constitutes not symbiosis but rather synecdoche and similitude: the assembly line worker *is* a motor, and becomes a part of the entire production machine (Rabinbach 1992; Armstrong 1998).[20] Moreover, an assembly line is always located in a building. The working body takes up space in a way that the thinking brain does not (or at least BBN did not conceive it that way). The notion of automation in hospitals, then, was more powerful than that of computerization, because linking the man, the machine, *and* the building was more effective than just linking the machine and the man.

There was also a crucial gendered difference between Licklider's vision of symbiosis and the way computational thinking could be applied in hospitals. Symbiosis was about men's cognition, but the machine-oriented hospital was about women's labor. Licklider promoted an intellectual use of computation between men and electronics, while the hospital implemented automation, a physical interaction between women and mechanics. In computerized hospitals, nurses and other staff took on the role of assembly line workers (Theodore 2013b: 273–298). As discussed below, BB&N's misunderstanding of these two differences, that is, the asymmetries between men and women and between computerization and automation, were key to the failure of the Hospital Computer Project. Licklider was interested in men and computers, while the hospital was striving to integrate women and automation.

Yet since the Hospital Computer Project was widely considered a failure when it wrapped up in 1968—even the hospital computer staff, you'll recall, called the research naïve—it perhaps also counts as the first *failure* of man-computer symbiosis (Gross 1969: 691–701). Of course, that's not the final evaluation of symbiosis—just the first. And failure can be productive (Imhotep 2012: 175–195). BB&N certainly profited financially and intellectually (McCarthy 1983).[21] And as historian Hallam Stevens points out, by working at the hospital on this project, BB&N gained both the technical knowledge and the reputation that supported their 1968 bid to set up that critically important early multi-computer network, the ARPANET, the forerunner of the Internet (Abbate 1999; H. Stevens 2010: 50–55).[22] And yet, the project's failure prompted deeper questions. Might symbiosis be the wrong way to conceive of man-computer (human-machine) relationships in the hospital? Did this first failure reveal a fatal flaw—a bug so critical that it could never be overcome through better machines or better design? Might man-computer symbiosis *always* fail?

Notes

1 The research team published ten memoranda on the project from 1963–1967. It is straightforward to locate these volumes in archives and libraries, except for the Appendix to Memorandum 6, consisting of 2,000 pages of source

First failure of man-computer symbiosis   109

language programs, which was published only on microfiche. Memorandum 9 gives a summary and overview of the project.

2 SAGE is one of four projects discussed in Thomas P. Hughes *Rescuing Prometheus: Four Monumental Projects That Changed the Modern World*.

3 John McCarthy recalled in 1983: "It was planned to ask NIH for support, because of potential medical applications of time-sharing computers, but before the proposal could even be written."

4 The Hospital Computer Project Memorandum from 1965 lists 20 staff members at the MGH involved, and 24 at BNN—so about 50 researchers at any one time.

5 For the most part, I consider the gender complications of Licklider's "man-computer symbiosis" implicitly. But note that there were important female employees at BB&N, including Donna L. (Lucy) Darling, who worked on speech and handwriting recognition; see *Culture of Innovation*, 35, 69.

6 For instance, heart transplant technology also entered the hospital in the postwar era.

7 The term "invention" belongs to Morris J. Vogel, *The Invention of the Modern Hospital: Boston 1870–1930*, (Chicago: University of Chicago Press, 1980). On the long development of the hospital, see John Henderson, Peregrine Horden, and Alessandro Pastore, "Introduction: The World of the Hospital: Comparisons and Continuities," in *The Impact of Hospitals: 300–2000* (Bern: Peter Lang, 2007), 15–56. On the postwar hospital, see Rosemary Stevens, *In Sickness and in Wealth: American Hospitals in the 20th Century* (Baltimore: Johns Hopkins University Press, 1989).

8 On the role of postcards, see Sara Anne Hook, "You've Got Mail: Hospital Postcards as a Reflection of Health Care in the Early 20th Century," *Journal of the Medical Library Association* 93, no. 3 (2005): 386–393.

9 The debate in Britain was especially contentious; see Jonathan Hughes, "Hospital City," *Architectural History* 40 (1997), 266–88; Jonathan Hughes, "The 'Matchbox on a Muffin': The Design of Hospitals in the Early NHS Medical History," *Medical History* 44 (2000a), 21–56; and Jonathan Hughes, "The Indeterminate Building," in *Non-Plan: Essays on Freedom, Participation and Change in Modern Architecture*, ed. Jonathan Hughes and Simon Sadler (Oxford: Architectural Press, 2000b), 90–103.

10 In 1962, 39 US hospitals used computers; by 1966, 586 hospitals had a computer or used computer services; Walter L. Bennett, Charles F. Stroebel, and Bernard C. Glueck, Jr., "Hospital Automation: Something More than a Computer," *Spring Joint Computer Conference* (1969): 709–714, 709.

11 One influential British advocate for operations research approaches to hospital planning was statistician Norman T. J. Bailey; see e.g. "Operational Research in Hospital Planning and Design," *OR* 8, no. 3 (Bailey 1957): 149–157. American planner John D. Thompson began a series of statistics-based planning studies at Yale University in 1956; some of his work on ward planning was included in John D. Thompson and Grace Goldin, *The Hospital: A Social and Architectural History* (New Haven: Yale University Press, 1975).

12 Initially, the American Hospital Association had hoped to convince David D. Rutstein, head of the Department of Preventive Medicine at the Harvard Medical School, to participate in the project. Letter, July 19, 1961, Madison B. Brown to Dean A. Clark, Massachusetts General Hospital Archives.

13 Action at a distance is an important trope in technology, thanks especially to underwater cables, telegrams, and of course the telephone and radio. See e.g. Roland Wenzlhuemer, *Connecting the Nineteenth-Century World. The Telegraph and Globalization* (Cambridge: Cambridge University Press, 2013);

110   *David Theodore*

P. M. Kennedy, "Imperial Cable Communications and Strategy, 1870–1914," *The English Historical Review* 86, no. 341 (1971): 728–752. J. Lyons & Co restaurants instituted a delivery and production management system using LEO I, the "first" office computer, linked to a telephone call center; see F. Land, "The First Business Computer: A Case Study in User-Driven Automation," *IEEE Annals of the History of Computing* 22, no. 3 (2000): 16–26.

14 Another demonstration took place the same year at the NIH headquarters in Maryland; see Hospital Computer Project Memorandum 5.

15 Barnett's laboratory at the MGH went on to develop MUMPS (Massachusetts General Hospital Utility Multi-Programming System), a successful programming language and database software, famously used by the US Department of Veterans Affairs electronic record system. See Morris F. Collen and Marion J. Ball, ed., *The History of Medical Informatics in the United States*, 2nd ed. (London: Springer-Verlag, 2015), 101–102, 201.

16 Paul Castleman, who started his career in medical computing by working on the Hospital Computer Project, wrote in a memoir that BB&N learnt from their exposure to medical professionals at the MGH that "successfully changing a corporate culture from government defense work to commercial activities is always difficult and often impossible. (As I was quoted in the *St. Louis Post-Dispatch* in 1992, 'It's not like changing your clothes; it's more like changing your sex')"; Castleman, "Medical Applications," 14. See also the exploration of prescriptive and descriptive technical work in Julian Orr, "Images of work," *Science, Technology, & Human Values* 23 (1998): 439–455.

17 A BB&N researcher recalled that, "The feelings at MGH ranged from 'very interesting' to 'it may kill my patients, get it out of here,' with a strong bias toward the latter," *Culture of Innovation*, 59.

18 For an extensive contemporaneous list, see Donald Longmore, *Machines in Medicine: The Medical Practice of the Future* (London: Aldus Books, 1969).

19 Friesen's work on American hospitals had a significant impact on British postwar hospital design; see John Weeks' address to the Royal Institute of British Architects in 1964, "Hospitals for the 1970s," *Medical Care* 3, no. 4 (1965): 197–203.

20 The classic account is Anson Rabinbach, *The Human Motor: Energy, Fatigue, and the Origins of Modernity* (Berkeley: University of California Press, 1992). See also Tim Armstrong, *Modernism, Technology, and the Body: A Cultural Study* (New York: Cambridge University Press, 1998).

21 Baruch remembers getting $1 million for the first grant from NIH; see *Culture of Innovation*, 58.

22 Hallam Stevens, *Life Out of Sequence: An Ethnographic Account of Bioinformatics from the ARPANET to Post-Genomics* (Ph.D. Diss., Harvard University, 2010), 50–55. BB&N's role receives less emphasis in Janet Abbate's *Inventing the Internet* (Cambridge, MA: MIT Press, 1999).

Bibliography

Abbate, J. (1999) *Inventing the Internet*, Cambridge, MA: MIT Press.

Abramson, D. (2016) *Obsolescence: An Architectural History*, Chicago, IL: University of Chicago Press.

Adams, A. (2008) *Medicine by Design*, Minneapolis, MN: University of Minnesota Press.

American Hospital Association (1970) *Report of a Special Committee on the Provision of Health Services, E. Perloff, Chairman*, Chicago: American Hospital Association.

Armstrong, T. (1998) *Modernism, Technology, and the Body: A Cultural Study*, New York: Cambridge University Press.

Bailey, N. T. J. (1957) "Operational Research in Hospital Planning and Design," *OR* 8, no. 3, 149–157.

Barnett, G. O. (1968) "Medical Progress: Computers in Patient Care," *New England Journal of Medicine* 279, no. 24, 1321–1327.

Barnett, G. O. and Greenes, R. A. (1969) "Interface Aspects of a Hospital Information System," *Annals of the New York Academy of Sciences* 61, 756–768.

Barnett, G. O. and Hoffman, P. B. (1968) "Computer Technology and Patient Care: Experiences of a Hospital Research Effort," *Inquiry* 5, no. 3, 51–57.

Baruch, J. (1960) "Doctor-Machine Symbiosis," *IRE Transactions on Medical Electronics ME&* 4, 290–293.

Baruch, J. J. and Barnett, G. O. (1966) "Real-Time Shared On-Line Digital Computer Operations," *Journal of Chronic Disease* 19, 377–386.

Barzansky, B. (2010) "Abraham Flexner and the Era of Medical Education Reform," *Academic Medicine* 85, Supplement 9, 19–25.

Bennett, W. L., Stroebel, C. F. and Glueck, B. C. Jr. (1969) "Hospital Automation: Something More than a Computer," *Spring Joint Computer Conference*, 709–714.

Brown, M. B. (1961) *Madison B. Brown to Dean A. Clark*, July 19. [Letter] Massachusetts General Hospital Archives.

Castleman, P. A. (1969) "A Time-Sharing Computer System for Hospital Information Processing," *Annals of the New York Academy of Sciences* 161, no. 2, 707–713.

Castleman, P. A. (2006) "Medical Applications at BBN," *IEEE Annals of the History of Computing* 28, no. 1, 6–16.

Collen, M. F. and Ball, M. J. (ed.) (2015) *The History of Medical Informatics in the United States*, 2nd ed., London: Springer-Verlag.

DeMicheal, D. (1969) "We're Practicing 20th-century Medicine in 19th-century Facilities!," *Actual Specifying Engineer* 21, no. 4.

Dos, G. (1982) "Technological Paradigms and Technological Trajectories: A Suggested Interpretation of the Determinants and Directions of Technical Change," *Research Policy* 11, no. 3, 147–162.

Eaton, L. K. (1950) "Charles Bulfinch and the Massachusetts General Hospital," *Isis* 41, no. 1, 8–11.

Edwards, P. N. (1996) *The Closed World: Computers and the Politics of Discourse in Cold War America*, Cambridge, MA: MIT Press.

Faxon, N. W. (1959) *The Massachusetts General Hospital, 1935–55*, Cambridge, MA: Harvard University Press.

Francis, S., Glanville, R., Noble, A. and Scher, P. (1999) *50 Years of Hospital Ideas in Health Care Buildings*, London: Nuffield Trust.

Gross, P. F. (1969) "Health Information and Planning Systems: The Need for Consolidation," *Spring Joint Computer Conference*, 691–701.

Henderson, J., Horden, P. and Pastore, A. (2007) "Introduction: The World of the Hospital: Comparisons and Continuities," in John Henderson, Peregrine Horden, and Alessandro Pastore (eds.)*The Impact of Hospitals: 300–2000*, Bern: Peter Lang.

Hook, S. A. (2005) "You've Got Mail: Hospital Postcards as a Reflection of Health Care in the Early Twentieth Century," *Journal of the Medical Library Association* 93, no. 3, 386–393.

112   *David Theodore*

Howell, J. (1995) *Technology in the Hospital: Transforming Patient Care in the Early Twentieth Century*, Baltimore: Johns Hopkins University Press.

Hughes, J. (1997) "Hospital City," *Architectural History* 40, 266–288.

Hughes, J. (2000a) "The "Matchbox on a Muffin": The Design of Hospitals in the Early NHS Medical History," *Medical History* 44, 21–56.

Hughes, J. (2000b) *"The Indeterminate Building,"* in Jonathan Hughes and Simon Sadler (eds.) *Non-Plan: Essays on Freedom, Participation and Change in Modern Architecture*, Oxford: Architectural Press, 90–103.

Hughes, T. P. (1998) *Rescuing Prometheus: Four Monumental Projects that Changed the Modern World*, New York: Pantheon.

IEEE Annals of the History of Computing (1992) 14, no. 1.

Imhotep, E. J. (2012) "Maintaining Humans," in Mark Solovey and Hamilton Cravens (eds.) *Cold War Social Science: Knowledge Production, Liberal Democracy, and Human Nature*, New York: Palgrave Macmillan, 175–195.

Kennedy, P. M. (1971) "Imperial Cable Communications and Strategy, 1870–1914," *The English Historical Review* 86, no. 341, 728–752.

Kirker, H. (1998) *The Architecture of Charles Bulfinch*, Cambridge, MA: Harvard University Press.

Land, F. (2000) "The First Business Computer: A Case Study in User-Driven Automation," *IEEE Annals of the History of Computing* 22, no. 3, 16–26.

Licklider, J. C. R. (1960) "Man-Computer Symbiosis," *IRE Transactions on Human Factors in Electronics* HFE-1, 4–11.

Licklider, J. C. R. (1965) *Libraries of the Future*, Cambridge, MA: MIT Press.

Licklider J. C. R. and Clark, W. E. (1962) "Online Man-Machine Communication," *Proceedings of the Joint Computer Conference* 21, 113–128.

Llewelyn-Davies, R. (1966) "Similarities and Differences in Hospital Design: International Trends," *AJPH* 56, no. 10, 1675–1683.

Longmore, D. (1969) *Machines in Medicine: The Medical Practice of the Future*, London: Aldus Books.

Lusted, L. B. (1966) "Computers in Medicine – A Personal Perspective," *Journal of Chronic Disease* 19, 365–372.

Massachusetts General Hospital Laboratory of Computer Science (1963) *Hospital Computer Project: Memorandum Five*, Boston, MA: The Hospital.

Massachusetts General Hospital Laboratory of Computer Science (1965) *Hospital Computer Project: Memorandum Eight*, Boston, MA: The Hospital.

Massachusetts General Hospital Laboratory of Computer Science (1966) *Hospital Computer Project: Memorandum Nine: Progress Report*, Boston, MA: The Hospital.

McCarthy, J. (1983) "Reminiscences on the History of Time Sharing," *Culture of Innovation* 56. Online. Available at: stanford.edu/jmc/history/timesharing/time sharing.html.

McCarthy, J., Boilen, S., Fredkin, E. and Licklider, J. C. R. (1963) "A Time-sharing Debugging System for A Small Computer," *Proceedings of the Spring Joint Computer Conference*, 51–57.

McKellar, S. (2018) *Artificial Hearts: The Allure and Ambivalence of a Controversial Medical Technology*, Baltimore: Johns Hopkins University Press.

November, J. A. (2011) "Early Biomedical Computing and the Roots of Evidence-Based Design," *IEEE Annals of the History of Computing* 33, no. 2, 9–23.

November, J. A. (2012) *Biomedical Computing: Digitizing Life in the United States*, Baltimore, MD: Johns Hopkins University Press.

Nuffield Provincial Hospitals Trust (1955) *Studies in the Functions and Design of Hospitals*, London: Oxford University Press.

Orr, J. (1998) "Images of Work," *Science, Technology, & Human Values* 23, 439–455.

Rabinbach, A. (1992) *The Human Motor: Energy, Fatigue, and the Origins of Modernity*, Berkeley, CA: University of California Press.

Rosenberg, C. (1979) "Inward Vision and Outward Glance: The Shaping of the American Hospital, 1880–1914," *Bulletin of the History of Medicine* 53, 3, 346–391.

Schlich, T. (2010) "The Technological Fix and the Modern Body: Surgery as a Paradigmatic Case," in Linda Kalof and William Bynum (eds.) *The Cultural History of the Human Body*, Ivan Crozier (ed.), Vol. 6, 1920-present, London: Berg Publishers, 71–92.

Stevens, H. (2010) Life Out of Sequence: *An Ethnographic Account of Bioinformatics from the ARPANET to Post-Genomics*. Ph.D. Diss. Harvard University.

Stevens, R. (1989) *In Sickness and in Wealth: American Hospitals in the Twentieth Century*, Baltimore, MD: Johns Hopkins University Press.

Theodore, D. (2013a) "Oedipal Time: Architecture, Information, Retrodiction," in Pablo Lorenzo-Eiroa and Aaron Sprecher (eds.) *Architecture in Formation: On the Nature of Information in Digital Architecture*, New York: Routledge, 73–77.

Theodore, D. (2013b) "'The Fattest Possible Nurse': Architecture, Computers, and Post-war Nursing," in Laurinda Abreu and Sally Sheard (eds.) *Daily Life in Hospital: Theory and Practice from the Medieval to the Modern*, Oxford: Peter Lang, 273–298.

Thompson, J. D. and Goldin, G. (1975) *The Hospital: A Social and Architectural History*, New Haven, CT: Yale University Press.

Vogel, M. J. (1980) *The Invention of the Modern Hospital: Boston 1870–1930*, Chicago, IL: University of Chicago Press.

Walden, D. and Nickerson, R. (eds.) (2011) A Culture of Innovation: Insider Accounts of Computing and Life at BBN. Online. Available at: www.cbi.umn.edu/hostedpublications/pdf/CultureInnovation_bbn.pdf.

Weeks, J. (1964) "Indeterminate Architecture," *Transactions of the Bartlett Society* 2, 83–106.

Weeks, J. (1965) "Hospitals for the 1970s," *Medical Care* 3, 4, 197–203.

Wenzlhuemer, R. (2013) *Connecting the Nineteenth-Century World. The Telegraph and Globalization*, Cambridge: Cambridge University Press.

7 The unclean human-machine interface

Rachel Plotnick

From the 1950s to 1970s, mainframe computers garnered notoriety not only for what they could do, but also for the *care* they needed in terms of manufacturing and use. These large, cumbersome devices were manufactured in hyper-clean spaces, and once they entered offices, they occupied whole rooms and sometimes even floors of buildings. From production through consumption, these computers required ongoing maintenance and repair to protect them from human/environmental contaminants. As journalist Dee Wedemeyer (1978) put it in an article on how workplaces were adapting to computers, "Housing one of the larger computers is still a bit like finding shelter for something as large as a horse and as fragile as a flower" (Wedemeyer 1978: R1). Wedemeyer's language here referenced two important points: first, the notion of "housing/shelter" implied domesticity, indicating that office workers cared for computers by providing them with safe spaces/environments. Second, the journalist's depiction of a computer as "fragile as a flower" suggested a common thread in discourse about early computing – that these machines required (hygienic) protection due to their vulnerabilities. The following pages attend to these two elements, care and hygiene, as traditionally overlooked aspects in histories of computing. In particular, this chapter is concerned with a gradual shift that occurred in the transition from mainframe computers to microcomputers – not in terms of these computers' technical features or uses – but rather in terms of how myriad stakeholders (from office workers and architects to furniture designers and advertisers) imagined that computers should be cared for, protected and situated in certain environments and not in others. Notably, in the early 1980s, these stakeholders began deliberating about how "personal" or micro-computers could graduate from the "clean room" or cordoned off "computer room" and into multipurpose offices, living rooms, kitchens, factories and other spaces for everyday use. Such a shift happened both rhetorically and materially to make computers less "clean" and sterile – to expose them to the messy practices of everyday life – and therefore more approachable. However, concerns persisted over these devices' vulnerabilities and the risks that could befall them at the hands of their users (from mundane contaminants like dust,

The unclean human-machine interface   115

fingerprints, spilled drinks, and smoking). Examining how computers emerged from highly controlled computing rooms (both for their manufacture and for early computation), this chapter argues that a comprehensive history of computing must attend to the materiality and embodied practices of computing that relate to caretaking, cleanliness, hygienic architectural spaces, and design/aesthetics.

Where most histories focus on newness and moments of invention, this project instead draws on scholarly literature about repair and maintenance in the perpetuation of practices and environments designed with a "clean" aesthetic in mind. In so doing, it unearths a history of computing characterized by fragility and vulnerability.[1] Technicians undertook a great deal of work not to make computers and their accessories more technically efficient and powerful, but rather to protect or repair them from bodies and spaces deemed unsafe, improper, or detrimental. Taking "broken world thinking" as its jumping off point, this chapter considers how sociotechnical systems inevitably "creak, flex, and bend their way through time," and it privileges moments of breakdown, conflict, and messiness (Jackson 2014). This approach suggests that we might shift our focus to understand interfaces not as stable, neutral "things" that always work and come into contact with people, but rather as fluid, dynamic points of contact that emerge only in the nexus between humans and machines as they meet and negotiate the terms of their relationship.[2] It is in these "assemblages" or "interminglings," then, that interfaces take shape – in the tangled webs of companies, technologists, advertisers, designers, users, and machines themselves (Slack 2013). Approaching interfaces from this vantage point allows us to see, in Suchman's (2007) terms, "how and when the categories of human or machine become relevant … " (Suchman 2007: 2). Indeed, discussions about cleanliness in computing often raised fundamental questions about what it meant to be "human" or "machine" as these shifting categories came into contact with one another.

A focus on computing hygiene and interfacing-as-process thus brings new computer practices to the fore. In a piece that aims to speak across disciplines of communication/media studies and science and technology studies (STS), Jackson (2014) rightly reminds scholars to put issues of technology maintenance and repair front-and-center, thereby "referenc[ing] what is in fact a very old but routinely forgotten relationship of humans to things in the world: namely, an ethics of mutual care and responsibility" (see also Slack 2013). Yet this "mutual" care looks strikingly unbalanced when considering the case of hygienic computing and the ways that computer workers' bodies were viewed as threats in the name of protecting computers – particularly prior to the 1980s. First, human bodies and their practices were often perceived as undermining the stability of the machines to which they tended. In order to work with computers – and their increasingly intricate and delicate layers of hardware – computing organizations constructed "virgin" kinds of environments untainted by smoking or

116   *Rachel Plotnick*

eating; they touted the value of pristine flooring free from the dents made by women's heels; and they warned of the dangers of human fingerprints and finger smudges ("Disc System" 1970). These requirements placed the burden upon users to "clean up" around computers in average computing rooms or offices across a variety of industries. Quite often, these caretaking practices (much as in domestic spaces) fell to women – as cleaning and cleanliness generally had long been associated with women's work (Cowan 1985; Kaplan 1998; Luxton 1980). This gendered cleaning often applied to the most hyper-clean computing environments, known as specially designed "clean rooms" for manufacturing computer parts, where women were hired to work in special suits, gloves, and masks to avoid any and all contamination in the assembly process.

Regarding these clean rooms, scholars have identified the great lengths to which humans have gone to conform to machines' needs. Harpold and Philip (2000) suggest that in clean rooms

> human labor is subject to principles of cleanliness in keeping with the demands of a machinic order: a grain of dust poses no threat to the human organism, but may be fatal to the computer chip; the most elementary human activities – simply breathing and moving about – must therefore be bracketed by the demands of manufacture.
>
> (Harpold and Philip 2000: para. 27)

In this regard, human-machine interactions must necessarily become less "human," in the sense that mundane and life-sustaining human behaviors (breathing, moving, and eating) and bodily functions are suppressed in order to protect machines. Bodies, when perceived as anathema to computers, must undergo policing and follow a specific set of protocols.

Beyond the clean room, historians of computing have noted that American society has long idealized computers as "reliable and rational," where "various types of accidents, deviations, errors, and mistakes stand out as anomalies" (Parikka 2007: 34–35). Yet, as a number of authors have shown, this myth of controllability and order has been belied by computer worms, viruses, and other breakdowns that characterize "normal" computing, and these "malfunctions" date back to the 1950s (Beniger 1986; Parikka 2007). The "virus" metaphor is biological in nature, too, suggesting how bodies and computers have long remained in tension with one another (Casilli 2010). To denaturalize myths of seamless, always-functioning technologies, both in computing and other industries, requires attending to "culturally, spatially and socially produced understandings of dirt and hygiene" (Campin and Cox 2007: 4). How concepts of "dirty" and "clean" get mobilized provides insight into the politics and concerns of designers, manufacturers, and various users alike.

Importantly, the drive to clean and to achieve cleanliness is neither a product of the mid-twentieth century nor isolated to the field of computing.

The unclean human-machine interface 117

In fact, Freud wrote in *Civilization and Its Discontents* (1930) that "Dirtiness of any kind seems to us incompatible with civilization" (Freud 2005: 77). Yet "dirtiness" remains through-and-through a social and historical concept bounded by geography and culture; one person's definition of dirt might differ significantly from another's. The task at hand becomes, then, to map how people mobilize concepts of cleanliness and dirtiness in specific contexts, using these concepts to determine the permissibility of certain habits, protocols, and designs. For example, what counted as "dirty" in a computer room differed significantly from what counted as dirty in a clean room, which differed significantly from what counted as dirty at a kitchen table – and yet computers existed in all of these spaces. Histories of computing have largely overlooked these elements, yet they can help us to understand how embodied interactions and material environments both have constrained and enabled human-machine relationships. Attending to such histories can also offer a window into the present, where clean practices, clean rooms, and clean aesthetics remain prominent in twenty-first century computing. From the stark white design style of Apple products to the flourishing clean room industry for semiconductor chips, it is impossible to ignore the centrality of cleanliness as aesthetic, metaphor, and technical imperative in the digital economy.

It becomes instructive, then, to examine the ways that computer users and organizations have constructed definitions of dirtiness and cleanliness around computing at different historical moments. From the late 1950s to the early 1980s, employee handbooks, marketing materials, advertisements, user guides/manuals, computing industry publications and news articles suggest that cleanliness in computing remained a central problem that required behavioral, procedural, environmental, and aesthetic solutions. Early efforts, for example, focused on isolating computers from potential contaminants – closing them off in specially constructed rooms, limiting who could touch and use them and under what conditions. A variety of relevant social groups at this time period remarked about the perceived vulnerabilities and sensitivities of computers, which mandated that people care for them much as they would an ill person or hospital patient. By defining computers as "fragile," it became necessary to put boundaries and protocols into place as a form of protection, and issues of control predominated in conversations about computer-friendly circumstances.[3] Later, in the 1970s and 80s, new conversations would center on how to encourage computers to adapt to humans' messiness rather than requiring humans to primarily make these adaptations.

Part I: clean enough for a computer

If even the slightest dust or dirt gets on the tracks during assembly, the disk is rejected. Obviously, air must be dust-free.

IBM 1966

118 *Rachel Plotnick*

Perceptions of computers as requiring intense cleanliness began first at the level of manufacture. In the late 1950s and early 1960s, manufacturers began opening plants with standards in line with hospitals, laboratories and aerospace facilities. Ball bearing plants, for example, produced bearings for everything from aircraft and missile guidance control systems to computers, and these plants took great pains to eliminate contaminants from their process. The manufacturing clean room vilified dust, with one report (1957) commenting that, "An invisible speck of dust (.00008 inches – fifty times smaller than can be seen with a human eye) can cause enough friction in such a bearing to throw a missile or aircraft off course" ("New Plant Reduces Dust" 1957: 38). Given that the human eye could not even detect dust this small, cleanliness had to exceed human faculties and to achieve stringency well outside the bounds of everyday environments.

The aerospace industry's involvement in computer manufacturing only further intensified clean room procedures, bringing with it a new set of tools and techniques to support cleanliness. Companies including Bendix Corporation, Fabri-Tex, Inc., Raytheon Company and Simmonds Precision Products, Inc. adopted aerospace methods or would use aerospace companies as subcontractors in the 1960s to solve thorny clean room problems. Others such as Sandia Corporation in Albuquerque, NM converted nuclear weapons manufacturing facilities into plants that could produce miniaturized components across a wide range of industries that required contamination-free assembly ("This Clean Room" 1965). In these new facilities, dirt was "excluded within the limits of human capability" (Smith 1965: F1). One book depicting 200 clean rooms across the world demonstrated tremendous overlap between aerospace companies, hospitals, and computer manufacturers in terms of their emphasis on hyper-clean environments (Austin 1967). In this regard, too, protocols in manufacturing spaces came to mimic those in hospitals, where computers came to play the role of patients cared for by doctor- and nurse-like workers.

For instance, employees went to great lengths to shield their bodies from the computer parts they produced. At the Barden Corporation in Danbury, Connecticut, "personnel in the critical areas wear lint-free garments and enter through air locks or high-velocity air showers" ("Cleanliness is the Soul" 1958: 26), while at the Fafnir Bearing Company of New Britain, Connecticut, "women cannot wear face powder or rouge, must work in lint-free Orion dresses and hats and must wear white kid gloves" ("New Plant Reduces Dust" 1957: 38). Similarly, according to a journalist (1965) visiting multiple clean room facilities, "workers in these areas are clothed in special nun-like, lint-free garb giving the rooms the appearance of a futuristic hospital" (Smith 1965). Images of these workers – usually female – showed human bodies entirely encased in fabric so as to come into minimal contact with machines. Similarly, IBM boasted about its workers' cleanliness in a full-page advertisement (1966) for its clean room facilities in San Jose, CA, remarking that, "When cleanliness is a must, there can't be any doubt.

The unclean human-machine interface 119

[...] A little dust is big trouble – no wonder air is filtered and everyone dresses like surgeons!" (IBM 1966). Using the surgeon analogy, the ad included colorful images of women dressed in gowns, caps and gloves, once again drawing attention to the medicalized and feminized practice of caring for computers. Harpold and Philip (2000) have called clean room suits, such as those mentioned above, "barrier technologies" to "eliminate[e] the messy specificity of the body" (Harpold and Philip 2000: para. 35). By treating the body as a hazard, this apparel aimed to create greater distance between human and machine by limiting their points of contact and modes of interaction. As discussed previously, it is notable, though perhaps not surprising, that women would often take on this kind of work, as clean room tasks mimicked housekeeping and caretaking responsibilities that would fall almost entirely to women in domestic spaces.

Although manufacturers could exert maximum control over the environments in which computers were manufactured – and police the behaviors of the people who produced them – a new set of problems manifested once computers went "into the wild" in offices. Outside of clean rooms, human and environmental "contaminants" posed persistent threats. To this end, references to computers in the popular press often described these machines as vulnerable, requiring significant care and dedicated facilities. One news account (1959) explicated IBM's efforts to protect its Raman 305, worth nearly $1 million, from construction happening in a German facility. In this case, the journalist reported that IBM "closed down and swaddled" the computer to protect it from cement dust ("Computer is Stymied" 1959: 2). Similarly, a *New York Times* article (1962) warned readers in its headline that "Computers Pose Many Problems." Chief among these, as more businesses turned to computing, they had to determine how to outfit their buildings and offices to house such large and delicate mechanisms. The journalist interviewed an architect to learn that "electronic brains, because of their sensitivity, frequently require their own air conditioning systems, specially constructed floors, added electric power, sealed chambers, extra cooling towers and special methods for cleaning the space they occupy" ("Computers Pose Many Problems" 1962: 315). Likewise, an associate for Emery Roth & Sons, who arranged tenant leases of office spaces, noted that those tenants with electronic data processing needs required special handling when outfitting their facilities, as computers could be, "sensitive to heat, humidity, dust particles, vibrations, unequal flow of electric current and an uneven floor" ("Computers Pose Many Problems" 1962: 315). These depictions of computers as "sensitive," as well as efforts to "swaddle" and close them off from surrounding hazardous elements, indicate how computing spaces were designed to accommodate vulnerable, patient-like machines that could only thrive under certain conditions.

Writers frequently warned about the deleterious effects of environmental contaminants – in particular, dust. According to Burton and Mills (1960), "Dust is another enemy of the computer, and must be eliminated from the

120   *Rachel Plotnick*

computer room to the maximum extent possible" (Burton, Mills 1960: 163). Similarly, an author writing in *The Building Services Engineer* (1968) threatened that, "Dust and dirt must be eliminated from computer rooms at all costs" (*The Building Services Engineer* 1968: 29). Other texts such as *Data Systems* (1973) referred to studies that demonstrated the sheer pervasiveness and perniciousness of dust. The journal noted that the US Post Office attributed 70% of its computer failures to dust, and it remarked that, "It has been estimated that, in the space of a year, each person brings with him into the computer room half a pound of dust ... " (*Data Systems* 1973: ii). This article described humans as carriers of this harmful agent, and therefore human bodies became a kind of threat to machines, a barrier to their proper functioning, and therefore antagonists.

Indeed, as difficult as it may have been to prepare for a computer to inhabit an office space, introducing human users into that space only added further potential hazards. And, unlike clean room workers required to clean up by virtue of their profession, it could be more difficult to police office workers to perform cleanliness protocols. As a result, computing texts often made proscriptive recommendations about how computer users should conduct themselves around these machines in an effort to encourage "good" behavior. Marketing materials for the Univac II (1957), for example, explained to sales people that fingernails and "abrasive dust particles" could destroy tapes and tape decks (Univac 1957: 1109). Likewise, an article in *Computers and Data Processing News* (1964) warned readers that " ... it is necessary to become familiar with the stringent demands of a computer room" (*Computer and Data Processing News* 1964: 15), while another piece on mainframe and minicomputer usage by Brumm (1965) cautioned that computer offices were "vulnerable to dust, fingerprints, coffee spills, ashes, sneezes, and other grime" (Brumm 1965: 82). These lists suggest that mundane and harmless behaviors in other arenas – sneezing, spilling, or placing one's fingers on something – were coded as catastrophic in computing. Humans' default state thus became dirty and unfit, and office hygiene became a source of frequent discussion. For instance, a May 1970 handbook on handling magnetic tape by Memorex outlined the dangers of careless (or simply everyday) user practices. In a section labeled, "Invitation to Trouble," Memorex illustrated poor hygiene in a photograph, wherein a man's hand held a cigarette next to an ashtray full of butts, alongside a cup of coffee, in close proximity to a computer. "Smoking and eating in the computer room are two of the most frequent causes of contamination," the handbook remarked (5/9). To this end, the company recommended that "good housekeeping really pays off" and advocated for "general computer room cleanliness" (5/10). In much the same vein, in a report on computer control to the Chemical Industries Association, Lowe and Hidden (1971) encouraged people to avoid producing dirt and dust, as "work is done better in a clean environment and on clean equipment" (Lowe and Hidden 1971: 113). These definitions of "clean" served as rejoinders to users carrying out their usual human routines in close proximity to their computers. To be clean, it seemed, meant to cater to the computer's perceived sensitivities by reducing one's "dirty" habits and "housekeeping" by performing tasks commonly associated with domesticity.

As office workers were encouraged to adjust their bodies and the spaces they inhabited to computers' demands, they recognized that such demands created a very specific computing aesthetic – related to computers themselves, their environment, and their placement – associated with cleanliness. Both in computing rooms and clean rooms, the absence of dirt created a qualitatively different spatial experience than working in other (dirtier) spaces. One writer (1967), explaining what it felt like to move from one office space to another, described leaving the "din of the key punch operation" to enter the "quieter, almost antiseptic atmosphere of the computer room" (*Management Accounting* 1967: 71). A magazine, *Technocracy Digest* (1970), used similar language, suggesting that "computer rooms are like emergency wards: white, antiseptic, enclosed." Workers in these environments, such as one computer programmer (1969), described a stark divide between workers in these clean computer rooms and the people who existed beyond them:

> Because others can't talk our language, we don't try to communicate – to management, to our non-computer-oriented friends, to the man on the street, or to anyone. But out there beyond our antiseptic computer rooms, beyond the service bureau, the software houses, the manufacturing plants, and the computer conferences are the people our actions are affecting – and those people are grumbling. This society is governed by those people.
>
> (*Journal of Data Management* 1969: 15)

This author depicted two kinds of worlds that seem to remain out of reach from one another. Like computers themselves, the computer worker perceived himself as isolated and disconnected from the flesh-and-blood grumbling society beyond the computer room's walls. The term "antiseptic," used again in reference to the computer room, suggests a close association between cleanliness, computing and medicine – recalling the strong ties between clean room manufacturing of computer parts and hospital environments. Here, "antiseptic" took on double meaning as a form of hypercleanliness and as an aesthetic quality that lacked character and warmth, reflecting an ideology that prioritized machines' wellbeing over humans' connectivity with more "natural" parts of the world.

A few years later, Allen and Hecht (1974), in a treatise on how to use computers in education, also pointed to a kind of inhuman computing environment:

122 *Rachel Plotnick*

> Typically, the setting is cold and impersonal, often painted stark white without a trace of art. It seems as if the most aesthetically unappealing area is carefully selected for the computer room (more often than not, the basement). Even in legitimate classrooms in schools and industry, the number and spacing of computer terminals evoke Orwellian images.
>
> (Allen and Hecht 1974: 242)

This clean aesthetic – white, devoid of artwork, physically separated – was interpreted not only as impersonal but even potentially dystopian and dangerous, as these spaces did not allow for self-expression or human agency. In these writers' estimation, clean also meant cold, not only aesthetically but also affectively. Thus, the pursuit of cleanliness involved aesthetics and affect as much as practical considerations. In many ways, to be clean meant to function like a machine rather than a human being.

Due to these negative perceptions of the cleanliness of computing, it is perhaps unsurprising that designers in the 1960s and 70s began considering ways to change both computers and their settings through aesthetic choices so as to destigmatize their hygienic associations. At this point, although computing primarily occurred in spaces only meant for computing (the "computing room"), designers and architects began to imagine the increasing centrality of computers in office life. Remarked one journalist (1967) to this end, "The problem faced by space designers is to create an environment that, while necessarily dominated by sophisticated and increasingly complex computers, does not overpower the people who must share working quarters with the machines" (Fowler 1967: 378). While these efforts were not widespread, they reflected a set of new ideas about design in computing. For example, Univac III designers (1962) experimented not only with producing computers in different colors, but also with offering decorator ideas for the computer's surrounding elements, such as wall colors, fluorescent lamps and floor coverings. To reimagine the aesthetics of computing meant also to think philosophically about the complicated nature of human-machine relationships. Indeed, journalist Glen Fowler (1967) poetically described the challenges of rethinking computer room aesthetics in these terms: "In this age of automation, architects are called upon for special efforts to promote the peaceful coexistence of machines and people in the office space they design" (Fowler 1967: 378). Fowler's words strikingly emphasized "coexistence" – creating environments where humans and machines (portrayed as being so unlike one another) could get along. He visited the Honeywell Education and Computing Center in New York to learn about space designer Robert Caigan's efforts to reimagine the 18-story office building. According to Fowler, Caigan designed the center to create a "pleasant setting" for the computers that would "reflect the vitality of advanced technology" (Fowler 1967: 378). At the same time, he noted that the "people" spaces such as conference rooms featured "subtle warmth" through fabric and texture. Caigan designed human spaces and

The unclean human-machine interface   123

machine spaces differently, acknowledging their points of contact yet emphasizing humans' humanness in contrast to machines.

Talcott also undertook similar efforts, later in 1974, by enlisting artists to design colorful computer cases that would resemble their user's tastes. According to Donald S. Alvin, vice president of Talcott, the artists could "reduc[e] what he says is an 'antiseptic look' in most computer rooms" (Reif 1974: 47). Yet again referring to the "antiseptic" computer room, Alvin recognized that an aggressive move toward artistically designed computers could not only augment popular perceptions of computing, but it could also give Talcott a unique market share. These movements toward rethinking aesthetics strove to remake the character of computing spaces, but they could not remedy the problems that would inevitably arise as computers graduated from computing-only rooms.

Part II: grappling with the messiness of everyday life

By the late 1970s, a constellation of forces – both technical and social – coincided that made computers more available outside of their carefully controlled, clean spaces (Ceruzzi 2003). MIT professor Nicholas Negroponte, an influential voice in the early years of computing, presciently noted (1978) to a journalist that, "The days of the hermetically sealed, glass-walled computer room are almost over," and that journalist likewise agreed:

> Most terminals – a keyboard and a means of feedback from the computer, usually a video screen or a printer – can get along nicely in the same environment as mortals. Because of the increased use of the so-called 'mini computers,' which can also survive in a less pampered environment, the entire office is becoming a computer room.
>
> (Wedemeyer 1978: R1)

New perceptions of computers as multipurpose and multi-sited emphasized that "mortals" (humans) and computers could get along in the same environment more easily. Wedemeyer's recognition that mini or microcomputers could "survive in a less pampered environment" also indicates that metaphors of caretaking were evolving to make computers less hospital patients and more co-habitants (Wedemeyer 1978: R1). Additionally, the author proposed that computers no longer required their own rooms – sealed off from the rest of office operations – and instead every room could serve as a computing room. Theoretically, then, users no longer needed to as stringently adapt their behaviors and embodied practices to computers; rather, computers could increasingly adapt to humans' working environments.

As *Computerworld* (1979) noted, "No longer is [data processing] done in sealed, air-conditioned, air-filtered, humidity-controlled, sanitized computer rooms away from the smoke and dust of the workaday world."

124   *Rachel Plotnick*

Rather, "Today computers are found in offices, warehouses, workshops, plants and garages." However, as computers emerged from highly controlled, intensely clean environments and into these diversely-used spaces, workplaces and workers had to grapple with new challenges in terms of cleanliness. Many noticed that regular people and places were *dirty*. John Read, principal engineer for Digital Equipment Corporation in Colorado Springs, CO surmised that office environments were "an order of magnitude or two dirtier" than computer rooms (Surden 1978: 67). Similarly, an article on data processing for computer professionals (1979) warned that "optimum levels of cleanliness are hard to achieve outside the sanitized computer room" and cautioned that "while one may think that a factory floor is an obvious example of an unclean area, even an office environment is many times dirtier than the traditional computer room" ("Disk Cleaners Invaluable" 1979: 66). One method to curb dirtiness thus involved trying to create consensus around "appropriate" versus "inappropriate" behavior amongst office workers. For example, an article in *Infosystems* (1978) reported that a survey it conducted of office employees found that, "Most queried [...] agreed that smoking and food and drinks should not be allowed ... " ("The Space" 1978: 58). This piece and others like it tried to maintain hygienic behaviors in office environments where computing had not occurred previously by delineating the boundaries of human behavior. While computers and "mortals" could get along, demands for cleanliness certainly did not cease to exist in these office environments where workplaces could not as easily enforce or control hygiene.

Given changes in computing technologies at this time period, many cleanliness concerns cropped up pertaining not as much to computers themselves, but rather to their disk drives and magnetic tape. Such worries about improper handling of disks and tape stood in contrast to the ways that these disks and their associated enclosures were manufactured – in facilities that utilized hyper-clean practices and spaces – much as computers were produced in clean rooms. The Digital Development Corporation in San Diego, CA (1968), for instance, boasted of its memory system, produced in a "controlled environment" that "completely protects the unit from dust, dirt, moisture, or any other contaminating elements, and provides the hydrodynamic gas bearing for the flying heads" (Digital Development Corporation 1968). Likewise, an ad for Ball Computer BD disk drives (1978) articulated that its disk packs were "sealed in a 'clean room' environment" and their process could eliminate "most of the reasons for loss of data; dust and dirt accumulation on precision mechanisms and the disk surfaces" ("High Data Reliability" 1978). These descriptions worked not only to assuage potential consumers' concerns about these disks' functionality, but they also served as reminders of disks' vulnerabilities, thereby entreating potential users to treat them with the utmost care. In this regard, advertisements functioned proscriptively to encourage proper cleanliness protocols.

The unclean human-machine interface   125

Yet despite how manufacturers might have tried to head off dirt and "bad" behavior at the pass, major questions arose about how to protect a computer's memory. Writers warned of typical scenarios where harm could befall disks at the hands of everyday users doing everyday things – especially when it came to data:

> You are a small systems user and your system is set up as part of the office's regular décor. The people in your office are normal – they sometimes spill coffee and soda, drop cigarette ashes and keep the windows open. Do you have a problem? You might, if all these conditions lead to dirty disks – and therefore to lost information and lost money.
> (Surden 1978: 67)

In this description, it is most noteworthy that the author described these people and their behaviors as "normal," thereby constructing "dirtiness" as an expected human trait. Yet this normality became a liability for offices at risk of losing data and finances. One company, The Software Works in Sunnyvale, CA, took out a large ad in *InfoWorld* (1980) to issue missives to users about their disk behaviors, writing that, "The single largest cause of user problems encountered by our service department is mishandling of floppy diskettes" (The Software Works 1980: 28). The Software Works then provided a series of rules for proper handling that included:

> Don't bend or fold a floppy disk. This sounds like a reasonable rule, but it is the one most violated by users.
>
> Don't touch the magnetic surface of the diskette. Fingerprints almost invariably destroy the readability of your data.
>
> Don't expect much sympathy from your computer shopkeeper or our service department if you ignore these rules.
> (The Software Works 1980: 28)

Not only did the company work to enforce certain behavior, and to mitigate the risks of the human element (in this case, fingerprints), but it also warned that service providers would not provide sympathy if users violated these rules. Such chastisements drew boundaries between less careful/informed computer users and the professionals that worked directly on broken machines and their accessories. Language about "contamination" frequented discussion of disk handling, with fear-mongering phrases such as, "Once contaminants enter the scene, data errors, headcrashes, lost data and lost time, frustration and increased [data processing] costs are the result" (*Computerworld* 1979: 66) and "like magnetic tape, floppies are very susceptible to contamination by foreign particles (dirt, dust, fingerprints)" (Rampil 1977: 26).

In addition to asking users to clean up their behavior, a market emerged for storing and cleaning one's memory devices so as to protect them. Kenneth

126 *Rachel Plotnick*

Eldred, president of International Minicomputer Accessories Corporation recommended a "'clean room' storage cabinet" that could hold up to 400 floppy disks and "incorporates an air filter to repel dust and other magnetic media contaminants" (Beeler 1979: 76). Likewise, disk cartridge cleaners became popular office accessories for repairing damage to disks. Advertisements implored potential purchasers to "Give your cartridge and your data all the protection they deserve" so as to avoid the cost of irretrievable data (*Computerworld* 1977: 10). Manufacturers targeted these cleaning mechanisms at the average user without any special skills, for "almost anyone can clean the disks" (Surden 1978: 67). In this regard, users could continue their stubbornly human and problematic practices, using disk cleaners as an antidote to these behaviors. These technologies meant for reactive repair, rather than proactive protection, reflected a shift from creating wholly controlled environments that could eliminate threats – to managing environments where undesirable behavior could occur with plans for future mitigation.

As moving from the clean room or computer room to the general office necessitated new kinds of thinking about hygienic computing, so too did the shift from office computing to domestic computing require another reimagining of how humans and computers should co-exist. It is noteworthy to consider that while advertisers and computing publications entreated office workers to take cleanliness seriously, they took a more relaxed approach to the home/amateur user. For example, advertisers of micro-computers in the late 1970s emphasized how these first domestic users could incorporate computers into their daily lives and spaces, breaching some of the boundaries previously in place for cleanliness. One ad in *Interface Age* for the Equinox 100 8080A CPU showed a casually dressed brunette woman sitting in a chair, holding a glass of red wine, with the Equinox 100 and a vase of brightly colored flowers atop a wooden desk in arm's reach ("Equinox 100" 1978). Far from vilifying her drinking near the machine, it depicted a warm, homey scene where the user could carry out an uninhibited nighttime activity while working with her computer.

A similar second advertisement argued for home computing as un-sanitized and instead integrated into users' mundane (and therefore sometimes messy) practices. An advertisement for Shugart minifloppy disks (1979) in *Byte* magazine featured the tagline, "My Shugart followed me home" ("My Shugart Followed Me Home" 1979). It featured a white man in a short-sleeved dress shirt and tie, sitting and smiling at his desk. The desk included a computer monitor and keyboard, as well as his books, a set of keys, a partially eaten sandwich on a plate, and a glass of milk. As with the woman holding a glass of wine, this ad encouraged potential buyers to imagine computers flowing seamlessly into their home environs. To do so, it proposed a harmonious domestic scene where drinks and food were not anathema to computers – quite in contrast to the "antiseptic" computer room of the past.

Another ad from *Byte* magazine (1980), in quite a turnaround from perceptions of computers as fragile and in need of caretaking in the 1950s and

The unclean human-machine interface   127

60s, depicted "domesticated computers" by portraying a cover scene that featured a martini glass, string of pearls and white gloves in close proximity to the computer, while the screen displayed the words: "Madam: Dinner is Served." Where once humans were implored to care for their computers, now, the magazine suggested, computers could care for their humans. If indeed the act of "domestication" was complete, then servants to computers could now perhaps become masters of those same devices.

Last, another ad in *Byte* magazine for the Apple II computer instructed the reader (and potential purchaser) to, "Clear the kitchen table. Bring in the color TV. Plug in your new Apple II ... " ("Introducing Apple II" 1978). These directions proposed that one could integrate the computer into a home space without any great effort; in this case, the kitchen table became a desk and the TV transformed into a computer component. Home and office functions, furniture and machines merged together unproblematically. However, it is worth noting that Apple did recommend to potential users that they *clear* the kitchen table before using it. Ads such as this one tapped into complications posed by bringing computers into domestic spaces. Indeed, *Interface Age* editor Terry Costlow (1979) noted that many users, in their excitement while bringing home a new computer, would forget to think about where to put that computer. Costlow remarked that, "Kitchen tables don't go over very well with other family members who occasionally find the need to eat [...] And these older desks don't often fit the modernistic look and feeling that a computer brings" (Costlow 1979: 138). Trying to *create* separation between eating/ family gathering spaces and computing spaces, Costlow recommended instead that new computer users invest in office furniture for their homes that would provide for clean computing practices. Furniture dealers worked to make these associations, too, to suggest that computer aesthetics no longer need evoke negative hospital-like connotations, yet the home user should set aside unique spaces for computing ("Furniture Completes" 1979). Such remarks worked to make sense of what kinds of rooms and furniture could and should house computers.

To a certain degree, newer personal micro-computers *were* more impervious to human and environmental elements when compared to their predecessors. Still, efforts to make computers unclean were often more rhetorical than practical – as personal computing became more common and popular, so too were new products, services and protocols created to manage home computer users so they performed appropriately with their machines.

Part III: cleanliness as a persistent virtue

In a successful man/computer system there must be empathy between the man and the computer system.

C. F. Reynolds 1977

128   *Rachel Plotnick*

In the period between the mid-1950s and the early 1980s, significant deliberations occurred about how to calibrate humans' and machines' interactions and environments so that they might "get along nicely" (Wedemeyer 1978: R1). The ability to get along depended not only on human understanding of how computing technologies worked (and computers' capacity to communicate with humans), but it also depended upon humans recognizing and responding to barriers to computers' efficient functioning that often took shape in the form of mitigating mundane human behaviors (eating, drinking, smoking, touching, etc.) and mundane environmental factors (dust, dirt, humidity, etc.) to whatever degree possible.

In the 1970s, as micro-computing and personal computing became increasingly possible and popular, manufacturers and designers endeavored to extract computers (both rhetorically and materially) from their clean environs. Advertisers portrayed users at home with computers, not only showing how computers could fit into domestic spaces, but also imagining how users could perform domestic activities such as eating and drinking alongside computers safely. Likewise, companies reconfigured offices to make all working spaces computing spaces, quite in contrast to physically separated computing rooms. These efforts to "humanize" computers and their spaces de-emphasized cleanliness in computing in order to perhaps reduce the stigma associated with computer use. However, a sizable industry devoted to cleanliness and repair continued to flourish, particularly in relation to peripheral computer hardware such as disks and magnetic tape. Now, cleanliness offered protection for one's data – for the computer's sensitive "brain" – and therefore the threat of fingerprints, fingernails and dust remained stubbornly in play.

Endeavors to rhetorically and materially reimagine where computing occurred and what people could do in computing spaces fit in with Silverstone and Haddon's (1996) theory of design and domestication. This theory involves a multi-part process in which designers imagine an ideal consumer/user and then that user finds ways to harmonize an information/communication technology so that it will fit into the patterns and spaces of everyday life. As Monteiro (2004) writes, "domestication is intended to emphasize the naturalization process, the way we cultivate and discipline artefacts when weaving them into the domestic sphere" (Monteiro 2004: 134). Advertisers worked to counter predominant attitudes about computing as sanitized, antiseptic, or contained in an office, by imagining a freed home consumer (and enthusiastic amateur user, given widespread technophobia about computers) whose bodily rhythms and routines (eating and drinking) could exist alongside the computer without fear of contamination or harm (Reed 2000). To make computers "natural" required advancing an argument that computers, like humans, could get dirty. However, as this article has demonstrated, computers also disciplined computer users at home and at work, in the sense that humans had to adjust to – and protect – these machines' vulnerabilities. Thus, "domestication" worked in both directions, as machines also "tamed" users

The unclean human-machine interface 129

to perform in particular ways. Historians have documented efforts toward domestication for objects from radios to televisions – and computers, too (Andrews 2012; Cummings and Kraut 2002; Habib and Cornford 2001; Reed 2000; Spigel 1992) – yet a focus on cleanliness adds another dimension to this literature by illustrating the friction that can exist between bodies, environments, spaces and technologies to make humans clean enough for machines and machines dirty enough for humans.

The case of cleanliness and dirtiness in computing offers much in the way of theorizing about human-machine interfaces and interfacing. This chapter has taken a cue from Black (2014), who argues that an interface "appears spontaneously during interaction, and does so *between* the surface of the machine and the surface of the human body" (Black 2014: 47) (emphasis in original). According to Black, interfaces materialize when humans and machines meet – and the most interesting and important aspects of these interactions occur in the liminal space between their surfaces. By putting the spotlight on caring and hygiene practices for computers, it becomes clear that sometimes this space is made large – when users are shielded in suits and gloves from their machines – and sometimes this space is made small, when users touch and eat and behave "humanly" in close proximity to their machines.

Given the ways in which newer technologies, particularly mobile technologies, become increasingly ingrained in the spaces and practices of everyday life, it is critical that we begin to attend to cleanliness as an ever-present consideration in human-technology interactions. Users of all kinds take on burdens of caring for their technologies in various ways – or, by breaching certain protocols – bear the cost and responsibility of repairing or replacing these technologies. To this end, a large and growing economy exists for repair, maintenance and new and of-the-moment products (from warranties to drop-proof cases and carriers) designed to unburden users from constant worry over damaging their data or harming their devices irreparably. The case of computing from the 1950s to the 1980s contributes to this narrative, suggesting the complexities of trying to fit machines into humans' rhythms and of trying to control humans so that they might behave responsibly around machines. These moments of interfacing, both historical and contemporary, help us to conceptualize how humans and machines negotiate their inherently messy (both literally and figuratively) relationship.

Notes

1 In science and technology studies (STS), particularly, a recent emphasis on "vulnerability" in technological systems has gained prominence. See, for example Kang, Jackson (2014); Denis and Pontille (2015); Hommels, Mesman and Bijker (2014).
2 My definition of "interface" builds on the work of Black (2014).
3 This emphasis on control fits in with broader discussions about control at this time period. See, for example, Beniger (1986).

130 *Rachel Plotnick*

Bibliography

Allen, D.W. and Hecht, J.C. (1974) *Controversies in Education*, Philadelphia, PA: W.B. Saunders.

Andrews, M. (2012) *Domesticating the Airwaves: Broadcasting, Domesticity and Femininity*, London and New York: Continuum.

Austin, P.R. (1967) *Austin's Clean Rooms of the World: Case Book of 200 Clean Rooms*, Ann Arbor: Ann Arbor Science Pub.

Beeler, J. (1979) "A Little Extra at the Start for Supplies, Accessories Seen Saving in Long Term," *Computerworld*, October 15, 76.

Beniger, J. (1986) *The Control Revolution*, Cambridge, MA: Harvard University Press.

Black, D. (2014) "Where Bodies End and Artefacts Begin: Tools, Machines and Interfaces," *Body & Society* 20, 1, 31–60.

Brumm, P. (1965) *The Micro to Mainframe Connection*, New York: Tab Books.

Burton, A.J. and Mills, R.G. (1960) *Electronic Computers and Their Business Applications*, London: Ernest Benn Limited.

Byte (1980) 5, 1. Available at: https://archive.org/details/byte-magazine-1980-01 [Accessed August 25, 2018].

Campin, B. and Cox, R. (2007) "Materialities and Metaphors of Dirt and Cleanliness," in B. Campin and R. Cox (eds.) *Dirt: New Geographies of Cleanliness and Contamination*, London and New York: IB Tauris & Co. Ltd, 1–8.

Casilli, A.A. (2010) "A History of Virulence: The Body and Computer Culture in the 1980s," *Body & Society* 16, 4, 1–31.

Ceruzzi, P.E. (2003) *A History of Modern Computing*, Cambridge and London: MIT Press.

"Cleanliness Is the Soul of New Ball Bearing Plant" (1958) *New York Times*, November 15, 26.

"Computer Gets Fashion Appeal" (1962) *New York Times*, November 4, F14.

"Computer Is Stymied" (1959) *New York Times*, July 29, 2.

Computers and Data Processing News (1964) 1, 15.

"Computers Pose Many Problems" (1962) *New York Times*, August 26, 315.

Costlow, T. (1979) "The Expanding Furniture Market," *Interface Age* 4, 11, 138–139.

Cowan, R.S. (1985) *More Work for Mother: The Ironies of Household Technology from the Open Hearth to the Microwave*, New York: Basic Books.

Cummings, J.N. and Kraut, R. (2002) "Domesticating Computers and the Internet," *The Information Society* 18, 3, 221–231.

Data Systems (1973) p. ii. London: Business Publications Limited.

Denis, J. and Pontille, D. (May 2015) "Material Ordering and the Care of Things," *Science, Technology, & Human Values* 40, 3, 338–367.

Digital Development Corporation (1968) "7301 Memory System," *Data Sheet*, April, Available at: https://archive.org/details/bitsavers_memorextaponMagnetic ComputerTapeMay70_24046744? [Accessed January 5, 2018].

"Disc System" (1970) *Business Automation* 17, 85.

"Equinox 100" (1978) *Interface Age* 3, 1, n.p.

"Everything an OEM Will Ever Need in Disk Drives" (1978) Available at: https://arch ive.org/details/bitsavers_ballBrotheskAd1978_3954096 [Accessed January 5, 2018].

The unclean human-machine interface 131

Fowler, G. (1967) "Designer Humanizes Computer Rooms," *New York Times*, September 10, 378.

Freud, S. (2005) *Civilization and Its Discontents*, New York: W.W. & Norton Company.

Habib, L. and Cornford, T. (2001) "Computers in the Home: Domestic Technology and the Process of Domestication," *The 9th European Conference on Information Systems*, Bled, Slovenia.

Harpold, T. and Philip, K. (2000) "Of Bugs and Rats: Cyber-Cleanliness, Cyber-Squalor, and the Fantasy-Spaces of Informational Globalization," *PMC* 11.1, 9: para. 1–39. Available at: http://pmc.iath.virginia.edu/text-only/issue.900/ 11.1harpoldphilip.txt.

"High Data Reliability" (1978) *Datamation*, 24, 116.

Hommels, A., Mesman, J. and Bijker, W.E. (eds.) (2014) *Vulnerability in Technological Cultures: New Directions in Research and Governance*, Cambridge, MA: MIT Press.

IBM (1966) "What's New in 'Clean Rooms'?" *Life* 11, n.p.

Industrial Design Magazine (1980) 27, 30.

Institution of Heating and Ventilating Engineers (Great Britain) (1968) *The Building Services Engineer*. 36, 29. London: Batiste Publications Limited.

"Introducing Apple II" (1978) *Byte*, 3, 4, n.p.

"Introducing Digital's New Disk Cartridge Cleaner" (1977) *Computerworld*, October 24, 10.

Jackson, S.J. (2014) "Rethinking Repair," in T. Gillespie, P. Boczkowski and K. Foot (eds.) *Media Technologies: Essays on Communication, Materiality and Society*, Cambridge, MA: MIT Press, 221–233.

Journal of Data Management (1969) 15.

Kang, L. and Jackson, S.J. (2014) "Breakdown, Obsolescence and Reuse: HCI and the Art of Repair," *CHI'14 Proceedings of the SIGCHI Conference on Human Factors in Computing Systems*, ACM, 449–458.

Kaplan, A. (1998) "Manifest Domesticity," *American Literature* 70, 3, 581–606.

Lowe, E.I. and Hidden, A.E. (1971) *Computer Control in Process Industries*, Chemical Industries Association, Instrumentation Advisory Committee, London: Peter Peregrinus Ltd.

Luxton, M. (1980) *More than a Labour of Love: Three Generations of Women's Work in the Home*, Toronto, ON: Women's Educational Press.

Management Accounting (1967) 48, 7–12, 71.

Mini-Micro Systems (1980) 13, 110 Boston: Cahners.

Monteiro, E. (2004) "Actor Network Theory and Cultural Aspects of Interpretive Studies," in F. Land (ed.) *The Social Study of Information and Communication Technology: Innovation, Actors, and Contexts*, Oxford: Oxford University Press, 129–139.

"My Shugart Followed Me Home" (1979) *Byte*, 4, 1, n.p.

"New Plant Reduces Dust to Minimum: Bearing Company Really Cleans Up" (1957) *New York Times*, May 13, 38.

Parikka, J. (2007) *Digital Contagions: A Media Archaeology of Computer Viruses*, New York: Peter Lang Publishing, Inc.

Rampil, I. "A Floppy Disk Tutorial." (1977) *Byte*, 2, 12, 24–45.

Reed, L. (2000) "Domesticating the Personal Computer: The Mainstreaming of a New Technology and the Cultural Management of a Widespread Technophobia, 1964-," *Critical Studies in Media Communication* 17, 2, 159–185.

132 Rachel Plotnick

Reif, R. (1974) "Art on Computers Aims to Cut 'Antiseptic Look'," *New York Times*, November 11, 47.

Reynolds, C.F. (1977) "Computers and Men," *New Scientist*, October 6, 45.

Silverstone, R. and Haddon, L. (1996) "Design and Domestication of Information and Communication Technologies: Technical Changes and Everyday Life," in R. Mansell and R. Silverstone (eds.) *Communication by Design: The Politics of Information and Communication Technologies*. Oxford: Oxford University Press, 44–74.

Slack, J.D. (2013) "Beyond Transmission, Models, and Media," in J. Packer and S. B. Crofts Wiley (eds.) *Communication Matters: Materialist Approaches to Media, Mobility and Networks*, London and New York: Routledge, 143–158.

Smith, W.D. (1965) "Aerospace Clean Rooms Aid Computer Field," *New York Times*, November 28, F1.

The Software Works, Inc. (1980) "Disk Treatment," *InfoWorld*, December 8, 28.

"The Space" (1978) *Infosystems*, 25, 58.

"The Software Works." Perhaps the in-text citation here, and a few lines down, should be changed to reflect that the author is The Software Works, whereas the title is "Disk Treatment."

Spigel, L. (1992) *Make Room for TV: Television and the Family Ideal in Postwar America*, London and Chicago, IL: The University of Chicago Press.

Suchman, L.A. (2007) *Human-Machine Reconfigurations: Plans and Situated Actions*, Cambridge and New York: Cambridge University Press.

Surden, E. (1978) "Office Environment Poses Problem with Dirty Disks," *Computerworld*, March 13, 67–68.

Technocracy Digest (1970) 215–216, n.p.

"This Clean Room Really Is Clean" (1965) *New Scientist*, July 15, 142.

Univac (1957) "Univac II Marketing Manual," May 15. Available at: https://archive.org/stream/bitsavers_univacunivgManualJun57_20214143/Univac_II_Marketing_Manual_Jun57#page/n0/mode/2up/search/fingernails [Accessed January 5, 2018].

Wedemeyer, D. (1978) "Adapting The Workplace To Computers," *New York Times*, April 23, R1.

"With DP Now Getting Dirtier, Disk Cleaners Seen Invaluable" (1979) *Computerworld*, May 14, 61–66.

Part III
Storage

8 Architectures of information

A comparison of Wiener's and Shannon's theories of information

Bernard Dionysius Geoghegan

On April 15th, 1963 Claude Elwood Shannon made his debut in *Vogue*. A crisp black and white photograph shot by Henri Cartier-Bresson shows him standing inside his home in Winchester, Massachusetts, cigarette in hand and a faraway look in his eyes. The accompanying article characterizes Shannon as "the authority on Information Theory at the Massachusetts Institute of Technology," adding that information "has been his lifelong study—'information' in the very special sense that word has come to have under the Theory of Information, his major contribution as a scientist and a mathematician ...." (Brower 1963: 89). Shannon's colleague Norbert Wiener had already appeared twice in *Vogue*, which heralded him as the great mathematician responsible for founding cybernetics. As if explaining their presence in a magazine oriented towards a fashion-focused female readership, one of the articles featuring Wiener's portrait explained that he and his contemporaries in science "know that science can not progress without generous public support" and that "to gain this support the scientist will have to learn how to create in the public an interest and an understandings of his strivings in research" (*Vogue* 1951: 97). A cynic might well regard the unctuous praise lavished on Wiener and Shannon as evidence of a broader uncritical enthusiasm towards science that swept the United States in the 1950s and 1960s as part of its mobilization in the anti-communist Cold War effort. Perhaps, however, it also reflects an insight that permeated that moment in American public culture that has waned in the intervening years: namely, that the authority of scientific theories rests in a peculiar way upon the manner in which their conception and elaboration interweaves with the broader fabric of the embedding culture. Scientific investigation was not simply the product of an ivory tower removed from the public but rather depended in a vital manner on public engagement to thrive. Such engagement was not the politicization of science but rather an element in its flourishing, with salutary effects upon the laboratory and the public alike.

The presence of both Shannon and Wiener in *Vogue* magazine also hints at the multiple itineraries and publics a scientific idea such as "communication" or "information" galvanized. To be sure, both works occupied

136   *Bernard Dionysius Geoghegan*

shared intellectual space. Wiener's *Cybernetics: Control and Communication in the Animal and the Machine* and Claude Shannon's "A Mathematical Theory of Communication," both published in 1948, offered far-reaching formulas for measuring and managing an elusive entity sometimes called "information"—a term only loosely understood but suspected to be of far-reaching importance in technical and social domains. But both theories also tended to reproduce the values of distinct research environments, ultimately giving genesis to different intellectual architectures for deduction, collaboration, and even ontology. Wiener embraced the study of information as part of a broad, interdisciplinary study of problems in physiology, social science, engineering and related fields—sometimes pursuing an audience in the media as part of his broader program of agitation in support of cybernetics. Shannon offered a more circumspect approach to the study of information, rooted in the values of engineering practice and the economic rationales governing his longtime employer, Bell Telephone Laboratories, the research arm of American Telephone and Telegraph (AT&T). Where the former identified the study of information with the greatest undertakings of Western science and philosophy since Leibniz (perhaps even Plato), the latter more closely associated his research with the development of rigorous scientific theories tailored to specific technical setups (though Shannon sometimes extrapolated ideas about communicating with extraplanetary life forms, the building of thinking machines, and some topics in psychology, based on his practical studies of efficient information transmissions). By the time Wiener and Shannon appeared in *Vogue*, their works had become classics appealing to broad but somewhat distinct audiences. Attractively illustrated articles in venues such as *TIME*, *LIFE*, and *Vogue*, and appearances in science documentaries on public and commercial television, fleshed out imaginary worlds for these theorists. Frequently they named fellow-travelers in thought, as well as predicting the building of infrastructures of future societies around these theories.

The present article examines the genesis of these two specific theories of information—their distinct practical and disciplinary origins, their wartime and institutional intersections, and the epistemological divergences—amidst a broader family of conceptual and professional problems embedding research on "information" in the 1940s and 1950s. It concludes with remarks on the wider uptake of these theories. In suggesting these theories embodied two different architectures, I underscore the extent to which scientific theories are not simply abstract concepts detached from history and place but, on the contrary, embody specific values and histories that give shelter to distinct communities and exercises. An idea is not only a tool to think with—as Sherry Turkle and Claude Lévi-Strauss before her suggested. It is also a kind of structure or environment within which particular thoughts and communities can gather. Even its most utilitarian elements reflect a certain set of values and aesthetic sensibilities peculiar to its place of origin (a place it almost at once preserves and aspires to

Architectures of information 137

transform). The consideration of these two theories and their milieus in some detail serves two more specific aims. First, I uncover the professional, ethical, and even cosmological concerns that structured the types of questions and solutions these two theories developed. Such a culturalist consideration aims at casting light on the diversity of factors that go into formulating a scientific question or problem and, thereby, set the stage for its later application and appropriation. That consideration leads to the second aim of this chapter— namely, to discern how the cultural origins of these theories shaped their subsequent appropriation, allowing Wiener's and Shannon's theories to be applied to different questions and problems.

Information theories and their sources

The 1940s and 1950s witnessed an unprecedented wave of scientific theories of information and its measurement, closely tied to the end of World War II and the rush of wartime research findings being declassified and refigured for wider scientific consumption. In 1948 alone at least eight competing accounts of information appeared in prestigious English, British, American, and French journals (Verdú 1998: 2058). Jerome Wiesner, director of MIT's Research Laboratory of Electronics, told a reporter in 1952 of the great anxiousness many engineers felt about the need to define the information. "Before we had the theory [of information] a lot of us were deeply troubled," he explained. "We had been dealing with a commodity that we could never see or really define. We were in the situation petroleum engineers would be in if they didn't have a measuring unit like the gallon" (Bello 1953: 140). It was to this desire—equal parts quantitative and ontological—that theories of information responded.

The years 1945 to 1960 witnessed the first concentrated wave of theories of information, spearheaded by engineers with wartime experience in cryptography, artillery fire-control systems (for targeting weaponry), and radar. Historian of computing William Aspray notes that the theorization of information included a wide array of researchers familiar with one another's work, who often did not conceive of their work as theorizing "information" per se (Aspray 1985: 117–140). As a graduate student Shannon studied under Wiener; Alan Turing met Shannon during consultations at Bell Labs during the war who, in turn met with Donald MacKay at the famed British "Ratio Club"; Warren McCulloch and Walter Pitts collaborated with Wiener at the early Macy Conferences (where they also debated the definition of information and redundancy with Shannon), Wiener and John von Neumann frequently exchanged letters and Shannon knew the latter from their shared time in Princeton, New Jersey during World War II. That this network of interrelations closely mirrored relationships and projects developed during World War II provides clues about the origins of information theory: it was not a *sui generis* discovery but the result of a wide scale mobilization that wove existing scientific strands into a composite scientific project.[1]

138 *Bernard Dionysius Geoghegan*

A few shared notions underlie most theories developed in that first wave of engineering-related theories of information. These included the notions that signals and relays manifest in communication systems could be described according to a unified system of mathematics and logic that mapped out their regularities, and that technical telecommunications systems—telegraphy, digital computers, telephony, or even artillery control systems—served as an excellent model for speculating more broadly about the laws of communication in non-technical systems. Such technical systems would therefore be suitable for developing a more general theory of the rules and constraints governing communications systems generally. Nestled within understanding of information technologies as paradigmatic of social communications was a conception of communications as composed of physical traces available for empirical and statistical scientific explanation. Theorists of information held that experimental study could reveal communications as a more or less physical entity governed by objectifiable laws.[2]

Perhaps most peculiar to information theorists was the idea that information and communication technologies provided the clues to the broader modes of communication that prevailed in the universe—that a study of the rules governing transmissions in a wire might also cast light on the rules governing elegance in a sonnet, provide clues for the mechanical translation between Russian and English, or cast light on the nature of scientific experiment. This conception appeared decidedly one-way in its application: rarely did information theorists derive rules from sonnets for governing the design of missile guidance systems or for improved transmissions in a noisy channel. In the decade following World War II, for engineers and swaths of the general public, computers, telephone lines, and telegraphs became privileged objects for envisioning broader features of biology, sociology, and cosmology. Where savants of the seventeenth- and eighteenth centuries looked to automata to model properties of human motion and the mind, and Darwin's theory of evolution provided a privileged model for social theory in the latter half of the nineteenth century, theorists of information in the middle of the twentieth century identified computing and telecommunications as the favored objects of epochal enlightenment.

Diverging theories of information

Divergences in theories of information reflected, in part, the spaces of their development. As historians including Ron Kline and Jérôme Segal have observed, scientific definitions of "information" reflected the specific constellations of objects, relations, and cosmic horizons informing the community doing the theorization (Segal 2003, Kline 2015). Defining information entailed a definition of these relations and the place of the theorist within that world's observation and management. Information theorists' professional and intellectual background framed their definition of a communicative cosmos.

Architectures of information 139

Consider the competing definitions of information put forth by Wiener and Shannon. For the polymath Wiener, who had studied philosophy as well as mathematics at Harvard University, to theorize information was also to posit something about order and organization, and the place of human observers within it. In the years that Wiener developed cybernetics, he famously walked the halls of MIT almost obsessively, travelling from department to department, building to building, picking the brains of colleagues and students he encountered as he walked. These "Wienerwegs," as they were called, reproduced the pre-1950s spatial dispositions of MIT itself, when the various disciplines and departments were gathered around a centralized campus. Cybernetics provided a kind of conceptual route between these disciplines, an architecture for their intellectual communication with one another. Shannon, by contrast, identified the problem of communications closely with the concerns of the Bell Telephone System where he was employed. His was a theory built on the possibility of formulating the most general and well-founded theory of communication as the problem presented itself to the communications engineer. Speaking at the Macy Conferences on Cybernetics, Shannon explained that the

> communication engineer can visualize his job as the transmission of the particular messages chosen by the information source to be sent to the receiving point. What the message means is of no importance to him; the thing that does have importance is the set of statistics with which it was chosen, the probabilities of various messages.
> (Shannon 2004 [1951] 248)

Such an analysis provided no obvious link across the disciplines but it did sketch the way towards solving a well-defined commercial problem. Indeed, though Bell Labs was not slavishly tied to applicability, its general culture favored commercial innovation and problem-solving.

With other intellectual milieus came other manners of defining information. The physicists Donald MacKay and Dennis Gabor, members of what Ron Kline (following Warren S. McCulloch) has termed "the English School of information theory," identified information with the ability to predict and measure the outcomes of physical experiments.[3] "Information theory," MacKay argued, "is concerned with this problem of measuring changes in knowledge" (MacKay 1953: 9). His effort to account for meaning through information constituted one component in this larger effort to develop a general theory of knowledge and scientific method based on communications.[4] Lecturing at MIT in 1952 Gabor took a subtle swipe at the industrially-oriented work of Shannon, declaring that "[c]ommunication theory owes its origin to a few theoretically interested engineers who wanted to understand the nature of the goods sold in communication systems" (Gabor 1952: 1). Gabor effectively recognized in Shannon's theory an approach to communication that reflected industrial imperatives of a

140 *Bernard Dionysius Geoghegan*

large-scale concern like the Bell Telephone system. The physicist Gabor sought a wider gamut for communications. He argued that information theory also included the ability to adduce the likelihood of certain outcomes from a pre-specified experimental setup; in this account informational analysis of transmitted signals modeled a future information theory that would measure the range of likely outcomes and changes in knowledge resulting from the inputs and outputs of scientific experiment (Gabor 1952: 29). Gabor's efforts to model such distributions in the case of light projections culminated in his successful invention of holography, for which he received a Nobel Prize in physics in 1971.

At public gatherings and in printed publications theorists of information engaged in friendly quarrels over the definition of information and its scope. Speaking on "The Redundancy of English" at the Macy Conferences on Cybernetics, Shannon expounded on the centrality of redundancy to his definition, explaining that a measurement of information in terms of redundancy allowed for the extraction of predictable content and the more economical transmission of a compressed signal. "[T]he communication engineer can make a saving [sic] by the choice of an efficient code," he explained, closely identifying information with the problem of economy (Shannon 2004 [1951]: 248). Throughout his address eminent scholars, including logician Walter Pitts, anthropologists Margaret Mead and Gregory Bateson, and psychoacoustician J. C. R. Licklider interjected questions concerning the relationship of information and redundancy to topics including emotions, jokes, marital habits, language learning, and, in one instance, the prospect that translating Kant's *Critique* into Chinese and English might improve its intelligibility by enhancing semantic redundancy. Shannon listened to these discussions with patience, diplomatically insisting that his own definition of information should be understood as a "mathematical dodge" based on defining information in reference to a pre-constituted set of symbols rather than anything so complicated as meaning or intelligibility (Shannon 2004 [1951]: 271). He explained:

> I never have any trouble distinguishing signals from noise because I say, as a mathematician, that this is signal and that is noise. But there are, it seems to me, ambiguities that come in at the psychological level. If a person receives something over a telephone, part of which is useful to him and part of which is not, and you want to call the useful part the signal, that is hardly a mathematical problem. It involves too many psychological elements.
>
> (Shannon 2004 [1951]: 269)

In this conception, psychology marked the site where a defined ensemble of selections fractured into an indefinite ensemble of ill-distinguished selections. At the following year's Macy Conference, the meanings of information continued to proliferate. At one point in discussions, when Shannon suggested that Alex Bavelas—a psychologist and student of Kurt Lewin who had established the Groups Network Laboratory at MIT—confused psychological and engineering definitions of information, MacKay argued for a more capacious theory of information capable of accommodating both definitions (Bavelas 2003 [1951]: 366). When MacKay expanded on this idea with his proposal for a semantic theory of information, a frustrated Shannon interjected that, "I think perhaps the word 'Information' is causing more trouble in this connection than it is worth, except that it is difficult to find another word anywhere near right."[5]

The 1950 London Symposium on Information Theory provided an occasion for even greater confusion over the scope of the nascent field.[6] Speakers including Shannon, Gabor, Wiesner, and MacKay, among others, convened to present research at this first-of-a-kind international conference dedicated to the emerging field of information theory. British academic and electrical engineer Jackson Willis convened the conferencing, having correctly identified communications research as a promising field capable of attracting funding and new researchers to the Imperial College's staid department of Electrical Engineering, which he had joined in 1946 (Gabor and Brown, 1971). In an opening address titled "Communication Theory, Past and Present," Gabor discounted the importance of coding theory (the centerpiece of Shannon's research), instead identifying the future of communication theory with machine translation, robots, and the replacement of faulty human sensory organs. These various alternatives distinguished his broader aspirations:

> ...the concept of Information has wider technical applications than in the field of communication engineering. Science in general is a system of collecting and connecting information about nature...Communication theory, though largely independent in origin, thus fits logically into a larger physico-philosophical framework, which has been given the general title of "Information Theory."
>
> (Gabor 1953: 4)

Gabor's Imperial College colleague Colin Cherry (a British engineer and wartime radar researcher) expanded information farther afield to the structures of Roman shorthand writing, the heritage of Leibniz, and the research of Ivan Pavlov (Cherry 1953: 22–43). Phonetician Donald Fry invoked the work of linguist Ferdinand de Saussure and MacKay linked information with "changes in knowledge" (Fry 1953: 120–124; MacKay 1953: 9). Shannon defended his narrower definition of information by an appeal to applied mathematics, where—he suggested—"vague and ambiguous concepts of a physical problem are given more refined and idealized meaning." Shannon urged his participants to distinguish invocations of information in terms of that scientific nomenclature from ill-defined commonsensical notions.

142 Bernard Dionysius Geoghegan

Wiener and Shannon on information and purpose

In the early 1950s Wiener's and Shannon's theories of information emerged as the most widely noted and influential theories of information, albeit with distinct emphases. Wiener's *Cybernetics* adapted his wartime studies of artillery fire-control into a broad account of how information and communication underpinned diverse aspects of physics, mathematics, computing, neurology and biology (Wiener 1961 [1948]). Its interspersing of dense mathematical chapters with speculative and philosophical commentaries on machines sold briskly and helped establish a new genre of futurological writing that would later flourish in the hands of a later generation of speculative scientific popularizers such as Hans Moravec, Marvin Minsky, and Ray Kurzweil. Articles and books that followed Wiener generalized cybernetics into a universal science that could restructure research across the university, industry, and political life.[7]

Shannon's 1948 two-part article "A Mathematical Theory of Communication," based on wartime studies of cryptography, offered a more focused analysis of the formal characteristics, statistical rules, and mathematical limits governing signals and their transmission. In response to the great excitement his work elicited, Shannon agreed to republish his essay as a book titled *The Mathematical Theory of Communication* (the substitution of "The" for "A" indexed the ambitions that the book's publisher, The University of Illinois Press, harbored for this work). An ebullient accompanying commentary by Weaver touted the book's importance for "Analytical Communication Studies," a field of communication study that encompassed engineering, literature, ballet, and ultimately "all human behavior" (Weaver 1964 [1949]). Through this book a wider audience of natural scientists, engineers and social scientists discovered Shannon's work and came to believe it might decipher mathematical and formal properties of communication governing their fields.[8]

Wiener's and Shannon's approaches to information intersected at a number of points. They both describe communications systems in terms of serial transmissions characterizable in terms of (often) semi-predictable patterns, distributed sequentially in time as distinct elements (such as letters of the alphabet) or sampled chunks (from an analog recording), and both focused on the potential of statistical quantification to predict and manage likely signals. These similar outlooks reflected the overlapping research milieus of the theories. As a graduate student in engineering and mathematics, Shannon studied under Wiener. Both worked on military command-and-control research for the National Defense Research Council (NDRC) during World War II, on studies that focused on the production and evaluation of communications for managing machine systems—artillery and fire-control in particular—and occasionally consulted with one another. In addition, Wiener and Shannon shared the same supervisor at the NDRC, Weaver, who—as noted above—also acted as a patron, funding research into cybernetics in Wiener's case and acting as the single most important popularizer of the mathematical theory in Shannon's.

On the topic of communication and its purposefulness, however, the accounts of Wiener and Shannon begin to diverge. For Wiener, communication stemmed from purposefulness rooted in the performances of goal-oriented collectivities guided by recursive feedback. His first and arguably most lucid account of the cybernetic perspective, the 1943 essay "Behavior, Purpose and Teleology" co-authored with Arturo Rosenblueth and Julian Bigelow, proposed a unified account of purposeful behaviors in organisms and machines. The authors draw on examples from target-seeking torpedoes to humans bringing glasses of water to develop an account of goal-directed behavior as a system of ongoing feedback guiding interactions between an entity and its environment. In this account, humans, machines, and ensembles of humans-and-machines, assume the character of willful, desiring subjects of communication, whose exploitation of information define their being in the world and their kinship to one another. Shannon's information theory stripped purposefulness from communication; examining streams of written language, electrical transmissions, and other streams of communication, he uncovered patterns operating independent of any particular subject.

Purpose or teleology—as least as Wiener defined it—was anathema to Shannon's measure of information. For one thing, as noted above, Shannon argued that psychology and meaning were irrelevant to the communication engineer's definition of information. That these communications might pass by way purposeful minds was incidental to his research. The presence in speech of patterns available for technical measurement and compression related to the properties of a language system rather than the intentions of an individual user. A cornerstone of Shannon's method, the identification of semi-predictable Markov series in most forms of communication, was named for Andrei Markov's 1913 study of 20,000 consecutive characters in the poem *Eugene Onegin* by Alexander Pushkin, wherein Markov showed a statistical regularity in the distribution of vowels throughout the text (Markov 2006 [1913]: 591–600). A subsequent study by Markov of 100,000 letters in *Childhood Years of Bagrov's Grandson* by Sergey T. Aksakoff confirmed these initial findings and demonstrated that such patterns operated independently of the author (Link 2006: 563). Such patterns did not even reflect that lowly form of human intentionality known as habit. These serial patterns belonged to the Russian language itself and repeated in similar forms across texts by diverse authors. If purposefulness had anything to do with this account, it was that of Russian itself which employed human speakers as the medium for its statistically patterned expressions.

Information and entropy

An even more decisive difference between the two theories was Wiener's and Shannon's respective accounts of the relationship of information to entropy. In the late nineteenth century, physicist Ludwig Boltzmann

144 *Bernard Dionysius Geoghegan*

demonstrated a statistical basis to this disorder and the tendency of particles in the universe to distribute gradually into less predictable, disorderly states, i.e., for entropy to increase. Entropy is therefore a measure or disorderliness in a system and, beyond that, the relative predictability of the likelihood as to whether a given state prevails at a given place and moment. Boltzmann was one of a number of late nineteenth-century physicists who developed reliable statistical mechanisms for predicting and quantifying entropy of a system. Wiener and Shannon both recognized a striking similarity between the entropy of a physical system described in statistical mechanics and that of a communication system that can occupy a given state at a given moment in transmission. The notion of statistical likelihood for whether or not a particular physical particle would appear at a given moment in the physical system and the definition of that likelihood in terms of entropy is comparable to the likelihood of whether or not a given transmission would present a particular state at a given moment in the communication system—say, a 0 or a 1 or perhaps a letter A or Z. If the notion of entropy could be used to quantify statistically the probability of order—both in a physical system and the state of a given point in that—so too, they reasoned, it could be used to quantify the probability of one message or another appearing at any moment in time. On the basis of this measure, other factors could be determined—for example, whether a highly unusual message would be more likely to be a signal or noise and how to develop systems of encoding that could add or subtract redundancy in accordance with the likelihood of noise and how to devise filters that could automatically recognize and subtract noise from a signal.

When it came to defining the relationship of information to entropy, Wiener and Shannon reached for inverted mathematical figures. Wiener identified the quantity of information with its overall orderliness, understood largely in terms of its intelligibility to an observer. "Just as the amount of information in a system is a measure of its degree of organization," he wrote in *Cybernetics*, "so the entropy of a system is a measure of its degree of disorganization; and the one is simply the negative of the other" (Wiener 1961: 11). On this basis, Wiener identified information with negative entropy, which is to say the predictability and orderliness of a communication system. Eager to emphasize the complete continuity among the communications problem and adjacent fields, he labeled this observation of information and entropy as part of the "essential unity of the set of problems centering about communication, control, and statistical mechanics, whether in the machine or in living tissue" (Wiener 1961: 11).

The identification of information with order (or negentropy) encoded in Wiener's theory a certain cosmological stance—Wiener assumed the universe itself was orderly and coherent, and that humans could observe, understand, and participate in that orderliness. Thus Wiener inscribed information with a series of spiraling cybernetic analogies, wherein the state of local information depended on its relation to a series of larger

Architectures of information 145

embedded contexts and actors. In *Cybernetics* Wiener discussed how information might be used by machines, organisms, and communities to produce orderliness—in accordance with the account of entropy given in statistical mechanisms—and to set these systems off from environments. The outcome of this approach was the field Wiener termed cybernetics (an "umbrella discipline" in the words of Ron Kline (Kline 2015: 185)), which sought to group the widest number of natural, technical, and social sciences together around a common theory of message transmission and feedback as techniques for governing living and non-living systems.

Shannon, by contrast, identified the quantify of information as a measure of the relative disorder of the message—or its entropy. For Shannon, the greater a message's entropy, the greater the information content contained in it. The measurement of information had nothing to do with knowledge, at least as a measure of understanding. Quantity of information measured the number of selections, exclusions, and differences that produce a given message, particularly as those differentiations are produced by a machine. Thus, disorder and complexity corresponded to a greater range of possibilities. Shannon argued the selection of one message from a larger, more unlikely set thus conveyed more information than the selection of a highly predictable message from a limited set. Greater entropy correlated with greater information. In the United States, Shannon's approach gave rise to "information theory," a highly specialized mathematical field dedicated to theorizing the measurement and transmission of information in communication networks, ones typically technological in character.

Architectures of information

The distinctions between Wiener's and Shannon's accounts of information are an artifact of the distinctive epistemological architectures generated in their work. As discussed above, dense disciplinary and technical milieus provided the framework within which information came to be denied. Information theory these consolidated these milieus into durable spaces for thinking, building, and experimenting. While discussions of information today often elicit notions of an abstract, immaterial entity circling global fiber optics, the formulation of a theory of information developed from concrete experimental setups and their conceptual affordances. Wiener's research into cybernetics, and the heart of his work on information, stemmed from his participation during World War II in a small group at MIT responsible for studying how to correct errors in aiming artillery fire (Galison 1994: 233–245). The crux of fire-control was twofold. First, in the extremely chaotic situation of war, how does one consistently correct for errors that creep into soldiers' targeting of artillery, for example by the quivering of a hand? Second, the great speed and distance of planes targeted by soldiers prevented reliable human prediction of where, exactly,

146 *Bernard Dionysius Geoghegan*

artillery should be fired. It was therefore necessary that artillery guns be equipped with mechanisms able to predict and compensate for the slowness of human perception. Here, errors constituting the appearance of noise confounded the reliable transmission of a signal. The solution reached by Wiener was to treat the information relayed between gunner and gun as a discrete series of signals bedeviled by consistent and regular distortions, i.e., noise, and to determine a method for quantifying and correcting the errors. In this schema, redundancies—namely, regularly repeating patterns—were the key to correcting a signal. The analyst assumed continuity to an airplane's path and extrapolated from that a smooth and orderly trajectory of flight.

In contrast, Shannon's major assignment during the war was an evaluation of the top-secret SIGSALY cryptographic telephone system, which allowed for encrypted real-time conversation among Allied elites across North America, Europe, and the Pacific (Rogers 1994). It was during this period that Shannon authored "A Mathematical Theory of Cryptography," large portions of which reappeared in "A Mathematical Theory of Communication." Unlike the fire-control problem that treated human and machine as a single system of communication, cryptography introduced a strict line of separation between human and machine affordance by enveloping natural language within mathematical transformations that eliminated all traces of orderliness. Shannon credited this text with laying the groundwork for information theory, explaining many years later "they are very similar things, in one case trying to conceal information, and in the other case trying to transmit it" (Price 1984: 124).

Where Wiener's aim during the war was to subtract noise into communications, Shannon's was to introduce it. The chief way of doing so, it turned out, was to quantify as precisely as possible all repeating patterns in an original message and find a way of removing them. This operation came to prominence since the primary manner of deciphering an encrypted message was to find recurring patterns that signal an underlying pattern, which could then be correlated with a fixed property of the original message—a commonly used letter, word, or even a phoneme with given regularity in English or German, for the context of wartime. These repetitions had the quality of redundancies, and a good encrypting system would remove and replace them with a code that produced what looked like an arbitrary series of units. In consequence, a perfectly encrypted message, i. e., a message with no redundancies or apparent patterns, was isomorphic with noise and demonstrated a high measure of entropy.

The technical details of these two tasks reveal the reasons for divergent conceptions of entropy, measurement, and order. While a significant degree of overlap encouraged both Wiener and Shannon towards a similar figure—that of entropy—in defining information, the exact relation of that figure to information varied in part according to what the problem at hand. Eager to remove confounding disorder and noise from messages,

Wiener sought out information in redundancy and patterns that could be magnified to increase the orderliness of the message. Shannon, on the other hand, placed the accent in his wartime work on producing mathematical randomness and expelling patterns from signals. When Wiener and Shannon adapted their work into theories of information after the war, this background research lead to distinct emphases—that of order, for Wiener, and that of measurement, for Shannon. Cybernetics became a science of identifying and restoring order to a transmitted signal, with information playing the part of subtracting the noise. For the telephone engineer Shannon, however, the problem of communication was one of measuring patterns and efficiently managing repetition and redundancy.

Wiener's entropic universe

The confines of wartime research provided support for Wiener's and Shannon's theoretical dispositions but a wider set of commitments to the order of science and nature informed their analyses. Wiener's 1948 *Cybernetics* imagined information as the broadest property of physical, technological, biological, and social systems. His is a communicative cosmology stretching from the Brownian motions of the smallest particles to the largest sweep of thermodynamic tendencies towards entropy in the physical universe (Wiener 1950: 12). Within Wiener's cosmology, entropy stood in for the misanthropic tendencies of a universe racing towards complete and total disorder. Information—the occasional appearance of orderliness—was the bulwark against universal annihilation. Living organisms embodied one form of negentropic orderliness, and human societies another. The informed organism and the informed society came together in the individual empowered producing order through techniques of cybernetic observation and feedback. "[A]ny organism," Wiener wrote in *Cybernetics*, "is held together ... by the possession of means for the acquisition, use, retention, and transmission of information" (Wiener 1961[1948]: 161). From this perspective, the definition of information and negative entropy is co-extensive with the problematic of life and order in the universe. Affirming the information coincides with order and continuity. To understand is, in effect, to assign to cybernetics the task of doing combat with the forces of decay in the universe.

Wiener identified the rise of modern communications with the actualization of a post-Newtonian, statistical universe as theorized by nineteenth-century scientists and mathematicians such as Josiah Willard Gibbs. In his popularization of cybernetics, *The Human Use of Human Beings*, Wiener averred, "we no longer deal with quantities and statements which concern a specific, real universe as a whole [as we did in the time of Newton] but ask instead questions which may find their answers in a large number of universes" (Wiener 1950: 11). Wiener saw the decline of Newtonian mechanics and its replacement by statistically founded thermodynamics in the

148 *Bernard Dionysius Geoghegan*

nineteenth century as compelling a conflict between science and the forces of randomness and disorder implied in thermodynamics and its offshoot: relativity. "The scientist," Wiener posited, "is always working to discover the order and organization of the universe, and is thus playing a game against the arch enemy, disorganization" (Wiener 1950: 34).[9] The identification of information provided a mechanism for scientists to combat statistical caprice. "In physics," he explained, "the idea of progress opposes that of entropy ..." (Wiener 1950: 38).

Wiener's tethering of information to a wider scientific and human context found a certain instantiation in his work during wartime but the broader ethical aspirations of cybernetics ultimately found their roots in Wiener's training in humanist philosophies, which positioned the natural sciences as a partner in the advancement of edifying positive knowledge. Insofar as the artillery control problem understood human and machine as a dynamic, open-ended system of mutual feedback, it lent itself towards an amalgamation of humanist and technicist styles of thought. By stripping away the random and erratic noise of complex communications to restore the purposefulness of a human operator, fire-control research sought to put human intention back in the saddle of large technical systems. The genius of Wiener lay in his ability to align that technical problem with his humanist training.

During his graduate studies at Harvard, Wiener studied with celebrated Harvard philosopher Josiah Royce. Between 1913 and 1915 he made his earliest mathematical and philosophical contribution of note (including notable innovations to the logic of Bertrand Russell and Charles Peirce), while undertaking postdoctoral studies in Europe under Edmund Husserl, Russell, and the mathematician G. H. Hardy (Masani 1990: 45–65). Wiener's thought in these years developed in the hothouse of interwar European philosophy—marked by the early work of the Vienna Circle and Husserl's studies of mathematics—which promoted scientific and philosophical synthesis as part of establishing a framework for cultural progress.[10] Wiener immersed himself not only in philosophy but also in the writings of Henri Bergson, Bohr's atomic theory, J. W. Gibbs' work on statistical mechanics, and the Einstein-Smoluchowski studies of Brownian motion (Masani 1990: 55). This formation deeply marked his longer scientific outlook; the work on statistical mechanics and Brownian motion became foundations of his studies of disorder and information, and Wiener came to embrace a deep skepticism of specialization in the modern sciences. Where the studies of statistics and Brownian motion grappled with the difficulties of erratic and chaotic events in the physical world, interwar European philosophies explored the possibility of establishing a supra-disciplinary science that overcame balkanization in the social and political world. In cybernetics Wiener forged a tentative resolution of these tendencies. It promised to introduce a new principle of intelligibility across the disciplines, founded on the idea that local, chaotic disruptions could be

Architectures of information 149

integrated into larger, organic systems of order via information and feedback. The decision to put information on the side of negative entropy—and with it on the side of life and knowledge—resounded with these broader aims.

Shannon's industrial information

Shannon's "A Mathematical Theory of Communication" did not pit information against the chaos of an expanding universe; rather, it presented the entropy of information as the condensed expression of reading and writing of machines operating independently of human consciousness and intentionality. Shannon's theory may be described as "posthuman" (in the sense N. Katherine Hayles has used that term), insofar as it dispensed with the centrality of humans in the communications process (Hayles 1999). However, it was also post-organic—it overturned the centrality living organisms played in most accounts of communications (including Wiener's), preferring to view communications as a kind of automatism inscribed in the broadest range of statistically based phenomena. As an industrial engineer employed by the research laboratories of AT&T, Shannon's theory focused on most economical modes for recording, processing, and transmitting communications. He also introduced elementary diagrams with the power to reduce the peculiarity of industrial communications to an apparently timeless, uncontestable law. It is in this same role that he published his 1948 essay, famously declaring,

> The fundamental problem of communication is that of reproducing at one point either exactly or approximately a message selected at another point. Frequently the messages have meaning; that is, they refer to or are correlated according to some system with certain physical or conceptual entities.\These semantic aspects of communication are irrelevant to the engineering problem. The significant aspect is that the actual message is one selected from a set of possible messages. The system must be designed to operate for each possible selection, not just the one which will actually be chosen since this is unknown at the time of design.
>
> (Shannon 1964 [1948]: 31)

The attention critics have devoted to the exclusion of semantics has often obscured the second, equally decisive aspect of this formulation—that is, *selection from a set* that is key. With this framing, communication ceases to be the expression of an interior being animated by passions, desires, and imagination; it is, rather, selections from a set of possibilities. In the field of language and speech, this set may include phonemes, letters, words, or phrases. The human as communicator slips to the margins in this account, and a mathematically governed system of communicative possibilities rises in its stead.

150   *Bernard Dionysius Geoghegan*

Shannon's posthuman communications theory found roots in the projects of nineteenth-century engineers to exclude redundancy from Morse code and other communications systems in order to economize on the statistical patterns in language. In these projects letters such as *e* were assigned short codes, infrequent letters such as *z* had long codes. In this perspective, a text low in redundancy and high in improbable patterns proved most economical to transmit. Statistical disorder coincided with economic efficiency. Language as expression of man gave way to language as a system of codes to be economically written and read by engineering systems. Within this schema, the entropy was the condensed expression of a highly efficient reading and writing of machines.

Already in graduate school, Shannon turned to the questions that would occupy his later "Mathematical Theory." The first known text to trace his interest in a theory of data transmission is a 1939 letter to his MIT graduate advisor Vannevar Bush. The 22-year-old Shannon described his ongoing search for fundamental properties that govern "the transmission of intelligence …" (Shannon 1993: 455–456). A year later, Shannon graduated with a Ph.D. in mathematics and, following a summer stint, returned to AT&T's Bell Laboratories as a full-time researcher (Gallager 2001: 2682).[11] When "A Mathematical Theory of Communications" appeared in the *Bell System Technical Journal*, in 1948, it realized the aims first outlined in the 1939 letter, but the term "intelligence" had been substituted for the more technical "information." This terminological shift from intelligence to information captured a conceptual one towards non-anthropocentric theories of communication, spearheaded by AT&T and its Bell Labs.

In 1924, Shannon's predecessor at the laboratories, Harry Nyquist, had in fact developed a logarithmic measure for the "transmission of intelligence" that Shannon would later adopt (Nyquist 1924: 324–346).[12] In this treatise, Nyquist showed that regardless of what users said or engineers did, a transmission itself was governed by physical limits relating to channel dimensions, encoding complexity, and delivery speeds. This analysis took an initial step towards describing communications in terms of an order available to technical machinery rather than human cognition. Nyquist's colleague Ralph Hartley followed up with a 1928 article on "The Transmission of Information," which substituted the term information for intelligence and argued the former should be measured without reference to human psychology. In noting that telegraph messages were often transmitted accurately based only on trained operators' ability to intuit an intended meaning from the garbled transmission, he maintained such interventions constituted an obstacle to producing a mathematical and scientific measurement of information. Only when symbols could be measured and discerned independent from the receiver's expectation and understanding could that information be called scientific and objective.

When Shannon turned to cryptographic research during the war, the long history of industrial efforts to eliminate man from the analysis of

Architectures of information   151

language came to the fore. As his classified wartime memorandum on cryptography explained, "A natural language, such as English, can be studied from many points of view—lexicography, syntax, semantics, history, aesthetics, etc. The only properties of a language of interest in cryptography are of statistical properties" (Shannon 1945: 10). For the cryptographer, any statistical patterns present in the source that re-appear within an enciphered text run the risk of enabling its decryption. Ideal cryptography thus depended on machines that could strip away human-readable patterns and substitute them for apparently random patterns readable only to the enciphering machine. Divorcing meaning, knowledge, and intuition from communications, this procedure replaced them all with techno-mathematical patterns appropriate for analysis, decomposition, and reassembly according to quasi-arbitrary coding systems. This outlook had the peculiar effect of expanding the powers of speech to include non-human actors of the most diverse forms. As Shannon wrote in the cryptography memo, "[w]e consider a language, therefore, to be a stochastic (i.e. a statistical) process which generates a sequence of symbols according to some system of probabilities" (Shannon 1945: 10–11). Any "ergodic source"—i.e. an entity that emitted signals with some statistical patterning—could be credited with producing a type of language. Changing stock prices over time, shifting weather patterns, and serially patterned radiation emissions assumed properties that mirrored human language. Under cryptographic scrutiny, knowledge as understanding gave way to knowledge as probabilities. Consequently, Shannon could declare,

> "[k]nowledge' is thus identified with a set of propositions having associated probabilities. We are here at variance with the doctrine often assumed in philosophical studies which consider knowledge to be a set of propositions where are either true or false"
>
> (Shannon 1945: 3)

Knowledge became one statistically patterned formation among others, nominally independent from referentiality and semantics.

Meaning for the profession

Wiener's and Shannon's rival visions of information as order and disorder, as holistic system or machinic code, implied two distinct kinds of communication professionals. Wiener's theory summoned the broadest range of experts to contribute to the task of cybernetic steering for the messy postwar world. Information assumed a central role in the production of cybernetic feedback necessary to preserving life and enhancing the social order within which it dwelled. Shannon's approach, by contrast, offered a much more circumspect theory of communication centered on the practical tasks confronting industrial engineers. Rather than integrate information into the

152 *Bernard Dionysius Geoghegan*

great traditions of humane science, it began a piecemeal reconsideration from machines that gradually and tentatively reached into the human sciences. This emphasis did not preclude the establishment of grander alliances in information sciences but it prioritized engineered communication networks governed by well-defined mathematical limits. Shannon's theory also suggested that signal economy and the elimination of noise were desirable goals.

In the 1950s, the Institute of Radio Engineer's *Transactions on Information Theory*—the journal that had become most associated with researchers who focused their work on the analysis of information—solicited subscribers' opinions on the proper limits for information theory. L. A. De Rosa, Chairman of the Professional Group on Information Theory (PGIT),[13] stated the concern in an editorial titled "In Which Fields Do We Graze":

> The expansion of the applications of Information Theory to fields other than radio and wired communications has been so rapid that oftentimes the bounds within which the Professional Group interests lie are questioned. Should an attempt be made to extend our interests to such fields as management, biology, psychology, and linguistic theory, or should the concentration be strictly in the direction of communication by radio or wire?
>
> (Bagno 1956: 96)

Notably, the *Transactions* editorial presumed a main audience of engineers and labeled applications outside these traditional fields "extensions." Responses reflected on that implied perspective. In an indignant letter to the editor, Max Hoberman of Bergen Laboratories wrote, "The argument that the applications of information theory to other fields be left to specialists in those other fields is further evidence of the parochial attitude of scientists who forget that their field began as the investigation of all knowledge" (Hoberman 1956: 96). Another irate reader defended the fields' more promiscuous tendencies by declaring, "we have as little right to disown our products as to disown our physical offsprings [sic]" (Bagno 1956: 96).

The implicit debate was between approaches to information theory that drew on Shannon or Wiener, respectively, for inspiration. It was thus with no small amount of anticipation and fanfare that Shannon fired his first shot in the I. R. E. *Transactions* showdown with an editorial he called "The Bandwagon." His comments marked the tirades' height of rhetorical sophistication. In cool measured tones, Shannon produced an objective account of the fields' present state, warning against its more promiscuous linguistic and disciplinary practices: "It will be all too easy for our somewhat artificial prosperity to collapse overnight when it is realized that the use of a few exciting words like information, entropy, redundancy, do not solve all our problems" (Shannon 1956: 3). He elaborated:

Architectures of information   153

workers in other fields should realize that the basic results of the subject are aimed in a very specific direction, a direction that is not necessarily relevant to such fields as psychology, economics, and other social sciences...the establishing of such applications is not a trivial matter of translating words to a new domain, but rather the slow tedious process of hypothesis and verification. If, for example, the human being acts in some situations like an ideal decoder, this is an experimental and not a mathematical fact, and as such must be tested under a wide variety of experimental situations.

(Shannon 1956: 3)

Shannon charged devotees of information theory with appreciating local disciplinary practices; the coordination of local techniques and fidelity to a narrow set of terminological deployments took priority over establishing a global meaning. In short, while information operated devoid of meaning and isolated from context, information theory required understanding.

In the following issue of *Transactions*, Wiener offered his own response, aptly titled "What is Information Theory?" (Wiener 1956: 48). Unlike Shannon, Wiener encouraged the application of theories of information to the broad range of fields to which it, historically and ontologically, properly belonged:

I am pleading in this editorial that Information Theory...return to the point of view from which it originated: that of the general statistical concept of communication...What I am urging is a return to the concepts of this theory in its entirety rather than the exaltation of one particular concept of this group, the concept of the measure of information into the single dominant idea of all.

(Wiener 1956: 48)

Strongly rejecting Shannon's narrow focus on differentiations distinct to the engineering problem, he insisted "information" remained part of a larger system of order and relations that cut across the sciences. In return, he offered the tantalizing promise that "all branches of science" might fall under communication theory. Local scientific claims became a global feature of modern technological society: "In my opinion we are in a dangerous age of overspecialization ... I hope that the Transactions may steadily set their face against this comminution of the intellect" (Wiener 1956: 48). Wiener's information theory, like his information, would produce its meaning by correlating local bits with global patterns, with the brains and nervous systems of purposeful scientists acting as enlightened mediators.

Among self-identified information theorists, Shannon's counsel won the day. Members of the PGIT and the editors at the I. R. E. *Transactions on*

154 *Bernard Dionysius Geoghegan*

Information Theory put aside the question "What is information theory?" and fabricated, instead, "the slow tedious process of hypothesis and verification" (Shannon 1956).

Editors urged authors toward narrowed research subjects that could be mastered through mathematically guided engineering. An acidic 1958 editorial by Peter Elias of the RLE mocked contributors for their regular submissions of papers re-treading earlier results or superficially extending information theory to new fields. "These two papers have been written—and even published—often enough by now. I suggest that we stop writing them ..." (Elias 1958: 99). In their place, proofs, revisions, refinements, and applications of Shannonian theorems became the order of the day. Articles on linguistics, biology, artificial intelligence, and "other" fields gradually disappeared. In their place came "correspondences," short articles that incisively critiqued and enriched recently published articles. These repetitions and entrenchments were complemented by progress reports and tutorials that summarized the best research in the field, divided into manageable sub-fields, and pointed out areas for future innovation. On the occasion of *Cybernetics*' second edition, in 1961, a reviewer for *Transactions* slyly commented, "It is ... not so much the great mathematician Wiener we meet in this book, as the man of universal knowledge for whom the unity of science is still a reality" (Stumpers 1962: 332). The reviewer also predicted such men's imminent extinction.

The socialization of information

Although sometimes presented as rivals, the theories of Wiener and Shannon responded to different kinds of problems that arose in distinct research contexts from which they and their work emerged. Wiener's systems-oriented theory of information aimed at correlating new findings in communications research with a broader view of nature and ethics in an informational era. From it sprang an account of information based on systems, collectivities, and recursive feedback. Shannon, by contrast, devised techniques for the efficient management and transmission of signals; in this framework of analysis the notion of code quickly emerged as a strategy for mapping out underlying patterns in communications that would allow for their most economical transmission. Interpreters elicited from Shannon's theory a vision of language freed from expression and human intentionality—as a code, automatic and machinic, driven by demonic impulses irreducible to consciousness. The distinction between an emphasis on systems or codes became manifest in the inverted interpretations put forth by Wiener and Shannon concerning the relationship of information and entropy. Wiener defined informational quantities in terms of negative

Architectures of information 155

entropy—negentropy—arguing that increases in information provided the basis for creating highly ordered, holistic systems of feedback. Shannon posited a positive correlation between informational quantity and entropy, arguing that the disordered, unpredictable parts of a message comprised the most essential content.

As reflected in their distinct orientations, the origins of Wiener's and Shannon's theories of information were both plural and contingent—reflecting divergent cultures of communication as much as they did any underlying technical or mathematical problem. Their respective definitions of information quantities in terms of negentropy and entropy balanced conceptual fidelity to the physical properties of communication networks with external factors such as training, tasks at hand, and intellectual disposition. Their competing definitions of information and its measurement encoded distinct philosophies about the place of communication among humans, animals, machines, and ultimately the cosmos, as well as competing conceptions of the tasks of scientific investigators. Wiener's theory of information coincided with an understanding of scientific practice as enhancing order, be it in cybernetic human-machine systems or the coordination of interdisciplinary research teams. Shannon's theory of information sprang from the demands of industrial economy and military secrecy, which found economic and tactical value in novelty and difference.

As these theories of information circulated more widely, particular elements proved more tractable for interpretation than others; analysts seized upon certain terms and equations and allowed others to slip to the side. From these sprang a range of competing research communities—engineers, theorists of mind, ecologically minded-designers, and experimental writers, among others. As these theories of information moved beyond engineering communities, Wiener's preoccupation with holistic communication systems and Shannon's analysis of automatic codes proved particularly salient. That interpreters seized upon these elements speaks to the local concerns of interpreters as well as the epistemological affordances of these theories themselves. The circulation of one theory over another was, in short, a social affair—produced by the stitching together of diverse communities' concerns around shared concepts.

This selective circulation and appropriation of Wiener's cybernetics and Shannon's information theory enacted a socialization of the theories. By means of this circulation isolated elements—particularly the concepts of system and code—were adapted and absorbed according to diverse communities' concerns. This circulation also permitted the formation of different societies—information theorists, students of statistical communications, countercultural ecological thinkers, and communities of experimental readers and writers. This circulation did not, however, merely permit a flourishing of societies on the basis of neutral technical and scientific concepts; this circulation and socialization also disclosed the social origins of the theories themselves. The appropriation of Wiener's and Shannon's two

156 *Bernard Dionysius Geoghegan*

approaches to information revealed the distinct contexts agendas that animated their respective research context. Engineers practicing "filtering theory" in the tradition of Wiener and Lee, as well as ecologists imagining designs for a whole earth, reactivated Wiener's dream for informational systems that combatted noise, decay, disruption through the negentropic "acquisition, use, retention, and transmission of information" (Wiener 1961 [1948]: 161)—which itself traced aspirations for intellectual unity that informed Wiener's philosophical education. So too William S. Burroughs' probing into automatic writing by viruses, machines, and cut-up uncovered the origins of Shannon's theory in a world of reading and writing machines that favored entropic industrial economy over the lush redundancies of everyday semantics (Hansen 2001). To be sure, both Wiener and Shannon confronted technical problems and developed mathematical techniques admirably suited to their solutions. And these theorists' analyses proceeded in close concert with the material affordances and practical concerns they encountered in educational, professional, and wartime engagements. But when they came down to defining information in terms of entropy, their conclusions did not spring from neutral technical constraints. Instead, they hinged on larger conceptions of natural order; of the place of man in the universe; and of the task of scientific investigation.

Acknowledgment

I thank Ron Kline, Paul Michael Kurtz, Olga Touloumi, Thedora Vardouli and Grant Wythoff for their invaluable feedback on drafts of this essay. I would also like to thank members of Columbia University's Theory and History of Media workshop for inspiring feedback on an earlier draft of this work.

Notes

1 Aspray identifies five distinct strands that contributed to the mid-twentieth century theorization of information: (1) The identification of information with thermodynamics, statistical mechanics, and the concept of entropy in particular, (2) the rise of control and communication—i.e. the modulation and control of patterned signals—as an area of electrical engineering, distinct from power engineering, (3) advances in the physiology of the nervous system, which identified electrical and homeostatic properties in the control of organisms, (4) behaviorism and functionalism, both of which modeled the organism as an information processing machine operating on algorithmic principles, and (5) the development of logics—particularly mathematical recursive function theory—that modeled a translation of human thought into computation. The scientific teams convened to win World War II convened skills from across these domains.
2 Literary critic N. Katherine Hayles has suggested that information theorists dematerialized information, reducing it to pattern without body; this tendency was only partly true, for information theorists held firmly to the idea that information resided in experimentally verifiable physical traces tied to a specific medium. Information theorists rejected the notion that intelligence, speech, meaning, and life as something metaphysical essence that eluded materialist explanation, theorists of information sought to describe each of these phenomena in terms of patterned inscriptions traveling neurons, vocal cords, language, and cell tissue. In view of this exclusion of immaterial agencies mathematician and computer scientist Turing famously declared that contests of intelligence between humans and machines "should be written, or better still, typewritten,"

Architectures of information   157

thereby excluding the metaphysics of the voice and human body from the equation, in favor of standardized material inscriptions. The techniques of information theorist identified information with the relations that existed among those traces. For Hayles' account, see Hayles (1999).

3 For more on the intellectual context and itineraries of MacKay and Gabor, and the "English School," see Kline (2015: 104–112).
4 On MacKay's theory of information, see MacKay (1969: 1–39); Hayles (1999: 54–64); and Hansen (2002: 69–78).
5 Shannon speaking in the discussion section of MacKay (2003: 507).
6 For more on this conference see Segal (2003: 306–310).
7 On the universal aspirations of cybernetics see Bowker (1994).
8 For example, Shannon Lecture award winners Thomas Cover and Robert Gallager have cited their encounters with the Shannon and Weaver's book as transformative experiences that drew them towards the field. See Cover (1998: 18); and Goldstein (1993: 2–3). On the importance of buzz in attracting early interest to the field see also Slepian (1973: 146).
9 Peter Galison discusses the implications of this agonistic vision in detail in Galison (1994).
10 On the later reappropriation of Wiener's work by the heirs of the Vienna Circle, see Galison (1998: 45–71).
11 See also Rogers (1994). Note that Rogers seems to misdate Shannon's arrival at Princeton.
12 Nyquist was actually in the Development and Research Department at AT&T. Mindell (2019: 125).
13 For more on the PGIT and its role in these debates, see Kline (2015: 102–104, 112–118).

Bibliography

Aspray, W. (1985) "The Scientific Conceptualization of Information", *Annals of the History of Computing* 7, no. 2, 117–140.

Bagno, S. (1956) "Comments on 'In Which Fields Do We Graze?'" *IRE Transactions on Information Theory* 2, no. 2, 96.

Bavelas, A. (2003 [1951]) "Communication Patterns in Problem-Solving Groups", in Claus Pias (ed.) *Cybernetics: The Macy-Conferences 1946–1953 = Kybernetik*, Zürich: Diaphanes, 349–381. [Originally published in 1951, republished in this version in 2003].

Bello, F. (1953) "The Information Theory", *Fortune*, December, 48, 140.

Bowker, G. (1994) "How to Be Universal: Some Cybernetic Strategies, 1943–70", *Social Studies of Science* 23, no. 1, 107–127.

Brower, B. (1963) "The Man-Machines May Talk First to Dr. Shannon", *Vogue*, April 15, 89.

Cherry, C. (1953) "A History of the Theory of Information", *IRE Transactions on Information Theory* 1, no. 1, 22–43.

Cover, T. (1998) "Shannon Reminiscence", *IEEE Information Theory Society Newsletter*, Golden Jubilee Issue, Summer 1998, 18–19.

Elias, P. (1958) "Two Famous Papers", *IRE Transactions on Information Theory* 4, no. 3, 99.

Fry, D. (1953) "Communication Theory and Linguistic Theory", *IRE Transactions on Information Theory* 1, no. 1, 120–124.

158 Bernard Dionysius Geoghegan

Gabor, D. (1952) "Lectures on Communication Theory", Technical Report, Cambridge: Research Laboratory of Electronics, Massachusetts Institute of Technology, 1.

Gabor, D. (1953) "Communication Theory, Past, Present and Prospective", *IRE Transactions on Information Theory* 1, no. 4, 2–4.

Gabor, D. and Brown, J. (1971) "Willis Jackson. Baron Jackson of Burnley, 1904–1970", *Biographical Memoirs of the Fellows of the Royal Society* 17, 385–386.

Galison, P. (1994) "The Ontology of the Enemy", *Critical Inquiry* 21, 233–245.

Galison, P. (1998) "The Americanization of Unity", *Daedalus* 127, 45–71.

Gallager, R. G. (2001) "Claude E. Shannon: A Retrospective on His Life, Work, and Impact", *IEEE Transactions on Information Theory* 47, no. 7, 2682.

Goldstein, A. (1993) *An Oral History with Robert Gallager, Electrical Engineer*, Rutgers, NJ: IEEE History Center.

Hansen, M. B. N. (2001) "Internal Resonance, or Three Steps Towards a Non-Viral Becoming", *Culture Machine 3*. http://svr91.edns1.com/~culturem/index.php/cm/article/view/429.

Hansen, M. B. N. (2002) "Cinema Beyond Cybernetics or How to Frame the Digital Image", *Configurations* 10, no. 1, 69–78.

Hayles, N. K. (1999) *How We Became Posthuman: Virtual Bodies in Cybernetics, Literature, and Informatics*, Chicago, IL: The University of Chicago Press.

Hoberman, M. (1956) "Comments on 'In Which Fields Do We Graze?'", *IRE Transactions on Information Theory* 2, no. 2, 96.

Kline, R. R. (2015) *The Cybernetics Moment: Or Why We Term Our Age the Information Age*, Baltimore, MD: Johns Hopkins University Press.

Link, D. (2006) "Chains to the West: Markov's Theory of Connected Events and Its Transmission to Western Europe", *Science in Context* 19, no. 4, 563.

MacKay, D. M. (1953) "The Nomenclature of Information Theory", *Transactions of the IRE Professional Group of Information Theory* 1, no. 9, 9–21.

MacKay, D. M. (1969) *Information, Mechanism and Meaning*, Cambridge: MIT Press.

MacKay, D. M. (2003 [1951]) "In Search of Basic Symbols", in Claus Pias (ed.) *Cybernetics: The Macy- Conferences 1946–1953 = Kybernetik*, Berlin: Diaphanes.

Markov, A. A. (2006 [1913]) "An Example of Statistical Investigation of the Text Eugene Onegin Concerning the Connection of Samples in Chains", *Science in Context* 19, no. 4, 591–600.

Masani, N. (1990) *Norbert Wiener: 1894–1964*, Basel: Birkhäuser Verlag.

Mindell, D. A. (2019) *Between Human and Machine: Feedback, Control, and Computing before Cybernetics*, Baltimore, MD: Johns Hopkins University Press.

Nyquist, H. (1924) "Certain Factors Affecting Telegraphy Speed", *Bell System Technical Journal* 3, 324–346.

"Our Future" (1951) *Vogue Magazine*, 97.

Price, R. (1984) "A Conversation with Claude Shannon", *Communications Magazine, IEEE* 22, no. 5, 124.

Rogers, E. M. (1994) "Claude Shannon's Cryptography Research During World War II and the Mathematical Theory of Communication", in *28th Proceedings of the Conference on Security Technology*, Carnahan: Institute of Electrical and Electronics Engineers, 1–5.

Rosenblueth, A, N. Wiener, and J. Bigelow (1943) "Behavior, Purpose, Teleology", *Philosophy of Science* 1, (January), 18–24.

Segal, J. (2003) *Le zéro et le un: Histoire de la notion scientifique d'information au 20e siècle*, Paris: Éditions Syllepse.

Shannon, C. E. (1945) "A Mathematical Theory of Cryptography - Case 10878", Technical Memoranda, Murray Hill: Bell Telephone Laboratories, Princeton Libraries.

Shannon, C. E. (1956) "The Bandwagon", *IRE Transactions on Information Theory* 2, no. 1, 3.

Shannon, C. E. (1993) "Letter to Vannevar Bush [16 February 1939]", in N. J. A. Sloane and Aaron D. Wyner (ed.) *Claude Elwood Shannon: Collected Papers*, Piscataway, NJ: IEEE Press, 455–456.

Shannon, C. E. (2004 [1951]) "The Redundancy of English", in Claus Pias (ed.) *Cybernetics: The Macy-Conferences 1946–1953 = Kybernetik*, Berlin: Diaphanes, 248–272.

Shannon, C. E. (1964) "The Mathematical Theory of Communication", in *The Mathematical Theory of Communication*, Urbana, IL: University of Illinois Press, 29–125.

Slepian, D. (1973) "Information Theory in the Fifties", *IEEE Transactions on Information Theory* 19, no. 2, 146.

Stumpers, F. (1962) "Review of 'Cybernetics, or Control and Communication in the Animal and the Machine' (Wiener, N.; 1961)", *Information Theory, IRE Transactions on* 8, no. 4, 332.

Verdú, S. (1998) "Fifty Years of Shannon Theory", *IEEE Transactions on Information Theory* 44, no. 6, 2058.

Weaver, W. (1964) "Recent Contributions to the Mathematical Theory of Communication", in C.E. Shannon (ed.) *The Mathematical Theory of Communication*, Urbana, IL: University of Illinois Press, 1–28.

Wiener, N. (1950) *The Human Use of Human Beings*, Boston, MA: Houghton Mifflin Harcourt.

Wiener, N. (1956) "What Is Information Theory?", *IRE Transactions on Information Theory*, June 1956, Vol. 2, 48.

Wiener, N. (1961) *Cybernetics: Or Control and Communication in the Animal and the Machine*, New York: MIT Press.

9 Bureaucracy's playthings[1]

Shannon Mattern

For more than half a century Jack Wilkinson's office supply store stood on the corner of Allegheny Street and Cherry Alley in my hometown of Bellefonte, Pennsylvania. When I was a little girl, we'd make frequent visits—not to stock up on supplies for my dad's hardware store or my mom's classroom and volunteer activities, but at *my* request. On birthdays and Christmas I'd go in with a list: invoices, restaurant order forms, cash box, label maker, rubber date stamp, accounting book. These were my toys.

The playroom in our basement housed many unlicensed businesses: a restaurant whose menu blended some of my favorites from the Amity House diner (home of the fish-bowl sundae) and McDonald's; a bank with a drive-through window for bikes; a Matchbox car dealership; a hospital for my Glamour Gals and my brother's G. I. Joes; and, because this was the era of Miami Vice, a drug-trafficking "shoppe" where we sold generous dime-bags of all-purpose flour. The neighborhood kids were both our staff and our patrons. Everybody—even those to whom we sold controlled substances—got a receipt, made out in duplicate. Everybody received exact, if fake, change. Everybody had a color-coded customer or employee file, with a nametag crafted on my hand-held Dymo label maker (which had its own label).

We were weird—delightfully so, I must say. And we were into the "aesthetics of administration" well before art historian Benjamin Buchloh coined the term in the early 1990s. Which explains why the burnt-orange copy of Mina Johnson and Norman Kallaus's 1967 *Records Management* textbook sang to me from the shelves of the Reanimation Library during a recent visit. From Johnson and Kallaus we learn immediately that the stuff of my childhood play is actually quite serious business:

> In the average business office, record making constitutes approximately ninety percent of the activity. Alert businessmen keep a constant check on their costs of doing business. One paper lost, mislaid, or delayed can and often does inconvenience and retard a dozen or more people in their work.
>
> (Johnson and Kallaus 1967: 1)

Figure 9.1 Vertical Files. Source: Johnson M. and N. Kallaus (1967) *Records Management*. Southwestern Publishing, unknown page

Furthermore, "few people realize that, of all the service activities of an organization, the creation and the storage of business records are the greatest consumers of space, salaries, and equipment"—in 1967, at least.

One thing that records management will likely *not* consume, however, is your rapt, undivided attention. I had to take the book up on my roof, and walk laps while reading, just to keep myself awake—particularly while slogging through chapters on the rules of alphabetization (e.g. how to handle hyphenated business names? wouldn't you like to know!) and on the differences among "terminal digit," Browne-Morse Service Index, and Soundex filing systems. This certainly wasn't as fun as rubber-stamping phony restaurant receipts, affixing glittered stickers to indicate that they'd been "processed," and filing them away in hot-pink folders.

Then it struck me: the flair of filing was still here in *Records Management*—but it was in the *implied* aesthetic nature of the filing enterprise: in the alignment of tabs and arrangement of drawers (see Figure 9.1). That pizzazz was to be found, too, in the style of the book itself—in its liberal use of diagrams and illustrations and photographs of state-of-the-art office equipment and fashionably dressed, well-coiffed office ladies. I figured, why not read *Records Management* against the grain, focusing less on the staid instruction and more on the aesthetic and even *ludic* nature of filing work? Why not read this textbook as a toy catalogue, or as a set of rules for a Monopoly-esque administrative game?

Toys for serious business

Filing tools—the spindle file, the pigeonhole file, the bellows file, the flat file, the Shannon file, the vertical file—have been around for centuries (see Figure 9.2). But the First World War gave rise to a new era of business

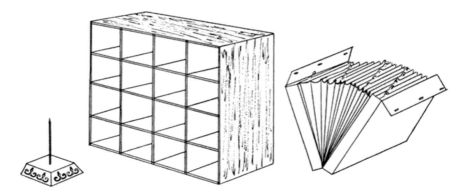

Figure 9.2 Spindle, Pigeonhole and Bellows File. Source: Johnson M. and N. Kallaus (1967) *Records Management*. Southwestern Publishing, p. 4–5

that generated an explosion of paperwork, and that paperwork needed to be filed away. "With the growth of businesses, the departmentalizing of activities, and the necessity of depending upon the written word rather than upon memory," Johnson and Kallaus write, "[t]he person who is responsible for the orderly arrangement of those papers has one of the most responsible positions in any business office" (Johnson and Kallaus 1967: 2). Those individuals who held the new and noble position of "Records Manager" had to know "where each piece of paper originates and why, how many copies of it are necessary, how these flow through the different offices and departments, where they are stored temporarily and how, and what their end may be," whether immediate destruction, destruction after being archived, or temporary or long-term retention (Johnson and Kallaus 1967: 9). How was anyone to keep tabs on individual forms as they floated through massive institutions? How could one find order in such seeming chaos?

Johnson and Kallaus explain how a file is processed: it's first inspected and "released" for filing; then it's indexed to determine where it should be filed; then it's coded or marked to indicate its placement within the file; then it's cross-referenced in case that file might be sought within the system under multiple names; and finally, it's filed away (Johnson and Kallaus 1967: 89–100). Yet how feasible is it to expect our Records Manager to oversee every invoice, contract, and letter as it passes through five stages from its creation to its ultimate placement within a cabinet drawer? Media and legal scholar Cornelia Vismann, in *Files: Law and Media Technology*, explains that institutions can develop ordering systems that *precede* the existence of the material files themselves. These procedures for "uniform and precise handling," documentation and archiving can "ensure that files

Bureaucracy's playthings   163

already assume an orderly shape when they are being compiled," rather than requiring that they be tidied up afterward (Vismann 2008: 100).

The files themselves display directions for their own movement through this chain of operations. "Address, location, and hold-file notes belong to the arsenal of operators that process the automobility of files," Vismann writes, and that allow those files to "move themselves from department to department" (Vismann 2008: 138). Sometimes even the *form* of the record embodies cues for its handling. Consider the McBee Key-Sort, which is used to organize filing cards (see Figure 9.3). The edges of the cards have holes, some of which are notched. When a long needle is inserted through one of those holes and lifted up, only the non-notched cards rise, thus filtering out the irrelevant records.

Once we get to the actual placement of records within the files, we can turn to other gadgets and techniques for directions on how to proceed. The architectonics and aesthetics of the filing mechanism can embody its filing logic or ontology—that is, its structural framework for organizing information. Consider Remington Rand's Variadex system, with its color-coding and tab-positioning (see Figure 9.4):

Figure 9.3 McBee Key-Sort. Source: Johnson M. and N. Kallaus (1967) *Records Management*. Southwestern Publishing, p. 213

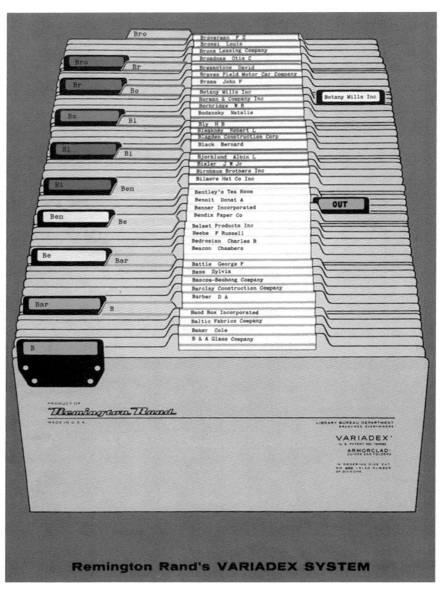

Figure 9.4 Variadex System. Source: Johnson M. and N. Kallaus (1967) *Records Management*. Southwestern Publishing, p. 10–11

Bureaucracy's playthings 165

[a]lphabetic guides are in first position, miscellaneous folders are in second position, individual folders are in third and fourth combined positions, and special guides for names having a large volume of correspondence or for names of frequent reference are in fifth position.

(Vismann 2008: 22)

Or take the Oxford Filing Supply Company's Speed Index, which adds tab *height*, *width*, and *materiality* into the filing ontology (see Figure 9.5):

The main alphabetic guides are numbered consecutively, are made with one-fifth-cut tabs, and are staggered in first and second positions. Their steel tabs and heavy construction afford prolonged life and usage. Individual name folders, with one-third-cut tabs are staggered in two positions, second and third. The folders tabs are at a lower level than the

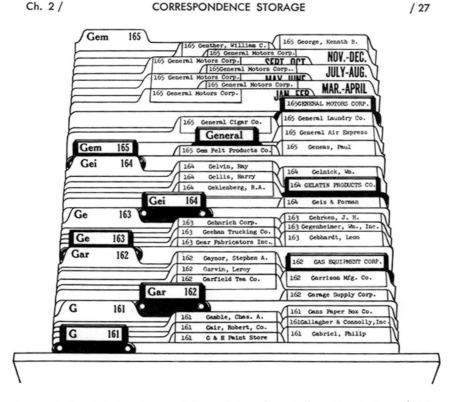

Figure 9.5 Speed Index. Source: Johnson M. and N. Kallaus (1967) *Records Management*. Southwestern Publishing, p. 27

guides, to protect them from becoming "dog eared." ... Salmon-colored one-fifth-cut miscellaneous folders have tabs in the first position, at the lower level of the other folders. Special heavy-duty folders ... for bulky correspondence have steel tabs and red windows; they have one-third-cut tabs and are in third position at high level for easy reference ...

(Vismann 2008: 27–8)

It's as if we've taken an alphanumeric outline we might sketch out on paper, and *dimensionalized* and *materialized*—and even *decorated*—it.

We have other aesthetic cues, or "signals," at our disposal, too; Johnson and Kallaus suggest that we use colored card stock, special printed edges, and removable metal or plastic tabs in a variety of colors and shapes—or what I like to call "file bling"—to make sure records are filed appropriately, and to aid in retrieval (see Figure 9.6). We can perforate our file edges to allow various colors to show through, or we can clip the corners of our files to code them. Even our filing furniture—our chests and bureaus and cabinets, some of which can spin around or release fold-out appendages—aids in directing files through the system: files are "ordered in a way," Vismann writes, "that furniture turn[s] into addresses, that is, into pointers for the retrieval of records that [are] counted by chests" (Vismann 2008: 98).[2] In other words, our filing containers help us gauge the size of our collections, and aid us in navigating through them.

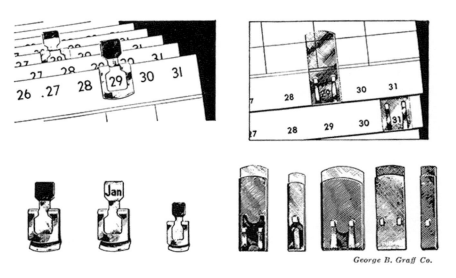

Figure 9.6 Card Signals. Johnson M. and N. Kallaus (1967) *Records Management*. Southwestern Publishing, p. 219

Particularly when records managers adopt filing systems based on reference numbers—alphanumeric sequences that indicate what's in each file, where it's located, when it was created, and which office is responsible for it—that number essentially embodies "the administrative macro-order." The reference number references not only a file's placement within a drawer, Vismann says, but also

> the topography of the shelves as well as the spatial arrangement of offices—until the entire administration is nothing but one big filing plan. Micro- and macro-order are interlocked in such a way that the individual file represents the entire universe of an office, while a 20th-century office building, in turn, turns into one "enormous file."
>
> (Vismann 2008: 145)[3]

There's a playful dollhouse/house of mirrors/Alice in Wonderland quality to this telescoping of scales: the file and the institution are micro and macro models of one another.

Johnson and Kallaus address the advantages and disadvantages of various systems—some systems are better or worse suited for firms whose geographic reach is expansive or limited, or who are involved in few or many lines of business, for example—but it's important to note that, sometimes, choosing a filing plan is simply a matter of cultural, or even aesthetic, preference. At the turn of the 20th century, for instance, Europeans and Americans clashed over their taste in binders. While all binders serve to "mechanize" a particular mode of organization—"Starting with the punch," Vismann writes, the record's "individual physical parts predetermine a clear order: *punch, open, fix, insert, close*"—and necessitate an alphanumeric arrangement of their contents, there are variations in how that mechanization takes form (Vismann 2008: 137). "Europeans cannot understand why the unnatural two-hand-pushing-on-the tongues movement would be preferred to the simple natural pulling motion needed to open two rings. Americans insist on the tongue and three rings" (Vismann 2008: 136).

And sometimes it's metaphysical. As the Leitz company acknowledged in a 1900 leaflet promoting its own biblorhaptes files, "The mechanism is the soul of the binder" (Vismann 2008: 133). At the same time, the spirit of the larger system—the file-keeping administration—is embodied in that tiny mechanism: in those rings and notches and tabs. The individual files, and even the individual components of each file, represent the "entire universe" of a bureaucracy. "Files are the mirror stage of any administration," Vismann argues (Vismann 2008: 92). "The entire order could be derived from the smallest element, that is, the state from a single file" (Vismann 2008: 133).

Bureaucratic puzzle pieces

Perhaps this is our game: to puzzle out the institutional order from its filed-away parts—or to move in the opposite direction, from the macro to the micro (see Figure 9.7). By studying the files of a governmental archive, for instance, as anthropologist Ann Stoler has done with Dutch colonial archives, we might be able to discern the state's means of defining and disciplining its subjects, or of justifying its own existence through the exercise of power. Yet by also acknowledging the aesthetic and ludic natures of filing, we might also come to appreciate the system's fissures—the spaces where play and resistance might take place. The very fact that files essentially direct their own processing, Vismann suggests, means that "those who work with [them] can easily be granted autonomy in their small world of files" (Vismann 2008: 137). What to do with this autonomy? Dadaist painter and poet Kurt Schwittzers, who worked for a German manufacturer of writing utensils, took inspiration from "abbreviated printed labels"—e.g., the "Roser-Rud; Schall; Scham-Schaz" tabs on individual folders—in creating his "Ur Sonata" sound poem (Vismann 2008: 185). And many conceptual artists embodied

Figure 9.7 Rotary files. Source: Johnson M. and N. Kallaus (1967) *Records Management*. Southwestern Publishing, p. 211

critiques of the bureaucratic system in their own explorations of the "aesthetics of administration."

What's more, the sheer scale and anonymity and lack of individual accountability embodied in bureaucracies offer opportunity for opposition. Ben Kafka, in his history of paperwork, suggests that late-18th-century French bureaucrat Augustin Lejeune might have sought to "slow down the pace of [the state's] political violence by burying it under paperwork"— drowning the Committee of Public Safety in excessively detailed reports— and by then burying that paperwork itself. Lejune recognized, Kafka writes, that

> the proliferation of documents and details presented opportunities for resistance, as well as for compliance ... The materiality of paperwork in fact presented unmistakable opportunities for resistance to the terrorist regime through everyday strategies of deferral and displacement.
> (Kafka 2012: 67, 74)

There's thus generative potential in losing and delaying files. And even the planned *disposal* of files offers opportunities for creative destruction. Johnson and Kallaus suggest that files can meet their demise through crushing, macerating, burning, shredding, or, least interestingly, by selling them to paper-collection agencies. Such a range of performative possibilities.

In addition to these opportunities for bureaucratic resistance, I suggest another: pure play—with stamps, label-makers, and file folders in all crazy colors. Creative experimentation with these tools of administration can show us that the file need not function as the building block of bureaucracy alone, but can instead serve as a modular unit for an imaginative universe, an experimental ontology. Or even an illegitimate basement business where kids can offer imaginary mortgages and serve up pretend hamburgers to their neighborhood friends, worrying not about proper routing or cross-referencing, but instead about the pleasurable aesthetics of paperwork.

Notes

1 This essay was first published by Reanimation Library. We would like to thank Word Processor and Andrew Beccone for giving us permission to reprint the essay. See: Shannon Mattern, "Bureaucracy's Playthings," *Reanimation Library*, October 28, 2013. www.reanimationlibrary.org/pages/wpmattern
2 In the mid 18th century Vincent Gournay ascribed so much agency to the bureau that he described the rise of a new form of government: "rule by a piece of furniture," or *bureaucracy* (quoted in Kafka 77).
3 See also Alexandra Lange on links between the standardization of filing and the rise of the skyscraper—particularly the work of Le Corbusier, who described his designs as "generated from the inside out, dimensioned by the path of standardized white paper" (60).

Bibliography

Buchloh, B. H. D. (1990) "Conceptual Art 1962-1969: From the Aesthetic of Administration to the Critique of Institutions," *October 55*, 105–143.

Johnson, M. M. and Kallaus, N. F. (1967) *Records Management: A Collegiate Course in Filing Systems and Procedures*, Cincinnati: South-Western Publishing Co.

Kafka, B. (2012) *The Demon of Writing: Powers and Failures of Paperwork*, New York: Zone Books.

Lange, A. (2002) "White Collar Corbusier: From the Casier to the cités d'affaires," *Grey Room 9*, 58–79.

Stoler, A. L. (2009) *Along the Archival Grain: Epistemic Anxieties and Colonial Common Sense*, Princeton, NJ: Princeton University Press.

Vismann, C. (2008) *Files: Law and Media Technology*, (Translated by Geoffrey Winthrop-Young), Stanford, CA: Stanford University Press.

Part IV
Computation

10 Imagining architecture as a form of concrete poetry

Matthew Allen

Computers arrived in architecture to a discipline caught up in longstanding agendas and contentious debates, and so architects began using them not for reasons of naïve curiosity or simple practicality but to further intellectual projects already in the works. The contours and directions of these projects were different in different locales, of course, but they were related in various ways. We now face the difficulty of sorting out how the idiosyncratic concerns nurtured in particular places are nonetheless indicative of broader shifts in architecture.[1]

Looking at the journal *Form* reveals a unique conceptual constellation involving algorithmic architecture, abstract art, and structuralist theory. Because it was founded at the University of Cambridge in the mid-1960s, *Form* fits most neatly within the lineage of British avant-garde art and architecture centered on London and its periphery. The very notion of architecture was up for debate. The architecture department at Cambridge had been headed since 1956 by Leslie Martin, a modernist architect and protagonist of the *Circle* group who in 1937 were reimagining architecture as a form of bureaucratic coordination.[2] Other related groups and publications are less well-known. *Data*, a publication of the Constructionist Group, modeled itself on *Circle* thirty years later, providing evidence that a neo-avant-garde around London was experimenting with computation while tweaking decades-old agendas of abstraction.[3] *Form* belongs to this loose set of artistic groups and publications, and it embodies a distinct conceptualization of architecture as essentially a form of concrete poetry.

Like other movements in art and architecture, *Form* eagerly drew contemporary theory into its mix. Thus we find French philosophers like Roland Barthes rubbing shoulders with British concrete poets and American computational devices. The lasting contribution of *Form* was to consolidate structuralist tendencies in the British artistic scene, serving as a testing ground for algorithmic dreams that would soon make their way to the mainstream of architecture.

174 *Matthew Allen*

Structuralist activity in *Form*

Unlike *Circle* or *Data*, *Form* was not only modeled on earlier avant-garde publications, but it was itself a true "little magazine," with ten issues appearing between 1966 and 1969.[4] It was aimed at a particular scene: *Form*'s three editors met at the Society of Arts in Cambridge. Two attended college together at the University of Cambridge (Moreno 2011: 223–224) where an influential center of experimentation in architectural science – the Centre for Land Use and Built Form Studies – opened in 1967.[5] The 1960s Cambridge ethos, with all its contradictions, was neatly captured in *Form*.[6] The *de facto* editor in chief, Philip Steadman, was an architecture student who supplied the technical and organizational acumen.[7] The two other editors, Stephen Bann and Mike Weaver, brought much of the artistic raw material and structuralist theory from their perspective as doctoral students in history and English (Grandal Montero 2015: 71). As students rather than artists or professional architects, the three editors reached widely – almost randomly – into the most interesting corners they saw in the surrounding artistic scene. One of their tasks in the arts society was to invite artists to give talks at Cambridge, and they appear to have relished the contact with notoriety and avant-garde ideas. Guests included Victor Pasmore, the central figure of the Constructionist Group; various other greats such as Allen Ginsberg and Karlheiz Stockhausen also passed through Cambridge in these years.[8] Part of the fun of *Form* was in the opportunity to continue such engagement with icons in the arts.[9] Contributions by Raoul Haussmann and Hans Richter from the older European avant-garde stand out as editorial coups that solidified an illustrious cast of characters over the journal's ten issues.[10] The editors' broad involvement with the artistic scene in and around London also led to a few elaborate events. In 1964 they pulled together the grandly-titled First International Exhibition of Concrete and Kinetic Poetry, which included 93 works from Latin America and Europe as well as from local artists.[11] By the end of its three-year run, *Form* was a focal point of the artistic avant-garde in Britain.[12]

A trial run of the project began when Steadman gained editorial control over a London-based arts magazine, *Image*, after having worked as its graphic designer (Moreno 2011: 507–509). The issues of *Image* from 1964 to 1966 thus served essentially as issues -2, -1, and 0 of *Form*. The enterprise began modestly, with a confusing mix of disconnected material from the previous editorial direction, but the final issue of *Image* was a coherent special issue on kinetic art and concrete poetry that remains a key document of the era. It offered two essays by two of *Form*'s editors – Bann and Weaver – that are among the clearest theoretical statements on their subjects (we will return to them later). Following a few other essays on the history and scope of current avant-garde artistic production and a thorough historical essay by Steadman on color music, the remaining

Imagining architecture as a form of concrete poetry   175

bulk of the issue consisted of more than a dozen examples of recent artistic experimentation. The arts appear to have been flourishing. The issue includes several of the hanging mobiles and shape poems that are now most readily associated with kinetic art and concrete poetry, but there are also Plexiglas boxes with moving blotches of light (by Frank Malina, who founded *Leonardo* three years later), images that look like paintings made of overlapping shards of colored glass (by Andree Dantu), text swirling in hallucinogenic graphic fields (by Sylvester Houédard), and an artist standing in a desert grinning beside a small rocket ready to launch (Frank Malina again[13]). Altogether, the final issue of *Image* presents contemporary artistic practice as a wide-ranging experimentation with forms, materials, and techniques.

The first issue of *Form* continues down parallel tracks of theoretical elaboration and artistic production, and the diversity is unabated. A reprint of a 1929 essay by Theo van Doesburg, "Film as Pure Form," leads off the issue. Van Doesburg begins with a classic statement of De Stijl motivation, setting the tone and ambition for what follows: "The problem of film as an independent creative form has made no great progress in the last decade" (Doesburg 1966: 5).[14] He elaborates a rather cryptic theory of space and its relationship to film, alongside which are presented fragments of works that take "elements" of film and "study" them using different techniques.[15] The fact that the editors found the essay worth reprinting four decades after it was written suggests that they thought progress had not been made in the intervening years: it was time to tackle "the problem of film" once again. And film was not the only "creative form" in need of revitalization. The following essays discuss (in order of appearance) the perception of graphic elements, the international style in architecture as it relates to the paintings of Fernand Léger, computers in design, historical examples of avant-garde poetry, and recent concrete poetry.

Exploration of these forms and many others continued in the following nine issues, but it was concrete poetry that was the most consistently theorized in *Form* – and the theory of choice was structuralism. Though the term "concrete poetry" groups together a wide variety of practices in the 1960s British poetry scene (Cobbing 1988), it is helpful to imagine it as a practice of taking the raw material of poetry – words on a page, in one definition – and expanding the field of possible things to do with that raw material in every conceivable direction. Poetry, generally, was of deep interest to the editors of *Form*. Bann had been winning medals for his poetry since childhood, and as an undergraduate student he had written for the literary journal *Granta* (the one poem he submitted, however, was rejected) (Grandal Montero 2015: 73–75). Weaver, for his part, was writing a dissertation on the modernist American poet William Carlos Williams. If poetry is approached as *words on a page*, one of the first expanded possibilities that suggests itself is to work with the page as a visual space. This sort of investigation was not new in the 1960s:

5/- (USA $1.00)

Form 8

Russian Exhibitions, 1904 to 1922 by John Bowlt: **'An Attaché at the French Embassy'**, short story by Thomas Bernhard: **Black Mountain College—Spectodrama, 'Play, Life, Illusion'** by Xanti Schawinsky: The work of **Pierre Albert-Birot**, including poems and extracts from **'Grabinoulor'**: **Great Little Magazines** No. 7: **SIC**

From 'SIC': 'Pablo Picasso' by Guillaume Apollinaire

PABLO PICASSO

Voyez ce peintre il prend les choses avec leur ombre aussi et d'un coup d'œil sublimatoire
Il se déchire en accords profonds et agréables à respirer tel l'orgue que j'aime entendre
Des Arlequines jouent dans le rose et bleus d'un beau-ciel Ce souvenir revit
les rêves et les actives mains Orient plein de glaciers L'hiver est rigoureux
Lustres or toile irisée or loi des stries de feu fond en murmurant.
Bleu flamme légère argent des ondes bleues après le grand cri
Tout en restant elles touchent cette sirène violon
Faons lourdes ailes l'incandesce quelques brasses encore
Bourdons femmes striées éclat de plongeon-diamant
Arlequins semblables à Dieu en variété Aussi distingués qu'un lac
Fleurs brillant comme deux perles monstres qui palpitent
Lys cerclés d'or, je n'étais pas seul! fais onduler les remords
Nouveau monde très matinal montant de l'énorme mer
L'aventure de ce vieux cheval en Amérique
Au soir de la pêche merveilleuse l'œil du masque
Air de petits violons au fond des anges rangés
Dans le couchant puis au bout de l'an des dieux
Regarde la tête géante et immense la main verte
L'argent sera vite remplacé par tout notre or
Morte pendue à l'hameçon... c'est la danse bleue
L'humide voix des acrobates des maisons
Grimace parmi les assauts du vent qui s'assoupit
Ouis les vagues et le fracas d'une femme bleue
Enfin la grotte à l'atmosphère dorée par la vertu
Ce saphir veiné il faut rire!
Rois de phosphore sous les arbres les bottines entre des plumes bleues
La danse des dix mouches lui fait face quand il songe à toi
Le cadre bleu tandis que l'air agile s'ouvrait aussi
Au milieu des regrets dans une vaste grotte.
Prends les araignées roses à la nage
Regrets d'invisibles pièges l'air
Paisible se souleva mais sur le clavier musiques
Guitare-tempête ô gai trémolo
O gai trémolo ô gai trémolo
Il ne rit pas l'artiste-peintre
Ton pauvre étincellement pâle
L'ombre agile d'un soir d'été qui meurt
Immense désir et l'aube émerge des eaux si lumineuses
Je vis nos yeux diamants enfermer le reflet du ciel vert et
J'entendis sa voix qui dorait les forêts tandis que vous pleuriez
L'acrobate à cheval le poète à moustaches un oiseau mort et tant d'enfants sans larmes
Choses cassées des livres déchirés des couches de poussière et des aurores déferlant!

GUILLAUME APOLLINAIRE

Figure 10.1 Cover of *Form 8*, 1968

Stéphane Mallarmé and Guillaume Apollinaire, for instance, had each worked with such things in strikingly different ways in nineteenth and early-twentieth century Paris. And concrete poets were well aware of this: the cover of issue eight of *Form* features a poem by Apollinaire that was similar to some contemporary work (see Figure 10.1).[16]

Concrete poets were interested in development and discovery within a preexisting space of possibilities, not in an attempt to define an entirely new field. In the first issue of *Form*, a poem by Pedro Xisto places the words *star*, *astro*, *rats*, and *ostra* in a field of white (the blank page), with a thin line between. The reader's eyes ping-pong between the words, spotting poetic implications in the process. The timeless vocation of poetry was not overthrown, but reimagined and revitalized.

Imagining architecture as a form of concrete poetry   177

There are other ways to define the elements of poetry, of course, and each suggests its own direction of vitality. Near the end of issue three of *Form* is a reprint of a poem by Kurt Schwitters, the German dada provocateur. It is a sequence of capital letters –

```
W W
PBD
ZFM
RF RF TZPF TZPF
MWT
RFMR
RKT PCT
SW SW
KPT
F G
KPT
R Z
KPT
RZL
TZPF TZPF
HFTL
```

– below which is printed a "trial guide to pronunciation." Alongside the poem is an essay, "Logically Consistent Poetry," in which Schwitters argues that "the basic material of poetry is not the word but the letter" (Schwitters 1966: 28). Other concrete poets used rhythms of dictation as their basic material. A poem by Ian Hamilton Finlay in the final issue of *Image* presents three rows of words that can be read as columns with different beats: the first column is a fast tick-tick-tick-tick; the second, a quick alternation of varying words; the third, a plodding sequence of heavy words. Sometimes the poetic structure was more elaborate. Weaver analyzes a poem with a looping structure oddly similar to a well-known universal formula for myth concocted by Claude Levi-Strauss (Weaver 1966: 308–309).[17] All of these experiments construe poetry as a practice that deals not in the meanings of words, but more broadly in perception and cognition.

Concrete poetry was one among many structuralist artistic practices in 1960s England, and the theoretical essays by Bann and Weaver in the final issue of *Image* apply to a much wider range than their ostensible subjects. Bann's essay on "communication and structure in concrete poetry" elaborates upon Ernst Gombrich's distinction between *communication* and *expression* in art. Against the vague (and popular) idea that artistic communication depends on "a kind of 'emotional contagion' between the artist and his public," Gombrich outlines a structuralist view (Gombrich 1962: 215–246). In Bann's words, "Gombrich's theory [...] involves two positions – that a fixed vocabulary of conventional signs is necessary for communication in art and that the emotional weight of individual elements

178 *Matthew Allen*

depends on their situation within a system of possibilities" (Bann 1964: 8). In Bann's interpretation, this means that artists work by setting up a "semantic space" and orchestrating the "exploration" of this space. Artistic practice is about striking a balance: deploying a "complex range of possibilities without overloading the expectations of the reader" (Bann 1964: 9). In his concern for the mental impact of complexity, Bann was building upon theories of cognition that were being developed in the 1960s.[18] In the end, Bann suggests that the goal of art is to produce charismatic moments: "occasionally a poet will surprise us by discovering a new possibility" within "the structure of the work." What Bann is imagining is a cycle between a "normal science" of the arts and periodic innovation, to use the contemporary terms of Thomas Kuhn (Kuhn 1962). Bann ends with a quotation from Gombrich that serves to contextualize the type of work that prevailed in *Form*: "What we call form in art, symmetries and simplicities of structure, might well be connected with the ease and pleasure of apprehension that goes with well-placed redundancies" (Gombrich and Shaw 1962: 226). Generalizing from this, Bann suggests that the goal of concrete poetry – and, we might add, structuralist art more generally – is "for us to perceive the mysteries of structure at a conscious level" (Bann 1964: 9).

In the tension between basic communication and mysterious, deeper meaning, however, structuralist art leans decisively toward the former. A characteristic anxiety of the editors of *Form* and many of its artists was the fear that, despite their efforts, nothing would be communicated at all. It is worth comparing concrete poetry in this regard to another formalist movement in poetry that flourished during the same period. A group associated with the so-called British Poetry Revival was also located in Cambridge (Sheppard 2005). Jeremy Prynne, a leading figure in this group, published an essay in 1961 titled simply "Resistance and Difficulty," in which "he laid out a theory of the two qualities that would later become the dominant characteristics of his poetry" (Witt 2011). The sort of resistance and difficulty Prynne advocated is not difficult to imagine – generally, it consisted of obscure word associations and complicated metrical qualities that only formalist poets like himself would be equipped to appreciate.[19] It was in this larger context of British poetry that concrete poets shifted their focus to the *everyday* perception of relatively *uninformed* audiences. Weaver, in his theoretical statement, discussed a possible lowest common denominator for poetry:

> All that is asked of the perceiver (the former "reader") is that he should possess unimpaired sensory organs and an undamaged brain; a capacity for fantasy, or self-stimulation of the notoriously "literary" kind, is not required. To participate in the concrete poem means no more (no less) than paying active attention in perceiving. Theo van Doesburg wrote, in matters of art, comprehension is always impossible; as soon as it is comprehended, art ceases to be art.
>
> (Weaver 1966: 295)

Imagining architecture as a form of concrete poetry 179

This shift from *reading* to *perception* served to move poetry into the realm of architecture – but only once architecture had been reimagined in terms of environmental effects.[20] This conflation of poetry and architecture can be seen most clearly in issue four of *Form*, which documents the Brighton Festival Exhibition of Concrete Poetry. Organized as an even more ambitious follow-up to the earlier First International Exhibition, the Brighton Exhibition was scattered across an entire town, and it used elements of the town as the medium of poetry. Edwin Morgan produced a set of "Festive Permutational Poems" that were placed in public buses, mimicking advertisements. This was kinetic art as well as concrete poetry, with the ambulation of the buses supplying the permutational shuffling (Grandal Montero 2015: 87). Claus Bremer installed a poem in the form of a banner above a park bench, and behind it Ian Hamilton Finlay installed a poem consisting of ampersands arranged over a yard, turning the grass into a "page" and enacting a desire for radical inclusivity: people and things standing in the grass among the ampersands would complete the poem – *this* & *that* & *that* & so on.

The resources of graphic design and advertising were fair game in the communication practices of concrete poets. A celebrated example is Décio Pignatari's 1957 poem, "Beba Coca Cola," which transforms its catchy title (translated "Drink Coca Cola") through a variety of immediately understandable permutations to arrive, in the end, at an opposite and equally blunt slogan: "cloaca" ("sewer") (Hilder 2016: 42–45). Aside from words, the symbols and logos of consumer culture sometimes made their way into poems, particularly those of Brazilian poets who felt a pressure to set aside Portuguese in order to engage with the hegemonic global-American culture (Hilder 2016: 63). Closer to Cambridge, at the Brighton Exhibition, Kenelm Cox set up a poem consisting of three words – BEAUTY, LOVE, PASSION – above the water a short distance out into the ocean. A photograph with a small boat in the foreground captures the intention perfectly: the words of the poem use the same graphic material as the symbols and numbers on the boat's sail, and they happily coexist in the same visual field (see Figure 10.2).

This was an *environmental* (and therefore architectural) intervention – poetry became part of everyday life, communicating with everyone. In a more constrained form, Steadman helped produce Augusto de Campos' "cubepoem," wrapping bold Helvetica text around four brightly-colored, collapsible panels (which, significantly, were in the same dimensions as *Form*).[21] This poem could be carried around and set up anywhere to create a communicating cube of space. We are reminded of the bright colors, simple forms, and bold graphics of Herbert Bayer's Bauhaus-era designs for cinemas and newspaper stands, the graphics of which were intended to cut through a cluttered visual environment to deliver their message (Brüning 2000: 332–341).

180 Matthew Allen

Figure 10.2 "Three Graces" by Kenelm Cox, photograph by Graham Keen, 1967

The cover of the final issue of *Form* features a project by Alexandr Rodchenko from 1923 that illustrates the underlying impulse: it is a project for a "cine-car," rendered using the bold simplicity of advertising graphics to communicate the revolution to the masses – even going so far as to drive it to them and project it directly into their everyday environment, on the sides of buildings (see Figure 10.3).

One insight that emerged from the concrete poetry scene but which found much wider application was the idea that artistic techniques are more important than the materials being worked with. Any material could

Figure 10.3 Cover of *Form 10*, 1969

serve the structuralist artist. Poetry, graphic design, and architecture were construed as fundamentally the same thing, united by a common structure (linguistic perception and cognition) and common techniques. In the first issue of *Form*, the second article is an essay by the literary theorist Roland Barthes on "the activity of structuralism," which serves as a manifesto for the structuralist artistic theory that underwrote the journal. Barthes says bluntly that "technique is the very essence of all creation" – not ideas, not meaning, but *technique* (Barthes 1966: 12–13). This was an inflammatory statement in Barthes' literary context; he was likely thinking about the Oulipo group in France (from Ouvroir de littérature potentielle, translated as "workshop of potential literature"), a group of writers and mathematicians whose work involved the formulation and excruciating application of rules (James 2009: 123–126). Georges Perec, for example, wrote a 300-

182 *Matthew Allen*

page novel, *La disparition*, without using the letter "e." Barthes explains that structuralists do not create *works*, but rather "dissect" some "material" and "arrange" it in a different way. In a definition very similar to the one offered by Gombrich, Barthes mentions that "it is through the regular return of units and associations of units that the work appears to have been constructed, that is to say, endowed with meaning; the linguists call these rules of combination *forms*" (Barthes 1966: 13). Structuralist artistic activity, then, leads to the construction of forms. Rather than forcing a choice between form and function, Barthes describes forms as "functional" units, and – looping back around – implies that function is generally about "fabricating meaning." This should be understood as the opposite of "creating" meaning: meaning, as Barthes describes it, is not something that exists inside the artwork to be transmitted to a passive spectator, but something the reader "fabricates" in her own mind. Agency is thus transferred from the artist to the reader – both engage in the same structuralist activity. The structuralist artist-technician constructs a sort of machine that the reader will use to build meaning, piece by piece, in a half-controlled manner, inside her own head. What sets Barthes' theoretical categories apart from each other is not always easy to decipher,[22] but at a practical level Barthes' message is clear: artists, the creators of lofty ideas, are out; technicians, who are inclined to tinker with the materials and effects of everyday life, are in.

Barthes' manifesto imparts new value to one type of humble technician in particular: the graphic designer. Thinking in the polemical vein of *Form*, we could see graphic design as the technique that is held in common between architects, concrete poets, painters, and many other artist-technicians. Steadman, the motivating force behind *Form*, produced few theoretical statements; instead, he carried out "structuralist activity" in the guise of editing, typography, graphic design, and a certain amount of less glamorous writing (summaries, captions, and the like).[23] In *Image*, this came together as a bricolage – some incongruous paintings at the beginning followed by a strange advertisement/statement (or poem?) by a production company, the editorial located awkwardly in the middle of the issue, and a lot of concrete poetry and kinetic art making up the remaining bulk. Using his full control of *Form*, Steadman engaged in a more holistic design effort. The journal was produced in an unusual square format, using Helvetica throughout. Advertisements were absent (in the first issues at least). The format of the table of contents – an epitome of contemporary modernist layout techniques – seems to have been lifted from *Studio International*. A rigorous but flexible grid system ruled the remaining pages, with text and images very often chopped and squished into place (see Figure 10.4).

The result pushed the agenda of "unification" inherited from the earlier British avant-garde (e.g. *Circle*) past its breaking point. Indeed, regular text is sometimes rendered indistinguishable from poetry in *Form*. The editors went to great lengths to find works that fit their mold, or could be made

Imagining architecture as a form of concrete poetry 183

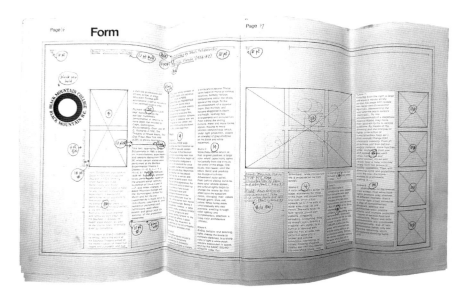

Figure 10.4 Paste-up of *Form*

to fit. Poems were generally re-designed in Helvetica, and resolutely idiosyncratic compositions like those of Sylvester Houédard (a father figure of British concrete poetry who had been included in *Image*) were left out entirely from *Form*. In its singularity of vision, *Form* stands in striking contrast to other little magazines: Ian Hamilton Finlay's fantastic *Poor. Old. Tired. Horse.*, for example, changed its layout and typography drastically to suit the content being published ("Poor. Old. Tired. Horse. (1962-68)" 2017).

The rigor of *Form* is likely attributable in part to the mindset Steadman had picked up as an architecture student under Leslie Martin, though he was also trained as a typographer.[24] In any case, *Form* is a clear example of the aesthetics of the technician at work. Following Barthes, the graphic designer supersedes the artist and the architect in importance, and the journal itself becomes a sort of structuralist assemblage that takes the place once occupied by individual artworks.

Form and algorithmic architecture

Interpreting *Form* from the point of view of the architectural criticism of the preceding period is revealing. Employing the well-known categories of Henry-Russell Hitchcock and Colin Rowe, Steadman's work on *Form*

184   *Matthew Allen*

presents an investigation into "natural beauty" in the mode of the "bureaucrat" – a direction which had been gaining momentum in England for two decades (Hitchcock 1947: 3–6; Rowe 1947: 101–104; Summerson 1957: 307–310). An impulse toward anonymity pervades the journal. In his theoretical statement, Weaver cites Jean Arp's wartime manifesto, "Abstract Art, Concrete Art":

> the works of concrete must not bear the signature of their author. These paintings, the sculptures – these things – should be as anonymous in the great workshop of nature as clouds, mountains, seas, animals, and men. Yes – men too should become part of nature.
>
> (Arp 1942)[25]

Arp's polemic resonated in the atmosphere of post-WWII reconstruction. As he described it, form is something found, not created. Weaver summarizes the theme nicely: "concrete is concerned with the discovery of form, the discovery of what Finlay calls 'an order *there*, somewhere, and not an order we can use (to save us, as it were) but more, that could use us, if we try'" (Weaver 1964: 15). The activities advocated by *Form* are altogether less polemical than was typical of modernist avant-garde production, but there is certainly a sense of a powerful force (the force of "nature") lurking behind their work, waiting to be channeled.[26] Structuralist activity thus sometimes comes across as a voluntary submission to *form* for access to its power over *life*.[27]

Though it evidently fit the broad concerns of its era, it is important to make one final conceptual step before the structuralist activity of *Form* can be seen to fit with computation in particular. If the artist is to become a technician, the artwork must become a machine or even a sort of computational device. "Techniques" (of the artist) and "effects" (of the artwork) usually went together in the practices collected in *Form*. The first essay in the first issue is about film, and the projector is presented by van Doesburg as an archetypal "machine" for producing artistic effects. László Moholy-Nagy's Light-Space Modulator (1930), which is featured in issue six, represents the apotheosis of this ambition: it projected dynamic, multicolor light compositions onto every surface of the room around it, replacing architecture with environmental effects (Kovacs 1967: 14–19).[28]

This approach could scale up into small buildings: issue five presents a project for an inhabitable space around which "a complex reflecting surface is distorted continuously by the action of rods from above; rotating cylinders of different colors, at floor level, are illuminated from the side, and mirrored in the surface above" (Lassus 1967: 14). Beyond such literal examples, any medium could be thought of as an abstract machine – the artist need only specify medium-properties and figure out their associated techniques and effects. If painting, for example, is about color on surfaces, an artist could add the element of time and put together a machine for producing "reflected light compositions." Or if music is about rhythms,

Imagining architecture as a form of concrete poetry 185

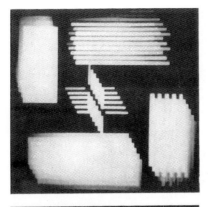

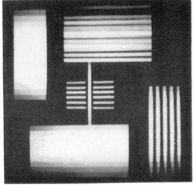

Figure 10.5 Reflected Light Compositions of Ludwig Hirschfeld-Mack, reproduced in *Form* 2, 1966

the same machine could be used to make "color music." Steadman wrote an essay about Lumia, which did the latter, and issue two of *Form* featured the work of Ludwig Hirschfeld-Mach, who did the former (see Figure 10.5) (Gilbert 1966: 16–25).

In this movement to analyze, systematize, and update prewar directions in art, however, the notion of creating singular, elaborate machines to produce specific effects was beginning, by the mid-1960s, to appear obsolete.[29] A new class of general-purpose "hardware" was now available. In a long essay on color music published in the same years as *Form*, Steadman suggests that problems of "randomness of effect" and limitation to "basic composition" could be overcome by new computer technology:

> The use of some techniques which are currently being investigated experimentally – the generation of images electronically using cathode-

186   *Matthew Allen*

ray tubes or electro-luminescent display panels – may offer to the artist control over mobile forms in color, and the possibility of rhythmic and "melodic" compositions perceived visually, of which the color-musician has dreamed.

(Steadman 2016: 24)

Steadman later remarked on his dream of making elaborate color music compositions using a computer.[30] It would have been obvious to anyone who had seen the technology, but not many had. In the computers of the 1960s, the cathode-ray tube was certainly the most important piece of hardware for the artist, but it was also the least known (Allen 2016: 637–668). The prevailing public imagination of the computer was of giant "electronic brains," not windows onto interactive environments (Edwards 1996).[31] But Steadman and his colleagues at Cambridge were slightly ahead of their contemporaries in this regard. Ivan Sutherland's famous demonstration of a proof-of-concept of general-purpose human-computer interactivity using screens and light-pens took place at MIT in 1962 (Cardoso Llach 2015), and only three years later Sutherland was invited to present his work at Cambridge (Steadman 2016: 291–306). A write-up on Sketchpad and its implications for design using computers was published in the first issue of *Form*, in 1966 (Gray 1966: 19–22). The text was somewhat bland in comparison to the essays by van Doesburg and Barthes that it followed, but the images resonated with their context: after the polemic about film and the theory of structuralist techniques and before a series of concrete poems, here was a technician pointing a light-pen at a glowing screen, creating what was, for all intents and purposes, a work of kinetic art (see Figure 10.6).

Here was a device and a procedure that could be applied to any art – a meta-medium to bring together all mediums.[32] The score of a reflected light composition on the cover of issue two would look, in this context, like a computer program (see Figure 10.7).

Conclusion

In the story of how a culture of computation found its way into architecture, computer hardware was little more than a convenient vehicle. In *Form* we see all the strands come together: a model of artistic production (using a medium-machine to produce perceptual effects), a figure who can carry out the work (the artist-technician), the backing of theory (van Doesburg and Barthes and many others), a medium (the interactive computer), and a technique (procedurality).[33] This socio-technical assemblage could be – and would be – applied anywhere and everywhere. This was the beginning of experimentation, not its end or even its culmination.

Perhaps one final strand should be added. The third essay in the first issue of *Form*, after van Doesburg and Barthes, is an essay on

Imagining architecture as a form of concrete poetry 187

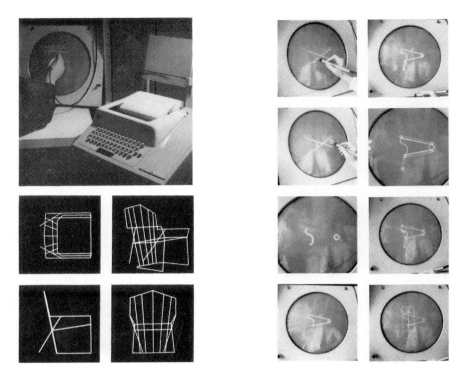

Figure 10.6 Sketchpad III and Lockheed-Georgia Co. CAD systems in use, reproduced in *Form 1*, 1966

"experimental aesthetics" that describes how to evaluate the structuralist activity that would follow. The advice is simple: create a controlled environment and test artistic techniques in the same way psychologists test perception (Cumming 1966: 14–15). Though this advice was rarely followed, it offered the final conceptual step in the bureaucratization of aesthetics: through controlled experiments, an artistic agenda could become a *research* agenda. From production through to evaluation, art and architecture could be both programmed and made programmatic. They could be taken out of the hands of the artistic genius and given over to the technician.

Much of the effect of structuralist theory in architecture came from its conflation of preexisting categories, and *language* was foremost among these. The prevailing view in architecture was that language is the realm of conventional meaning. Thus when John Summerson wrote about "the classical language of architecture," he meant "language" in a somewhat prestructuralist sense: language as an evolving set of meaningful elements

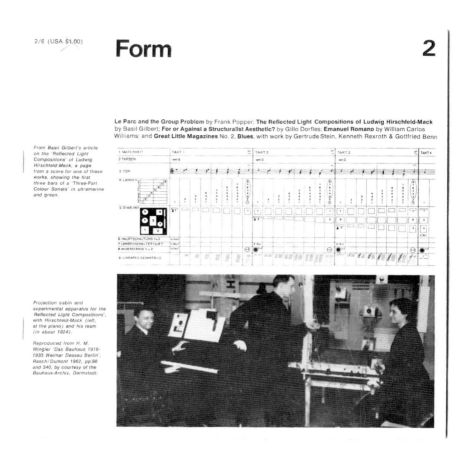

Figure 10.7 Cover of *Form 2*, 1966

rather than language as a synchronic structure of rules and relationships (Summerson 1963). The pathbreaking insight of structuralism was to suggest that a "classical language" could be approached in a modern way, just as one would approach any other formal system. Besides the *language of form*, structuralism suggested that architects should pay attention to the *form of language*. In other words, structuralism offered a generalized formalism – a formalism of form, a piling-up and recursive looping of abstraction upon abstraction (Jameson 1972). From a structuralist point of view, the longstanding distinction between architectural program and architectural form tended to disappear.

After a structuralist mindset had been adopted and a set of elements had been chosen came the task of working with them. This was when the computer – a structuralist device if there ever was one – entered the scene.

Imagining architecture as a form of concrete poetry 189

There is a saying that *if all you have is a hammer, everything looks like a nail*. With a computer in the room, everything began to look like structured data. Structuralism tagged along wherever there was institutional pressure to use computers. Fantasies of structuralist activity seeped into ever-wider habits of thought. Architects almost everywhere would soon enough learn to dream computationally.

Notes

1 A brief timeline: the first computer-aided design software was demonstrated in the early 1960s (Sketchpad, 1962); the first computer "laboratories" and "centers" opened in architecture schools in the mid-1960s (Harvard University, 1965; the University of Cambridge, 1967); the first successful architectural software companies formed in the late 1960s, and architecture firms began investing in computation in those same years (Applied Research of Cambridge, 1969; SOM writes its Building Optimization Program, 1968).

2 Compare, for example, the negative characterization of bureaucracy by Henry-Russell Hitchcock and the positive portrayal by Martin: Henry-Russell Hitchcock, "The Architecture of Bureaucracy and the Architecture of Genius," *The Architectural Review* 101, no. 601 (January 1947): 3–6; Leslie Martin, "The State of Transition," in *Circle: International Survey of Constructive Art*, ed. Leslie Martin, Ben Nicholson, and Naum Gabo (London: Faber & Faber, 1937), 215–19.

3 Anthony Hill, ed., *DATA: Directions in Art, Theory and Technology* (London: Faber & Faber, 1968).

4 For context, see R. J. Ellis, "Mapping the United Kingdom Little Magazine Field," in *New British Poetries: The Scope of the Possible*, ed. Robert Hampson and Peter Barry (Manchester: University of Manchester Press, 1993), 72–102. More generally, see Beatriz Colomina, *Clip, Stamp, Fold: The Radical Architecture of Little Magazines, 196X to 197X* (Barcelona: Actar, 2011); Steven Heller, *Merz to Emigre and Beyond: Avant-Garde Magazine Design of the Twentieth Century* (London: Phaidon, 2003).

5 On the Centre for Land Use and Built Form Studies, see Theodora Vardouli, "Graphing Theory: New Mathematics, Design, and the Participatory Turn" (Massachusetts Institute of Technology, 2017).

6 For context, see Mary Louise Lobsinger, "Two Cambridges: Models, Methods, Systems, and Expertise," in *A Second Modernism: MIT, Architecture, and the "Techno-Social" Moment*, ed. Arindam Dutta (Cambridge, Mass.: MIT Press, 2013), 652–85.

7 The editorial archive of *Form*, now at Princeton, shows Steadman to be the central organizing figure.

8 On the Constructionist Group, see Grieve 2005.

9 Author's interview with Philip Steadman, March 2017.

10 The correspondence in the *Form* archive shows the results of Steadman's attempts to solicit work from various artists.

11 A list is in *Granta* 68, no. 1240 (28 November 1964).

12 The *Form* archive contains dozens of unsolicited contributions from British artists. When Steadman shut down the journal after its tenth issue, letters poured in mourning the community's loss.

13 Malina was an aeronautical engineer and pioneer of rocketry as well as an artist and editor.

14 On the place of van Doesburg in architecture theory in this period, see Bois 1987: 102–130.

190 *Matthew Allen*

15 For an insightful discussion, see Richard Difford, "Developed Space: Theo van Doesburg and the Chambre de Fleurs," *The Journal of Architecture* 12, no. 1 (2007): 79–98.
16 See also Draper 1971: 329–340.
17 Compare with Lévi-Strauss 1955: 428–444.
18 See the Introduction in Strauss, Quinn 1997 and Chapter 1 of Reddy 2001. For an example of widely-read psychology on this topic from the era, see Miller 1955: 343–352.
19 "The difficulties this poetry poses for readers are potentially daunting. Complex hierarchies of syntactical dependence have to be followed and retraced, highly condensed and thoroughly dislocated references to the social world and its myriad discursive fields have to be followed up – and all the while readers' efforts are sabotaged by bathetic collapses, pratfalls, and aggression" (Ladkin and Purves 2007: 10).
20 This was a reconceptualization that had long been in the works. For the avant-garde polemical version, see Mondrian 1937: 41–56. For a version generalized for architects, see Summerson 1959, 11–28.
21 Design iterations can be found in the *Form* archive. Helvetica was a rare and difficult font to use in Britain at the time (Moreno 2011: 508). Steadman imagined at one point that *Form* would be published until a stack of them formed a cube (Author's interview with Philip Steadman, March 2017).
22 Barthes typically throws together similar terms in radical contradiction and in rapid succession: structuralism, he says, "seeks to relate to history not simply contents (a thing which has been done a thousand times), but also forms, not simply the material, but also the intelligible, not simply the ideological but also the aesthetic" (Barthes 1966). The meaning of this would be almost impossible to untangle – which is of course the point.
23 This is evident in the *Form* archive in the correspondence with authors – particularly the poets and artists – and the paste-up work of creating the journal's pages. One poet congratulated Steadman on the way his layout suited his concrete poems (Grandal Montero 2015: 224).
24 Author's interview with Philip Steadman, March 2017.
25 Quoted in Weaver 1964: 14–15.
26 For one polemical manifestation, see March, Echenique, Dickens 1971. Generally, the artistic scene under discussion was notable for its even-keeled (even dryly historical) perspective; see, e.g. Hill 1966: 140–147. None reach anywhere near the level of Filippo Tommaso Marinetti's "Manifesto of Futurism" of 1909: "Take up your pickaxes, your axes and hammers and wreck, wreck the venerable cities, pitilessly!"
27 This ominous implication of management and control would soon render structuralism unpalatable to developing tastes. For a revealing case study, see Skrebowski 2008: 54–83.
28 Moholy-Nagy was a pivotal figure between prewar German aesthetics and the more wide-reaching (and ultimately ubiquitous) aesthetics of "technology" in the postwar period (Williams 2014).
29 Machine metaphors were being widely replaced by systems metaphors. See, e.g. Meltzer 2013; Broeckmann 2016.
30 Author's interview with Philip Steadman, March 2017.
31 Christopher Alexander, an early computer-using architect, was adamant that computers were nothing but calculating machines (Alexander 1964: 52–54). See also Upitis 2013: 474–505.
32 On the dream of meta-media, see Manovich 2013. On the history of the media concept, see Guillory 2010: 321–362.
33 For a longer discussion of procedurality/algorithmics in architecture, see the author's dissertation: Allen 2019.

Bibliography

Alexander, C. (1964) "A Much Asked Question about Computers and Design," in *Architecture and the Computer: Proceedings of the First Boston Architectural Center Conference, December 5, 1964*, Boston, MA: Boston Architectural Center.

Allen, M. (2016) "Representing Computer-Aided Design: Screenshots and the Interactive Computer circa 1960," *Perspectives on Science* 24, 6, 637–668.

Allen, M. (2019) *Prehistory of the Digital: Architecture becomes Programming, 1934-1990*, Cambridge, MA: Harvard University.

Arp, J. (1942) "Abstract Art, Concrete Art," in P. Guggenheim (ed.) *Art of This Century: Objects, Drawings, Photographs, Paintings, Sculpture, Collages, 1910 to 1942*, New York: Art of this Century, 29–31.

Bann, S. (1964) "Communication and Structure in Concrete Poetry," *Image*, Kinetic Art: Concrete Poetry, 8–9.

Barthes, R. (1966) "The Activity of Structuralism," *Form* 1, 12–13.

Bois, Y. A. (1987) "Mondrian and the Theory of Architecture," *Assemblage* 4, 102–130.

Broeckmann, A. (2016) *Machine Art in the Twentieth Century*, Cambridge, MA: MIT Press.

Brüning, U. (2000) "Herbert Bayer," in J. Fiedler and P. Feierabend (eds.) *Bauhaus*, Cologne: Könemann, 332–339.

Cardoso Llach, D. (2015) *Builders of the Vision: Software and the Imagination of Design*, London: Routledge.

Cobbing, B. (1988) *Changing Forms in English Visual Poetry: The Influence of Tools and Machines*, London: Writers Forum.

Colomina, B. (2011) *Clip, Stamp, Fold: The Radical Architecture of Little Magazines, 196X to 197X*, Barcelona: Actar.

Cumming, C. (1966) "Experimental Aesthetics," *Form* 1, 5–11.

Difford, R. (2007) "Developed Space: Theo van Doesburg and the Chambre de Fleurs," *The Journal of Architecture* 12, 1, 79–98.

Doesburg, T. van (1966) "Film as Pure Form," *Form* 1, 5–11.

Draper, R. P. (1971) "Concrete Poetry," *New Literary History* 2, 2, 329–340.

Edwards, P. N. (1996) *The Closed World: Computers and the Politics of Discourse in Cold War America*, Cambridge, MA: MIT Press.

Ellis, R. J. (1993) "Mapping the United Kingdom Little Magazine Field," in R. Hampson and P. Barry (eds.) *New British Poetries: The Scope of the Possible*, Manchester: University of Manchester Press, 72–103.

Gilbert, B. (1966) "The Reflected Light Compositions of Ludwig Hirschfeld-Mack," *Form* 2, 10–13.

Gombrich, E. H. and Shaw, R. (1962) "Symposium: Art and the Language of the Emotions," in *Proceedings of the Aristotelian Society, Supplementary Volumes* 36, 215–246.

Grandal Montero, G. (2015) "From Cambridge to Brighton: Concrete Poetry in Britain, an Interview with Stephen Bann," in S. Bodman (ed.) *Artist's Book Yearbook*, Bristol: Impact Press.

Gray, C. (1966) "Computers and Design," *Form* 1, 19–22.

Grieve, A. (2005) *Constructed Abstract Art in England After the Second World War: A Neglected Avant-Garde*, New Haven: Yale University Press.

Guillory, J. (2010) "Genesis of the Media Concept," *Critical Inquiry* 36, 321–362.

192 Matthew Allen

Heller, S. (2003) *Merz to Emigre and beyond: Avant-Garde Magazine Design of the Twentieth Century*, London: Phaidon.

Hilder, J. (2016) *Designed Words for a Designed World: The International Concrete Poetry Movement*, Montreal and Kingston: McGill – Queen's University Press.

Hill, A. (1966) "Constructivism – The European Phenomenon," *Studio International* 171, 876, 140–147.

Hill, A. (1968) *DATA: Directions in Art, Theory and Technology*, London: Faber & Faber.

Hitchcock, H. R. (1947) "The Architecture of Bureaucracy and the Architecture of Genius," *The Architectural Review* 101, 601, 3–6.

James, A. (2009) *Constraining Chance: Georges Perec and the Oulipo*, Evanston, IL: Northwestern University Press.

Jameson, F. (1972) *The Prison-House of Language: A Critical Account of Structuralism and Russian Formalism*, Princeton, NJ: Princeton University Press.

Kovacs, I. (1967) "Totality through Light: The Work of Laszlo Moholy-Nagy," *Form* 6, 14–19.

Kuhn, T. (1962) *The Structure of Scientific Revolutions*, Chicago, IL: University of Chicago Press.

Ladkin, S. and Purves, R. (2007) "An Introduction," *Chicago Review* 53, 1, 6–13.

Lassus, B. (1967) "Environments and Total Landscape," *Form* 5, 13–15.

Lévi-Strauss, C. (1955) "The Structural Study of Myth," *The Journal of American Folklore* 68, 270, 428–444.

Lobsinger, M. L. (2013) "Two Cambridges: Models, Methods, Systems, and Expertise," in A. Dutta (ed.) *A Second Modernism: MIT, Architecture, and the "Techno-Social" Moment*, Cambridge, MA: MIT Press, 652–685.

Manovich, L. (2013) *Software Takes Command*, New York: Bloomsbury Academic.

March, L., Echenique, M. and Dockens, P. "Models of Environment: Polemic for a Structural Revolution," *Architectural Design*, 41.

Meltzer, E. (2013) *Systems We Have Loved: Conceptual Art, Affect, and the Antihumanist Turn*, Chicago, IL: University of Chicago Press.

Miller, G. (1955) "The Magical Number Seven Plus or Minus Two: Some Limits on Our Capacity for Processing Information," *Psychological Review* 101, 2, 343–352.

Mondrian, P. (1937) "Plastic Art and Pure Plastic Art (Figurative Art and Non-Figurative Art)," in L. Martin, B. Nicholson and N. Gabo (eds.) *Circle: International Survey of Constructive Art*, London: Faber & Faber, 41–56.

Moreno, J. (2011) "Interview with Stephen Bann," in B. Colomina (ed.) *Clip, Stamp, Fold: The Radical Architecture of Little Magazines, 196X to 197X*, Barcelona: Actar, 223–224.

"Poor. Old. Tired. Horse. (1962–68)," (2017) *Ubuweb*, Available at: http://ubu.com/vp/Poor.Old.Tired.Horse.html [Accessed November 5, 2017].

Reddy, W. M. (2001) *The Navigation of Feeling: A Framework for the History of Emotions*, Cambridge, UK: Cambridge University Press.

Rowe, C. (1947) "The Mathematics of the Ideal Villa: Palladio and Le Corbusier Compared," *The Architectural Review* 101, 101–104.

Schwitters, K. (1966) "Logically Consistent Poetry," *Form* 2, 28.

Sheppard, R. (2005) *The Poetry of Saying: British Poetry and Its Discontents, 1950-2000*, Liverpool: Liverpool University Press.

Skrebowski, L. (2008) "All Systems Go: Recovering Hans Haacke's Systems Art," *Grey Room* 30, 54–83.

Steadman, P. (1966) "Colour Music," in S. Bann (ed.) *Kinetic Art*, St. Albans: Motion Books, 16–25.

Steadman, P. (2016) "Research in Architecture and Urban Studies at Cambridge in the 1960s and 1970s: What Really Happened," *The Journal of Architecture* 21, 2, 291–306.

Strauss, C. and Quinn, N. (1997) *A Cognitive Theory of Cultural Meaning*, Cambridge, UK: Cambridge University Press.

Summerson, J. (1957) "The Case for a Theory of Modern Architecture," *The Journal of the Royal Institute of British Architects* 64, 8, 307–310.

Summerson, J. (1959) "Introduction," in T. Dannatt (ed.) *Modern Architecture in Britain*, London: Batsford, 11–28.

Summerson, J. (1963) *The Classical Language of Architecture*, London: Methuen & Co.

Upitis, A. (2013) "Alexander's Choice: How Architecture Avoided Computer-Aided Design c. 1962," in A. Dutta (ed.) *A Second Modernism: MIT, Architecture, and the "Techno-Social" Moment*, Cambridge, MA: MIT Press, 474–505.

Vardouli, T. (2017) *Graphing Theory: New Mathematics, Design, and the Participatory Turn*, Cambridge, MA: Massachusetts Institute of Technology.

Weaver, M. (1964) "Concrete and Kinetic: The Poem as Functional Object," *Image, Kinetic Art: Concrete Poetry*, 14–15.

Weaver, M. (1966) "Concrete Poetry," *The Lugano Review* 1, 5–6, 100–125.

Williams, A. (2014) *Movement in Vision: Cinema, Aesthetics, and Modern German Culture, 1918–1933*, New York: Columbia University.

Witt, E. (2011) "That Room in Cambridge," *n+1* 11.

11 The axiomatic aesthetic

Alma Steingart

In 1958, *Scientific American* published a special issue on "The Creative Process" dedicated to innovation in science (Bronowski 1958: 58–65). Edited by Jacob Bronowski, the volume included articles on the physiology and psychology of the imagination, as well as the role of innovation in mathematics, physics, and biology. Bronowski, who would later become famous for his work on the BBC television series *The Ascent of Man*, was committed to the idea that the sciences and the arts were not, as C. P. Snow would famously declare the following year, opposed to one another. Rather, they were parallel activities united by their creativity and innovation.[1] Bronowski was not alone in trying to bridge the gap between the sciences and the arts. Other intellectuals such as metallurgist-turned-historian of technology and art Cyril Stanley Smith, developmental biologist and philosopher Conrad H. Waddington, and designer and artist Gyorgy Kepes were similarly committed to a mid-century scientific humanism that emphasized creativity and aesthetic considerations as qualities shared by the sciences and the arts (Waddington 1970; Smith 1980, 1983). Whereas Bronowski's vision was an all-encompassing one that treated the sciences and the arts as unified wholes, his writings are inflected by his personal training in mathematics. His notion of creativity clearly bears the marks of the high modernist mathematical epistemology in which he was steeped. Bronowski's creative mind reflected values held in common by many modern mathematicians, who conceived of their field as a self-contained and autonomous body of knowledge.[2]

Bronowski held that in both art and science, creativity was fundamentally a question of *identification*, meaning the ability to recognize common features across separate spheres:

> a man becomes creative, whether he is an artist or a scientist, when he finds a new unity in the variety of nature. He does so by finding the likeness between things which were not thought alike before, and this gives him a sense both of the richness and of understanding. The creative mind is a mind that looks for unexpected likeness.
>
> (Bronowski 1958: 63)

The axiomatic aesthetic 195

Bronowski's description of creativity as the recognition of "unexpected likeness" in the search for unification and understanding is a testimony to the structural conception of mathematics that dominated mathematical research at the time. Mathematicians postulated that diverse mathematical subfields could be analyzed and approached from a unified perspective by turning their attention to the study of abstract mathematical structures. They sought universal theories that would enable them to describe mathematics as one unified whole. As historian Leo Corry has noted, by the mid-1940s "the idea soon arose that mathematical structures are the actual subject matter of mathematical knowledge in general" (Corry 2004: 10).

Bronowski directly identified structuralist mathematics as a shared model for both scientists and artists.

> Science is pictured as preoccupied less with facts than with relations, less with numbers than with arrangements. This new vision, the search for structure ... is also marked in modern art. Abstract sculpture often looks like an exercise in topology, exactly because the sculpture shares the vision of the topologist.
>
> (Bronowski 1958: 64)

That is, it was not simply that the nature of creativity operated similarly in both science and art. More fundamentally, they shared an underlying approach, "the search for structure." It is thus not surprising that Bronowski called upon topology, as opposed to geometry, to unite the sciences and the arts. By mid-century, topology was concerned more with the arrangement of an object than with its metrical qualities, and thus became symbolic of structuralist methods writ large.

Surveying the twentieth-century literature on science and art, Linda Henderson has noted that "by mid-century a focus on structure and form had become a more fundamental means to compare the two realms" (Henderson 2004: 426). Bronowski was not alone in identifying structure as a common denominator. One of the best examples of the attention to structure as a uniting concept in both science and arts is Kepes's 1965 edited volume *Structure in Art and in Science*.[3] Its cover, graced by the names of the preeminent artists, scientists, and architects who contributed essays, from Pier Luigi Nervi to Buckminster Fuller, gestures toward Kepes's definition of structuralism in its distribution of rectangles suggestive of decussating lines: "structure, in its basic sense, is the created unity of the parts and joints of entities. It is a pattern ... of interacting forces perceived as a single spatio-temporal entity" (Figure 11.1). It was the product of several seminars Kepes organized at MIT in which he hoped to foster interdisciplinary discussions around the notion of structure.[4] It serves as such as an uncommonly rich source with which to interrogate the structuralist vision that undergirded mid-century scientific humanism and as a testimony to its prevalence.

196 *Alma Steingart*

Kepes and his colleagues were not the only ones calling upon mathematical structure to unite the arts and the sciences. Throughout the postwar period, mathematicians advanced a parallel claim arguing that mathematics was simultaneously an art and a science. They did so as a reaction to the

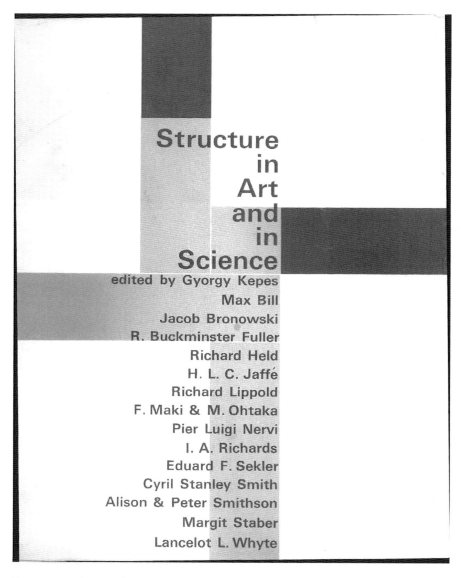

Figure 11.1 Cover of *Structure in Art and Science*. Kepes G. (ed) 1965. *Structure in Art and Science*. New York: Braziller.

The axiomatic aesthetic   197

militarism of the day, seeking to ensure the place of mathematical research in the postwar humanistic order. And, like their humanist colleagues, they pointed toward *creativity* and *aesthetics* in their claim to the arts, construing both concepts according to the structuralist vision of the field.

Yet, the structuralist visions advanced by mathematicians and scientific humanists were also fundamentally at odds with one another. Mathematicians' universe was not one of images and illustrations. One of the main characteristics of high modernist mathematics was that it was inherently non-visual. Kepes's books were bursting with images. The only way to reunite modern science and art, according to Kepes, was to reclaim the place of the senses: "the sensed, the emotional, are of vital importance in transforming its [the world's] chaos into order" (Kepes 1956: 19). For Kepes, it was precisely the invisible nature of modern scientific knowledge, "invisible viruses, atoms, mesons, protons, cosmic rays, supersonic waves," that demanded a new vision (Kepes 1956: 19). Access to this new world, he insisted, cannot be limited to rational thought. What was needed was a new structural vision that would attune the eye of the artist to the world of the scientist (and vice versa).[5] However, this was not so for mid-century mathematicians. To be sure, theirs was a richly symbolic world, with graphs and diagrams, but it was not the world of visible forms or of human perception. Mathematicians were after the topology of the infinite, not that of the world around them. Indeed, for pure mathematicians, the aesthetic nature of mathematics was inversely proportional to its boundedness in reality. Only by closing their eyes to the world, they suggested, could their creativity be expressed.

The mid-century attention to structure in both art and science is rooted in the turn of the twentieth century. During that period, transformations in mathematics, logic, science, linguistics, and the arts called into question the meaning of representation. The rise of non-Euclidean geometry, the discovery of general relativity, and the flowering of abstract art, alongside a renewed interest in symbolic logic and semiotics, put pressure on the role of abstraction in depictions of the world, whether scientific or artistic.[6] As Lorraine Daston and Peter Galison have shown, an adherence to a structuralist objectivity first emerged at the end of the nineteenth century among mathematicians and logicians, who argued that only relations can be known generally and without reference to subjective experience (Daston and Galison 2010: Ch. 5). By mid-century, mathematicians had severed their structuralist vision from its original epistemological context, turning it into a full-fledged research activity in its own right. This entailed a predilection for the abstract and general rather than the concrete and particular, as well as an ongoing search for governing structures. At the same time, structuralism had become an intellectual movement in a broader range of fields. In anthropology, psychology, sociology, and linguistics, a similar concern for relations and arrangements drove research and analytic activities.[7]

198   *Alma Steingart*

When Kepes and his colleagues turned to structure as a unifying concept across the arts and the sciences, they were building upon these diverse trajectories. Still, their understanding of structure was undoubtedly indebted to mathematics. What made structure such an appealing concept was that it reflected a precision associated with mathematics, while at the same time being ill-defined and open to multiple interpretations. Appeals to structure, whether in mathematics, science, or the arts, were as much rhetorical stances as they were a description of a particular methodology – for in all of these fields, structure above all was concomitant to modernism. Ironically, at the same time that scientific humanists turned to structure to make science and art more *visibly* connected, mathematicians insisted that it was structure's inherent *invisibility* that joined art and science.

Structure

Whereas the only mathematically trained contributor to Kepes's *Structure in Art and in Science* was Bronowski, the meaning of structure articulated by many of the contributors was clearly indebted to mathematics. The clearest example comes from Buckminster Fuller's contribution to the volume, which Kepes described as "providing an inspiring bridge between our comprehension of the structural principles of nature and the potential application of this knowledge to the creation of man-made forms" (Kepes 1965: v). Fuller, who by that point was already well known for his design work, especially his geodesic domes, quoted a 1953 report by MIT's Department of Mathematics in order to explicate his own use of the word structure: "Mathematics, which most people think of as the science of number, is, in fact, *the science of structure and pattern in general*" (Fuller 1965: 68). The emphasis on mathematics as the science of structure *in general* resonated with Fuller. Mathematics, he explained, was unique because it was the most generalized of all scientific disciplines, the most "comprehensive and abstract," and thus, it clearly indicated that "structure is not a 'thing' – it is not 'solid'" (Fuller 1965: 68).

What then was the structural conception of mathematics, and how did it emerge? The structural vision of mathematics is predicated on one particular method: modern axiomatics. If structure was the vision, axiomatics was the practice. Although by mid-century it was impossible to separate the structuralist vision of mathematics from the axiomatic method, axiomatics emerged first. It was formulated as a means by which to answer the most philosophical of all questions: how do we know what we know? Galvanized by the discovery of non-Euclidean geometry and similarly counterintuitive ideas such as space-filling curves, toward the end of the nineteenth century, mathematicians, philosophers, and logicians turned to study the foundations of mathematics (Grattan-Guinness 2011). Wanting to ensure that mathematical knowledge rested on a sound base, they reevaluated the most basic mathematical concepts, such as numbers and points. Axiomatics emerged from these investigations.

While several mathematicians contributed to this endeavor, the work of David Hilbert stands outs for its influence on the future of mathematical research. In his investigations into the foundation of geometry at the end of the nineteenth century, Hilbert suggested that trying to define the meaning of basic elements such as points and lines by appealing to intuition was fundamentally futile. All past attempts had demonstrated, according to him, that such a project was bound to fail. Instead, Hilbert suggested that all one can know with absolute certainty is the relations that hold true between the given elements in a system. Hilbert therefore proposed dispensing with the idea that an axiom presents something that is self-evidently true, and instead should be taken to be arbitrary. In his own analysis, the "truth" of a given axiomatic system does not follow from the correctness of its principles, but from the consistency of the system as a whole. For Hilbert, such complete and consistent axiomatic systems were the only way to secure the foundations of mathematics (Hilbert 1910; Hilbert 1996: 1105–1115).

These early roots of axiomatics are clearly evident in the conception of structure that dominated the 1950s and 1960s discourse on structure in art and science. Take for example physicist Lancelot Whyte's contribution to Kepes's volume. Whyte writes of Bertrand Russell's and Alfred Whitehead's *Principia Mathematica*. They, like Hilbert, were concerned with the foundation of mathematics, and sought to place the foundation of mathematics on logic. Whyte comments:

> The philosophy of structure is monistic, relational, precise, and potentially comprehensive. Unlike those ontologies of existence which seek permanent substances beneath appearances, such as extended matter or thinking mind, it accepts as a lone objective a changing pattern of relations. Isomorphic structures are indistinguishable; structure is all there is.
>
> (Whyte 1965: 22)

A structural approach required one to focus on relations as the only "objective" account of that which exists. Like mathematicians believed, a structuralist approach promised to reveal what was hidden beneath the surface of things.

Hilbert's ideas had far reaching implications for mathematicians. Although Hilbert originally proposed axiomatics as a foundational tool, by the turn of the century it turned into a research tool in its own right. A small community of American mathematicians first embraced axiomatics, but the work of Bourbaki popularized axiomatics and coupled it with structuralist mathematics.[8] A pseudonym for a group of French mathematicians who first gathered in the 1930s, Bourbaki advanced the conception of mathematics as the study of structures in a series of textbooks they published over the following decades.[9] Bourbaki's textbooks aimed to

200 *Alma Steingart*

modernize mathematical education in France, but Bourbaki's influence reached much further. Many members of the group taught in the United States, and budding mathematicians in the postwar period considered Bourbaki's publications mandatory reading. In Bourbaki's hands, modern axiomatics was wed to structuralist approaches. While not all mathematicians subscribed to Bourbaki's comprehensive vision of the field, most adhered to axiomatics, so much so that by 1950, one exasperated mathematician complained, "For the past fifty years, it has been axioms, axioms, axioms all the way, until axiomatics, to some of its practitioners, appears as the only mathematics there is and the answer to all the mathematicians' prayers" (Bell 1950: 425–426).

In 1950, Bourbaki published "The Architecture of Mathematics," in which they provided the most comprehensive charter of the group's vision for mathematics. Bourbaki celebrated axiomatics for its ability to peer beneath the surface of things, "to find the common ideas … buried under the accumulation of details properly belonging to each of them, to bring these ideas forward and put them in their proper light" (Bourbaki 1950: 223). But they also emphasized that axiomatics offered not just a method, but a comprehensive vision of mathematical knowledge. According to Bourbaki, the "whole of the mathematical universe" could be described in terms of structures. "It is clear," Bourbaki wrote,

> that we shall no longer recognize the traditional order of things, which, just like the first nomenclatures of animal species, restricted itself to placing side by side the theories which showed greatest external similarity … The organizing principle will be the concept of a hierarchy of structures, going from the simple to the complex, from the general to the particular.
>
> (Bourbaki 1950: 228)

This structural architecture became one of defining characteristics of Bourbaki's mathematics.

Kepes's conception of structuralist vision shares some of the major tenets of Bourbaki's. Whereas for Bourbaki the promise of structuralism was a comprehensive view of the whole "mathematical universe," Kepes believed that the "sense of *structure*" artists and designers needed to cultivate held a similar potential – "the power to see our world as an interconnected whole" (Kepes 1965: ii). Furthermore, in explaining the motivation behind his work, Kepes added that he had "a long-standing, stubborn belief that, all signs to the contrary notwithstanding, we may build, from our rich, many-faceted range of structural knowledge, *a structure of structures*, a new sense of interdependence between knowledge and feeling" (Kepes 1965). Namely, the structuralist vision Kepes advocated entailed both a methodology, which emphasized relations and uncovering that which hides beneath visible surfaces, and a comprehensive theory of knowledge, which promised to join the rational and the sensual.

The axiomatic aesthetic 201

Another similarity between mathematicians' appeal to axiomatics and Kepes's structuralist vision was their common conviction in the source of its utility. "The most powerful imaginative vision is structure-oriented," Kepes wrote, explaining that "as old connections crumble away, inevitably our creative efforts seek out new ordering principles to replace the old" (Kepes 1965: ii). A structuralist vision offered a way to break free from deeply ingrained conventions – a belief that was shared by mathematicians. Describing modern axiomatics, Hilbert's student Hermann Weyl explained,

> the axiomatic approach has often revealed inner relations between, and has made for unification of methods within, domains that apparently lie far apart ... It is as if you took a man out of a milieu in which he had lived not because it fitted him but from ingrained habits and prejudices, and then allowed him, after thus setting him free, to form associations in better accordance with his true inner nature.
>
> (Weyl 1951: 524)

A structural approach, in other words, forced one, whether an artist or a mathematician, to see anew.

Finally, calling upon a structuralist approach was not just a theoretical position advocated by Kepes and others to unite the arts and the sciences, but also a practical approach to doing so in practice. Artist Anthony Hill, who contributed to one of Kepes's volumes, appealed explicitly to structuralist mathematics in his work.[10] Hill, who was affiliated with a British group of postwar Constructionist artists, called upon artists to incorporate science and mathematics in their work. Hill was also one of the main contributors to *Structure*, a journal published between 1958 and 1964. As Hill explained in one of his earliest contribution to *Structure*, "to be mathematical – which can mean geometric, arithmetic or topological – is to think and work *structurally*" (Hill 1959: 5). Hill not only sought to integrate structural mathematics in his own art, but also in his analysis of other artists' works. For example, in 1968 he published an article on Mondrian's work, in which he established a "*set* of Mondrian axioms" (Hill 1968: 234). In an appendix, Hill invokes Bourbaki's concept of structure, though is careful to note that he had discovered it only after he had already completed his own analysis.

Thus, across the arts and mathematics the concept of structure stood for an emphasis on relational similarities, and the belief that true understanding required one to look beneath the visible surface to discover common features and configuration. What structure entailed in each case might have seemed vague, but the structuralist vision was all-encompassing, a structure of structures. Mathematical structure, however, not only served as a common feature and relay between science and art, but also as a fundamental aspect of mathematicians' own claims to creativity.

202 *Alma Steingart*

Creativity

"Creative work in this field," explained mathematician Adrian Albert in 1960, "has the same kind of a reward for the creator as does the composition of a symphony, the writing of a fine novel, or the making of a great work of art" (Albert 1960). Writing eight years later, mathematician Paul Halmos concurred that mathematics "is a creative art because mathematicians create beautiful new concepts; it is a creative art because mathematicians live, act, and think like artists; and it is a creative art because mathematicians regard it so" (Halmos 1968: 389). Such claims about the creative aspects of mathematical work and its close affinities to artistic creation were a common refrain in the postwar period. At a time when mathematics was dispersing into ever growing domains of intellectual activity from the natural sciences to the social sciences, pure mathematicians ferociously insisted that mathematics was akin to art and as such must be pursued according to its own internal logic as opposed to external demands.

In making such claims, they did not call upon the formal similarities between mathematics and art, despite the fact many artists of the day readily invited it. Rather, they forged an *operational* bond between the two. That is, mathematicians cast math and art as kin because they were parallel creative pursuits. No one made this case more forcefully than Marston Morse. An elder statesman by the end of World War II, Morse was well respected among American mathematicians. He was one of the first faculty appointed to the Institute for Advanced Studies upon its creation in 1930. Beyond his various mathematical publications, he was known for his tireless advocacy on behalf of the mathematical community. In 1950, Morse published "Mathematics and the Arts" in the *Yale Review*. Pointing to the work of Dürer, Michelangelo, and Vitruvius, Morse acknowledged that geometry has long served as an inspiration to artists. However, his goal in pointing to the bond between mathematics and art was different: "*the basic affinity between mathematics and the arts is psychological and spiritual and not metrical or geometrical*" (emphasis his) (Morse 1951: 607). Unlike his teacher George Birkhoff and his colleague Hermann Weyl, who wrote about symmetry and patterns in seeking to breach the gap, Morse insisted that their affinity lay in *practice* rather than product.[11]

Morse's paper was based on a talk he had given at Kenyon College, then the hotbed of New Criticism, as part of a conference in honor of Robert Frost. Before an audience of mid-century humanists, Morse maintained that discovery, in mathematics as in art, was not a matter of logic, but of intuition. Anticipating Bronowski's own analysis a decade later, Morse insisted that as an artist, the mathematician's goal was to create and to understand. The mathematician "wishes to understand, simply, if possible – but in any case to understand; and to create, beautifully, if

The axiomatic aesthetic   203

possible – but in any case to create."[12] Although Morse appealed to historical examples to support his argument, his emphasis on the role of creation was fundamentally indebted to structuralist and modern axiomatics.

Axioms were the means by which mathematicians defined the structures they wished to explore, and in its modern incarnation the axiomatic method provided mathematicians with complete freedom as to how to choose their axioms. As such, axiomatics refashioned mathematicians as *creators*. Rather than describing the world around them, mathematicians brought to life the mathematical realms, or structures, they wished to study. Bourbaki member André Weil made this case in a letter to his sister, philosopher Simone Weil, in which he praised the importance of axiomatics: "when I invented (I say invented, and not discovered) uniform spaces, I did not have the impression of working with resistant material, but rather the impression that a professional sculptor must have when he plays by making a snowman" (Krieger 2005: 341). Mathematician J. Weissinger argued similarly in describing the nature of modern axiomatics:

> Above all, the "possibility of mathematical composition" has been expanded by this freedom to an extraordinary degree. In free artistic play, guided only by a sense for mathematical values, one can modify, omit, and add individual axioms – or for that matter, *create* and examine entirely new systems of axioms.
>
> (Weissinger 1969: 18)

Like the painter's paint, a musician's notes, or the sculpture's stone, axioms were the raw material from which mathematicians built their structures. They were the medium with which they worked.

Bronowski similarly stressed the link between creation and creativity as a bond between science and art. Science, he insisted, was not merely an act of discovery or invention, but fundamentally one of *creation*. "The man who proposes a theory makes a choice – an imaginative choice which outstrips the facts. The creative activity of science lies here" (Bronowski 1958: 62). Theory construction was not a mechanical process that could be automated, he explained.

> To the man who makes the theory, it may seem as inevitable as the ending of *Othello* must have seemed to Shakespeare. But the theory is inevitable only to him; it is his choice, as a mind and as a person, among the alternatives which are open to everyone.
>
> (Bronowski 1958: 62)

Bronowski did not suggest that constraints did not exist in scientific work (as they also did in artistic production), but rather that it was in the freedom allowed within these constrains that the creative aspects of science could emerge.

204   *Alma Steingart*

For high modernist mathematicians, the case for creativity was more compelling than for scientists. Unlike physicists, chemists, or biologists, whose theories inevitably had to agree with experimental knowledge, mathematicians were unbound by the world. This view was advanced not only by some philosophically inclined mathematicians, but was also forwarded in a 1954 national report presented before the National Academy of Science:

> The axiomatic approach has emancipated mathematics from its bound state in science ... At the same time, it develops a deeply artistic aspect in its own nature. The *structures* which the mathematician axiomatizes are, in final analysis, his to choose and to change, modifying, dropping, or adding an axiom here and there – much as a score evolves under the composer's hand. There is no longer a need to scan the shifting reflections in the pool of his mind for the features of an alien reality forever looking over his shoulder. Instead, there unfolds a new and richly fascinating world.
>
> (Weyl 1956: 11–12)

In claiming mathematics as both a science and an art, pure mathematicians called upon the structuralist vision of the field. The structures mathematicians created were not bound by the world, nor did they correspond to some existing phenomenon. Rather, they were free creations, a "new and richly fascinating world." The "emancipation" of mathematics from science conferred on mathematicians free artistic play. It also redefined the meaning of mathematical aesthetics.

Aesthetics

In 1963, Bernard Friedman, chair of the Department of Mathematics at the University of California, Berkeley, sought to explain the difference between pure and applied mathematics and settled on an analogy: "Most Madison Avenue artists do work they don't consider art," Friedman explained to the reporters around him. "I'm an applied mathematician myself, but I must admit that the best work is being done these days by the pure mathematicians" ("Mathematicians" 1963).[13] The distinction, Friedman continued, is similar to the one "between Jackson Pollock and Norman Rockwell ... The students today find the same excitement in pure mathematics that artists do in Abstract Expressionism, because, you see, neither study has any necessary connection with the real world" ("Mathematicians" 1963).

Twenty years later, another applied mathematician, Peter Lax, found himself once again referring to Abstract Expressionism when commenting on postwar mathematical research:

The axiomatic aesthetic 205

Next to Bourbaki, the greatest champions of abstraction in mathematics came from the American community. This predilection for the abstract might very well have been a rebellion against the great tradition in the United States for the practical and pragmatic, the postwar vogue for Abstract Expressionism was another such rebellion.

(Lax 1986: 15)

Whereas Friedman claimed that pure mathematicians and abstract expressionist artists were united by the so-called break between their work and the physical world, for Lax it was their common stance against Cold War utilitarianism. Distance from the material world and politics defined the meaning of mathematical aesthetics for postwar American mathematicians.

Mid-century mathematicians adhered to a theory of aesthetic autonomy, whereby aesthetic considerations came to the fore as a theory became increasingly abstract. John Von Neumann, for example, explained that criteria such as elegance, beauty, and simplicity determined how new mathematical knowledge was constructed.

As a mathematical discipline travels far from its empirical source, or still more, if it is a second and third generation only indirectly inspired by ideas coming from "reality," ... It becomes more and more purely aestheticizing, more and more purely *l'art pour l'art*.[14]

Put differently, the aesthetic quality of mathematics correlated inversely with its empirical content.

Aesthetic judgment enabled mathematicians to evaluate the structures they created when experimental verifications were unavailable. Statistician John Tukey made this point in a letter to his colleague Lipman Bers. Trying to account for the difference between pure and applied mathematics, he explained:

In the inner citadel, both chains of symbolic reasoning and the results reached by these chains are mainly judged by aesthetic and intellectual standards of beauty, universality, economy, etc. ... At the outer fringes, although beauty, universality and economy are still valued, progress toward the empirically verifiable, especially toward the prediction or control of events in the real world of objects and men, becomes the prime criterion.

"John Tukey to Lipman Bers, 23 March 1964, John W Tukey Papers, Series I. Corrsepondence, Box 23, Folder "National Research Council (U.S.) – Committee on Support in the Mathematical Sciences."

206   *Alma Steingart*

For mathematicians, aesthetic considerations became one way to distinguish between pure and applied mathematics, between that which was free and that which was constrained.

Thus, in calling upon the artistic and aesthetic quality of mathematics, mid-century mathematicians were not just reflecting on the nature of contemporary research, they were also reacting directly against what they perceived to be the increasing emphasis placed on pragmatics in mathematical research. Defense research has not only drawn attention to applied mathematical theories, but also gave rise to a host of new subfields such as computing, operation research, and communication theory. For some pure mathematicians, this increased attention to mathematical applications had the potential of redefining all intellectual activity in the United States. This concern was especially clear in Morse's writing. In a series of speeches and articles, Morse explained that it was not science per se that he rebelled against, but what had become of science after the war. In his 1951 article, he remarked that when he listened to students discuss art and science he found himself "startled to see that the 'science' they speak of and the world of science in which I live are different things." A mechanistic vision of science, one which is motivated more by the pursuit of power than the pursuit of knowledge was, according to Morse, the intellectual ailment of the time.

Calling upon the artistic quality of mathematics and science, for Morse, was one way to redeem both. "I shun all monuments that are coldly legible," he concluded,

> I prefer the world where the images turn their faces in every direction, like the masque of Picasso. It is the hour before the break of the day when science turns in the womb, and, waiting, I am sorry that there is between us no sign and no language except by mirrors of necessity. I am grateful for the poets who suspect the twilight zone.
>
> (Marston 1951: 612)

For Morse and his colleagues, the aesthetic quality of mathematics was concomitant to freedom, both as the inspiration for their theories and as a countermeasure to cold rationality.[15] This vision of mathematical aesthetics was novel. The aesthetic quality of mathematics was no longer associated with symmetry and pattern-making, but was instead internal to mathematical thought. It was here that mathematicians broke from their humanist colleagues.

For both mathematicians and scientific humanists appeals to structure served in part as a reaction to the militarism of postwar scientific knowledge and an appeal to a new humanistic order in which the sciences and the arts would stand on equal ground. However, their understandings of aesthetics were fundamentally at odds with one another. The contributors to Kepes's edited volume sought structure with their eyes wide open. Whether it was the structure of a crystal, of a Pier Luigi Nervi building, or a Max Bill sculpture, structural vision was available to the senses. This,

The axiomatic aesthetic 207

after all, was exactly what was missing from the rationalistic worldview advanced by modern science. Yet in linking creativity with axiomatics, the aesthetic dimension of mid-century mathematics was inherently non-visualizable. The aesthetic can only be attained by turning away from the world, not towards it. The difference between the two is best appreciated in the invocation of topology, which came to replace geometry as the common inspiration for both mathematics and art.

Unlike geometry, topology does not revolve around the metrical qualities of forms. From a topological perspective, a square and a circle are the same, since one can be smoothly deformed into the other. Topologists are interested in exactly those characteristics of space that remain the same under continuous transformation. Thus, when Bronowski suggested that "Abstract sculpture often looks like an exercise in topology," his emphasis was on the way in which artists investigated the general shape of their subject as opposed to its exact proportions. In his article for Kepes's edited volume on *Structure*, Bronowski concludes with a discussion of Henry Moore's sculptures:

> The shapes which Henry Moore gives to the human form are strong and highly organized, but they are not organized on the frame of the skeleton. He is saying something else about the body than that it has bones in it; he is saying that the limbs are connected by a geometry which is characteristically human ... The shapes that he makes owe their humanity to their characteristic topology.
>
> (Bronowski 1965: 60)

This topological perspective, which Bronowski reads in Moore's work as the basis of the structuralist vision of art, sought not to reproduce that which appears on the surface, but to elucidate the underlying structure beneath it.

Bronowski was not alone in calling on topology to join the arts and sciences. In his 1971 article "Structure and Patterns in Science and Art" and in his later book *Space Structure*, Arthur Loeb similarly homed in on topology (Loeb 1971: 339–346, 1976). Trained as a physical chemist, Loeb's interest in design and the arts made him an influential figure in the early days of Harvard's Department of Visual and Environmental Studies. Loeb explained that the word structure can have a double meaning as both a collection of entities which bear a "well-defined relation to each other," and as "the set of relations between entities of a pattern." For Loeb, like Kepes, the structural approach was hierarchical: "when we deal with the relation *between* as well as *within* patterns, we study a *structure of structures*." Topology was one of the prime tools with which such structures could be investigated. Thus, as Loeb explained, "a topological description of a pattern is concerned *not* with exact values of distances and angles but rather with the number of connections" (Loeb 1971: 339). This shift from distance and angles to connections, by Loeb's view, gives rise to a better

208 *Alma Steingart*

categorization of pattern. Yet the topology that Loeb, Bronowski, and their colleagues were after was distinct from that which interested mid-century mathematicians.

By the mid-1940s the dominant approach to topology was algebraic. Mathematicians were no longer concerned with the inherently visualized conception of the field. Rather, their studies revolved around the algebraic structures that one can construct to distinguish between topological spaces. Whereas the field had its origin in inherently geometric questions, by the 1950s a mathematics student could be introduced to topology without ever considering its original motivations. For example, when Solomon Lefschetz published *Algebraic Topology* in 1942, one reviewer remarked that the book presents the material with "full accuracy and with clarity, but it has also largely lost touch with geometry." The reviewer continues that whereas the book "gives far reaching results, in very abstract style, from quite a unified point of view; the reader must largely furnish for himself the appropriate geometric interpretations … Most striking of all, there is not a single figure" (Whitney 1942). By the 1940s, not only was it possible to publish a book about topology with no illustrations whatsoever, in the following decade, it had become the norm.

The topology hailed by Bronowski and Loeb was the topology of the 1920s and 1930s. As such, while both mathematicians and critics called upon a structuralist vision to reunite the sciences with the arts, their worlds were distinct. Kepes insisted that scientific rationality on its own was insufficient, the artists and the poets had much to contribute, and the world of the senses had to be reasserted within this new landscape. To do so he called upon a new vision, a structuralist vision, that would bring artists, designers, and architects into direct conversation with the sciences of the day. Here *vision* was understood as a new theory of perception. Yet mathematicians who similarly claimed structure as a bond between science and art were happy to leave behind the sensual realm. The structural vision they called upon was a pragmatic one – a *vision* upheld not by sight, but by the mind alone. Indeed, in Cold War America, they considered it imperative to do so.

CODA

In the 1970s and the 1980s, the growth of computer graphics spurred several mathematicians to challenge the dominant mathematical approach and its emphasis on axioms and structures. In computer graphics, they saw hope of reclaiming the concrete, and above all the visual. For this group of mathematicians, the computer became an experimental tool precisely because it could be programmed to represent different geometries. As I have argued elsewhere, these mathematicians sought to manifest mathematics in order to open it to the world of the senses (Steingart 2015: 44–77). As mathematician Richard Palais explained,

The axiomatic aesthetic 209

it is only in recent years that remarkable improvements in computer technology have made it easy to externalize these vague and subjective pictures that we "see" in our heads, replacing them with precise and objective visualizations that can be shared with others.

(Palais 1999: 647)

The computer became a tool with which to translate the symbolic and algebraic into pictorial language.

As such, these later mathematicians seemed to be in tune with scientific humanists. However, the mathematical world they wished to explore was fundamentally not structural. Indeed, they conceived of their work as a reaction to the dominant structuralist conception of the field. Describing

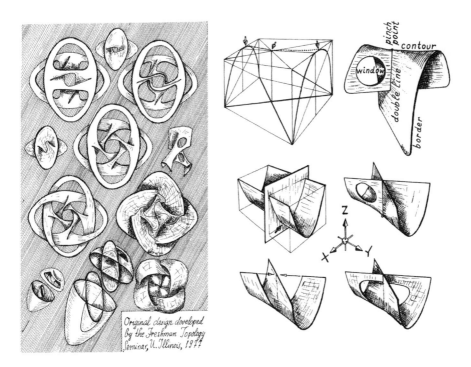

Figure 11.2 a. Sketch by the freshman Topology Seminar at the University of Illinois, reproduced in George Francis' Topological Picturebook (1987). Reprinted/adapted by permission from Springer Nature: *A Topological Picturebook* by George Francis 2007. b. Whitney Umbrella from George Francis' *Topological Picturebook* (1987). Reprinted/adapted by permission from Springer Nature: *A Topological Picturebook* by George Francis (2007).

210   *Alma Steingart*

his own path toward mathematical visualization, mathematician George Francis, explained that despite his early love of pictures, "this was the era of Bourbaki, and for a decade I erred blindly in higher dimension" (Francis 1983: 589–599). It was only once he was willing to turn his back on the axiomatic method of the field, once he left Harvard and chose to pursue his PhD in Ann Arbor, that he felt comfortable to turn his attention to the "concrete, the particular," and "visible topological analysis" (Francis 1983). In his research and mathematical practice, he aimed to develop a visual grammar for representing topological problems, as evidenced in his hand-drawn Topological Picturebook (Figure 11.2). Together with various other colleagues, Francis became involved in advocating for the use of computer graphics in mathematical research. Their world was full of images and illustrations, their senses were alert. And so, as the axiomatic method which aligned mathematics with the arts by reference to structuralist thinking waned, computer graphics offered a new method of experimenting with and collaboratively imagining seemingly unthinkable spaces.

Notes

1 On Bronowski see Emmitt (1982); Desmarais (2012: 573–89).
2 On this view, mathematics was no longer understood to be a descriptive science, which was bounded by the physical world. On the modernist transformation in mathematics, see Mehrtens (1990); Gray (2008).
3 The book was the second in Kepes's series. It followed Kepes's earlier volume *The New Landscape in Art and Science*, which arose out of an exhibition he organized under the same name.
4 On Kepes, see Terranova (2015: Ch. 2–3); Goodyear (2004: 611–635).
5 Orit Halpern has argued that Kepes's work represents a transformation in the "histories of visuality when perception gained autonomy as a material process and the image was no longer understood as representational (a language) but rather as a landscape or environment" (Halpern 2012: 329).
6 Several scholars across various fields have questioned the relation between transformations in science and art at the turn of the century. Linda Dalrymple Henderson has shown how mathematicians' investigations into higher dimensions influenced artistic practice: Henderson (2013). John Adkins Richardson points to similarities between scientific thought and artistic vision, while Paul C. Vitz and Arnold B. Glimcher have focused on perception as a common concern for both scientists and artists: Richardson (1971); Vitz and Glimcher (1984). Robert Brain similarly points to perception, but focuses more directly on experimental physiology and instrumentation: Brain (2015). In *Inventing Abstractions*, scholars from various fields homed in on the changing meaning of abstraction to think through artistic and scientific practice at the turn of the century: Dickerman (2012). More recently, Andrea Henderson has focused on Victorian society, demonstrating how mathematical formalism influenced literature, poetry, and photography: Henderson (2018). Focusing on mathematics, Jeremy Gray has also pointed to the similarities between mathematics and the arts: Gray (2008).
7 David Aubin has called upon the notion of a "cultural connector" to describe the influence of Bourbaki on structuralism in France. Aubin (1997): 297–342.
8 On the early adaptation of Hilbert's ideas in the US, see: Scanlan (1991: 981–1002); Corry (2007: 21–37).

The axiomatic aesthetic   211

9   On Bourbaki, see: Beaulieu (1994: 241–42); Corry (1992: 315–348).
10 As Theodora Vardouli demonstrated, the influence of Bourbaki's structuralist vision is also evident in the work of architects such as Lionel March, Christopher Alexander, and Yona Friedman. Vardouli (2017).
11 Birkhoff offered a mathematical analysis of aesthetic based on symmetry and pattern, while Weyl offered an investigation into symmetry. (Birkhoff 1933; Weyl 1952).
12 It is no surprise, therefore, that Morse's writing found appeal with others who similarly wished to rehabilitate a humanistic vision of science. In 1958, Cyril Stanley Smith contacted Morse and requested to republish his essay in a special issue of the Bulletin of Atomic Science on Science and Art. Like Bornowski's special issue on creativity, it brought artists and scientists together to discuss the commonalities between both endeavors. Morse (1951: 610).
13 Friedman was quoted in a *New Yorker* "Goings On About Town" listing ("Mathematicians" 1963).
14 Von Neumann did not support this tendency. He believed that mathematicians must continuously search for inspiration in the world around them. Von Neumann (1947: 180–96).
15 Fredric Jameson argues that late modernists' insistence on the autonomy of the aesthetic was not concomitant with the modernist movement itself, but rather was advanced by postwar critics who set their sights on theorizing modernism. It was, in his words, the ideology of modernism. A particularly "American invention," late modernism, Jameson writes, is "a product of the Cold War." This distinction between method and ideology is useful, for in mathematics as well, mathematicians' insistence on the autonomy of mathematics and its identification with artistic creativity was symptomatic of the period, when fears of pervasive utilitarianism pushed mathematicians to couple creativity with disinterested inquiry.

Bibliography

Albert, A. (1960) "Mathematics as a Profession," *Youth Conference on the Atom*, October 20, 1960, Adrian Albert Papers, Box 2.

Aubin, D. (1997) "The Withering Immortality of Nicolas Bourbaki: A Cultural Connector at the Confluence of Mathematics, Structuralism, and the Oulipo in France," *Science in Context* 10, no. 2, 297–342.

Beaulieu, L. (1992) "Bourbaki's Art of Memory," *Osiris* 14, 219–251.

Beaulieu, L. (1994) "Dispelling a Myth: Questions and Answers about Bourbaki's Early Work, 1934–1944," in S. Chikara, S. Mitsuo, and J. W. Dauben (eds.) *The Intersection of History and Mathematics*, Boston, MA: Birkhäuser-Verlag.

Bell, E. T. (1950) "Expertly Dissected. (Book Reviews: The Anatomy of Mathematics)," *The Scientific Monthly* 71, no. 6, 425–426.

Birkhoff, G. D. (1933) *Aesthetic Measure*, Cambridge, MA: Harvard University Press.

Bourbaki, N. (1950) "The Architecture of Mathematics," *The American Mathematical Monthly* 57, no. 4, 223.

Brain, R. M. (2015) *The Pulse of Modernism: Physiological Aesthetics in Fin-de-Siècle Europe*, Seattle, WA: University of Washington Press.

Bronowski, J. (1958) "The Creative Process," *Scientific American* 199, no. 3, 58–65.

Bronowski, J. (1965) "The Discovery of Form," in G. Kepes (ed.) *Structure in Art and in Science*, New York, NY: G. Braziller, 55–65.

Corry, L. (2004) "Modern Algebra and the Rise of Mathematical Structures," *Springer*, 10.

212 *Alma Steingart*

Corry, L. (2007) "Axiomatics between Hilbert and the New Math: Diverging Views on Mathematical Research and Their Consequences on Education," *International Journal for the History of Mathematics Education* 2, no. 2, 21–37.

Corry, L. (1992) "Nicolas Bourbaki and the Concept of Mathematical Structure," *Synthese* 92, no. 3, 315–348.

Daston L. J. and Galison, P. (2010) *Objectivity*, Cambridge, MA: Zone Books.

Desmarais, R. (2012) "Jacob Bronowski: A Humanist Intellectual for an Atomic Age, 1946–1956," *The British Journal for the History of Science*, Cambridge Core 45, no. 4, 573–589.

Dickerman, L. (ed.) (2012) *Inventing Abstraction, 1910-1925: How a Radical Idea Changed Modern Art*, New York, NY: The Museum of Modern Art.

Emmitt, R. J. (1982) *Scientific Humanism and Liberal Education: The Philosophy of Jacob Bronowski*, University of Southern California.

Francis, G. (1983) "Drawing Seifert Surfaces That Fiber the Figure-8 Knot Complement in S 3 Over S 1," *American Mathematical Monthly* 90, no. 9, 589–599.

Fuller, B. R. (1965) "Conceptuality and Fundamental Structures," in G. Kepes (ed.) *Structure in Art and in Science*, New York, NY: G. Braziller, 66–81.

Goodyear, A. C. (2004) "Gyorgy Kepes, Billy Klüver, and American Art of the 1960s: Defining Attitudes Toward Science and Technology," *Science in Context* 17, no. 4, 611–635.

Grattan-Guinness, I. (2011) *The Search for Mathematical Roots, 1870–1940: Logics, Set Theories and the Foundations of Mathematics from Cantor through Russell to Godel*, Princeton, NJ: Princeton University Press.

Gray, J. (2008) *Plato's Ghost: The Modernist Transformation of Mathematics*, Princeton, NJ: Princeton University Press.

Halmos, P. R. (1968) "Mathematics as a Creative Art," *American Scientist* 56, no. 4, 389.

Halpern, O. (2012) "Perceptual Machines: Communication, Archiving, and Vision in Post-War American Design," *Journal of Visual Culture* 11, no. 3, 329.

Hassler, W. 1942 "Review: Solomon Lefschetz. Algebraic Topology," MR0007093 (4,84f).

Henderson, A. K. (2018) *Algebraic Art: Mathematical Formalism and Victorian Culture*, Oxford, UK: Oxford University Press.

Henderson, L. D. (2004) "Editor's Introduction: I. Writing Modern Art and Science–An Overview; II. Cubism, Futurism, and Ether Physics in the Early Twentieth Century," *Science in Context* 17, no. 4, 426.

Henderson, L. D. (2013) *The Fourth Dimension and Non-Euclidean Geometry in Modern Art*, Cambridge, MA: MIT Press.

Hilbert, D. (1910) *The Foundations of Geometry*, trans. E. J. Townsend, Chicago, IL: Open Court Publishing Company.

Hilbert, D. (1996) "Axiomatic Thought," in W. Ewald (ed.) *From Kant to Hilbert: A Source Book in the Foundations of Mathematics, Volume II*, Oxford: Clarendon Press, 1105–11114.

Hill, A. (1959) "On Construction, Nature and Structure," *Structure* 2, no. 1, 5.

Hill, A. (1968) "Art and Mathesis: Mondrian's Structures," *Leonardo* 1, no. 3, 234.

Kepes, G. (ed.) (1956) *The New Landscape in Art and Science*, Chicago, IL: Paul Theobald and Co.

Kepes, G. (ed.) (1965) *Structure in Art and in Science*, New York, NY: G. Braziller.

Krieger, M. H. (2005) "A 1940 Letter of André Weil on Analogy in Mathematics," *Notices of the AMS* 52, no. 3, 341.

Lax, P. D. (1986) "Mathematics and Its Applications," *The Mathematical Intelligencer* 8, no. 4, 15.

Loeb, A. L. (1971) "Structure and Patterns in Science and Art," *Leonardo* 4, no. 4, 339–346.

Loeb, A. L. (1976) *Space Structures*, Boston, MA: Springer Science & Business Media.

"Mathematicians," *The New Yorker* November 16, 1963.

Mehrtens, H. (1990) *Moderne Sprache Mathematik: Eine Geschichte Des Streit Um Die Grundlagen Der Disziplin Und Des Subjekts Formaler System*, Frankfurt am Main: Suhrkamp.

Morse, M. (1951) "Mathematics and the Arts," *Yale Review* 40, 607.

Palais, R. (1999) "The Visualization of Mathematics: Towards a Mathematical Exploratorium," *Notices of the American Mathematical Society* 46, 647.

Richardson, J. A. (1971) *Modern Art and Scientific Thought*, Chicago, IL: University of Illinois Press.

Scanlan, M. (1991) "Who Were the American Postulate Theorists?," *The Journal of Symbolic Logic* 56, no. 3, 981–1002.

Smith, C. S. (1980) *From Art to Science: Seventy-Two Objects Illustrating the Nature of Discovery, Parental Advisory Edition*, Cambridge, MA: MIT Press.

Smith, C. S. (1983) *A Search for Structure: Selected Essays on Science, Art and History*, Cambridge, MA: MIT Press.

Steingart, A. (2014) "A Four-Dimensional Cinema: Computer Graphics, Higher Dimensions, and the Geometrical Imagination," in A. Carusi, A. Sissel-Hoel, and T. Webmoor (eds.) *Visualization in the Age of Computerisation*, New York, NY: Routledge.170-196.

Steingart, A. (2015) "Inside: Out," *Grey Room* April 1, 44–77.

Terranova, C. N. (2015) "Art as Organism: Biology and the Evolution of the Digital Image," *I.B.Tauris*.

Vardouli, T. (2017) "Graphing Theory: New Mathematics, Design, and the Participatory Turn," Dissertation, Massachusetts Institute of Technology.

Vitz, P. C. and Glimcher, A. B. (1984) *Modern Art and Modern Science: The Parallel Analysis of Vision*, New York, NY: Praeger.

Von Neumann, J. (1947) "The Mathematician," in R. B. Heywood (ed.) *The Works of the Mind*, vol. I, no.1 Chicago, IL: University of Chicago Press, 180–196.

Waddington, C. H. (1970) *Behind Appearance: A Study of the Relations Between Painting and the Natural Sciences in This Century*, Cambridge, MA: MIT Press.

Weissinger, J. (1969) "'The Characteristic Features of Mathematical Thought', in Thomas Lorie Weyl, H. (1951) 'A Half Century of Mathematics'," *The American Mathematical Monthly* 58, no. 8, 524.

Weyl, F. J. (1956) *Report on A Survey in Research and Training in Applied Mathematics in the United States*, Philadelphia, PA: Society for Industrial and Applied Mathematics.

Weyl, F. J. and Saaty, T. L. (ed.) (1969) *The Spirit and the Uses of the Mathematical Sciences*, New York, NY: McGraw-Hill Book Company.

Weyl, H. (1952) *Symmetry*, Princeton, NJ: Princeton University Press.

Whyte, L. (1965) "Atomism, Structure and Form: A Report on the Natural Philosophy of Form," in G. Kepes (ed.) *Structure in Art and in Science*, New York, NY: G. Braziller, 20–28.

Index

abstract art 10, 173
Abstract Art, Concrete Art 184
Abstract Expressionism 204, 205
abstract machines 184–185
abstract sculpture 195, 207
abstraction 9, 10, 60, 197, 205, 210n6
action at a distance 109–110n13
administration: machine-aided 105; *see also* management
Advanced Research Projects Agency (ARPA) 94
advertising: in poetry 179
aerospace industry: cleanliness in 118
aesthetic(s): of administration 160, 161, 163, 166, 167, 168–169; architectural 9; autonomy 205, 211n15; of computing spaces 123, 127; in structuralist art 183, 187, 197; *see also* axiomatic aesthetic; clean aesthetic
agency 4, 122, 182
Aksakoff, Sergey, T. 143
Albert, Adrian 202
Alexander, Christopher 6, 7, 21, 22, 23–24, 26, 28, 58, 59, 60, 61–63, 64, 65, 66, 68–69, 70–71, 72, 190n31
algebraic topology 208
Algebraic Topology 208
algorithmic architecture 10, 173, 183–186
algorithmic thinking 95, 97, 98, 104
Allen, D.W. 121
Almanacco Letterario Bompiani 35
alphanumeric filing systems 166, 167
Alquati, Romano 7, 50, 51, 52, 53, 54
Alt, Casey 2
Alvin, Donald S. 123
American Hospital Association 94, 97, 100

analysis (design problem) 72
Analytical Communication Studies 142
Andersen, Christian Ulrik 92
antagonism: of human bodies to machines 120; *see also* worker antagonism
antiseptic computer rooms 121, 123
Apollinaire, Guillaume 176
Apple 117, 127
applied mathematics 141, 204, 205, 206
arbitrariness 59, 61, 62, 63, 66, 199
Archaeologies of the Digital 4
architect(s): augmented 80–81; as co-producers of the digital landscape 1; need for sensory involvement 87
Architectural Forum 60
architecture: and computing, conceptual and operational entanglement 1; imagining as a form of concrete poetry 173–190; of information 145–147; modernist 7, 19, 21, 23, 61, 173; postwar research 63; rational 61; *see also* algorithmic architecture; computer architectures; digital architecture
Architecture and the Computer (1964 conference) 6, 26–29
Architecture Machine Group (MIT) 83, 85, 86, 87, 88, 89
architecture machines 85–89, 90, 91
The Architecture of Mathematics 200
architecture-as-interface 8
Arp, Jean 184
art(s): critique of administration systems 168–169; and design 37, 49, 123; and mathematics 10, 202–203, 210n6; research agenda 187; and science 7, 23, 194, 195–198, 203, 210n6; structuralist 10, 174–183

Index 215

Art for Ecology's Sake 23
Arte Programmata 55n1
artifacts: and augmented intellect 81, 86
artificial intelligence 83, 84, 85, 87, 96, 154
Artificial Intelligence Laboratory (MIT) 85
artillery fire control 142, 145–146, 148
artistic techniques 184, 185; importance of 180–181
As We May Think 81
Aspen Movie Map 87–88, 89
Aspray, William 137, 156n1
assemblages (interface) 115
assembly lines 36, 50, 51, 52, 54, 107, 108
attentional control 91
Auctor NC machine 46, 47
augmentation and interface 79–92; architecture machines 85–89, 90, 91; augmented human 80–83, 91, 92; Engelbart demo 79–80; enhancement through dialogue 83–85, 91; ubiquitous computing 90–91
Augmenting Human Intellect: A Conceptual Framework report 80, 82, 86, 91
automated computing machinery 7, 36; *see also* numerically-controlled (NC) machines
automation 8, 54, 104, 107, 108
autonomy 168, 205, 211n15
avant-garde art 10, 173, 174, 182, 184
axiomatic aesthetic 10, 194–208; creativity 202–204, 207; mathematics 204–208; structure 10, 198–201

Ball Computer BD 124
Bann, Stephen 174, 175, 177, 178
Barden Corporation 118
Barnett, G. Octo 104, 106, 107
barrier technologies 119
Barthes, Roland 173, 181, 182, 183, 186, 190n22
Baruch, Jordan J. 94, 95, 102, 110n21
Bateson, Gregory 140
Bauhaus/Bauhauslers 15–17, 19, 20, 23, 29, 44, 61, 179
Bavelas, Alex 141
Bayer, Herbert 16, 20, 179
Beba Coca Cola 179
Bedeaux system of management 51
behaviour 120, 124, 125, 142

Behaviour, Purpose and Teleology 143
"being in the interface" 87
Bell Telephone Laboratories 136, 137, 139
Bell Telephone System 139, 140
Bergson, Henri 148
Bernal, J. Desmond 19
Bers, Lipman 205
Bigelow, Julian 143
binders (file) 167
bioclimatic discomfort 21, 66
biology 19, 138, 142, 152, 154, 194
biomedical computing research 100
Birkhoff, George 202, 211n11
Black, D. 129
Blake, Peter 22
bodily interfaces 88
body(ies): and artificial intelligence 87; as hazards/threats to machines 116, 119, 120; shielding, in computer production 118; undermining of machine stability 115; *see also* embodiment
Bolt, Beranek and Newman Inc. (BB&N): Hospital Computer Project 94–110
Bolt, R.A. 89
Boltzmann, Ludwig 143–144
Bonetto, Rodolfo 46
Boston Architectural Center 6, 26
Bourbaki, Nicholas 199–200, 210n7, 211n10
Brain, Robert 210n6
Brand, Stewart 87, 88
Bratton, Benjamin 92
Brazilian poets 179
Bremer, Claus 179
Brescia, Riccardo 51
Breuer, Marcel 16, 17, 19
bricolage 182
Brighton Festival of Concrete Poetry 179
Brines, William 100
British avant-garde 10, 173, 182
British Poetry Revival 178
Bro Pold, Søren 92
Brodey, Warren M. 83–84, 85, 91
Bronowski, Jacob 194, 195, 198, 202, 203, 207, 208
Brownian motion 147, 148
Brumm, P. 120
Bruner, Jerome 62
Building Research Institute (BRI) 68
Building Research Station 61, 63

216 *Index*

Building Services Engineer 120
Bulfinch, Charles 98
bureaucracy: in structuralist art 173, 184, 187
bureaucratization of aesthetics 187
Burling, Francis P. 18
Burton, A.J. 119
Bush, Vannevar 81, 150
Byte 126–127

Caigan, Robert 122–123
Calcolatrice Elettronica Pisana (CEP) 37, 38
calculative/rule-based rationality 59, 60, 61, 64–65
Campos, Augusto de 179
Canada Land Inventory 28
Cape Cod: environmental conservation at 15–19
Cape Cod National Seashore Park 6, 15, 17, 18, 19
capital re-structuring 50
capitalism 7, 36, 50, 52, 54
The Capitalist Use of Machinery: Marx versus the Objectivists 52
card filing systems 163
card signals *166*
Cardoso Llach, Daniel 86
care/caretaking 114, 115, 116, 117, 119, 123, 126
Carson, Rachel 18, 22
Castleman, Paul 110n16
cathode-ray tubes: and electronically-generated images 185–186
central console (Elea 9003) *41*, *44*, 45
Central Research Laboratory (Olivetti) 49
Centre for Land Use and Built Form Studies 174
Chermayeff, Serge 6–7, 15, 16, 17, 18, 19–21, 22, 23–24, 26, 27, 28, 60, 62, 63, 65
Cherry, Colin 141
Chicago School of Design 19
Childhood Years of Bagrov's Grandson 143
choice: design rationality and need for 61–63
cine-car 180
Cipriani, Christine 16
Circle 173, 182
Civilization and Its Discontents 117
classification 9, 65, 66, 68

clean aesthetic 9, 115, 117, 121, 122
clean rooms 114, 116, 117, 118, 119, 121, 124, 126
cleanliness 8–9, 115, 116, 117–123, 124, 126, 127–129
climatic factors 21, 66
codes/coding 9, 141, 155
coexistence (humans-machine) 122
cognition: concrete poetry 177, 178; miscasting of women's labor as men's 8, 108
cognitive capacity 8, 96
cognitive ergonomics 8
cognitive interaction 106
Cold War rationality 61, 64
collaboration(s) 6, 21, 37, 63, 65, 70, 83, 85, 90
color music 174, 185, 186
color-coded console (Elea 9003) 43
command and control research 89, 142
common ground(s) 1, 5, 10, 60
communication(s)se: in art 177–178; human-machine 45; information theories 9, 138–140, 142, 143, 144, 146, 147, 149; interpretive system 95, 103–104; materialities of 3; in poetry 179; posthuman communication theory 149, 150; symbolic 43; technicians and 53; *see also* dialogue; language(s); speech
communication theory 136, 139, 141, 142, 149, 150, 153, 206
Community and Privacy: Toward a New Architecture of Humanism 6, 22, 25–26, 26–27, 28, 65
complexity: computers and environmental 28; informational 27, 81, 145
composite diagrams 72
Composizione organica del capitale e forza-lavoro alla Olivetti (Organic composition of capital and labor) 51
computation 6, 10; axiomatic aesthetic 194–208; and design 1, 45; imagining architecture as a form of concrete poetry 173–190
computer architectures: architecture of 6; *see also* computation; input/output; program; storage
computer cases 123
computer graphics 208–210
computer rooms 114, 117, 121, 122, 123; *see also* clean rooms

Computer Software 2
The Computer for the 21st Century 90–91
computer workers 115, 121
computer-aided design 73, 80, 98, 189n1
computers: and design 1, 21, 23–24, 122, 123; idealization of 116; as medium 2, 3; role in architecture (1964 conference) 6, 26–29; *see also* mainframe computers
Computers and Data Processing News 120
"Computers Pose Many Problems" 119
Computerworld 123
computing: and architecture, conceptual and operational entanglement 1; environment 121–122, 124, 126
concrete poetry: imagining architecture as a form of 10, 173–190
conflicts: in problem's logical structure 68
connections: and patterns 207–208
conservation/protection (environmental) 15–19, 20, 22
construction: of the digital landscape 1
Constructionist Group 173, 174, 201
contaminants/contamination 117, 119–120, 125, 126
continuity 5, 10, 147
continuous numerically-controlled (CNC) machines 45
control/controllability 116, 119, 124, 126, 129n3
conversational space: in history writing 5–6
cooperative game 63–65
correlation (machine-worker) 51
Corry, Leo 195
cosmology 138, 144, 147
Costlow, T. 127
Cox, Kenelm 179
CRC102A mainframe computer 37
creation: and creativity 203
The Creative Process 194
creativity 10, 53, 169, 194, 195, 197, 201, 202–204, 207, 211n15
Critique 140
cryptography 142, 146, 150–151
"cubepoem" 179
cultural connector 210n7
cybernetics 9, 44, 51, 52, 60, 83, 97, 139, 145, 147, 148

Cybernetics: Control and Communication in the Animal and the Machine 136, 142, 144–145, 147, 154
Cybernetics Technology Office 88

Dantu, Andree 175
Daston, Lorraine 197
Data 173
Data Space project 89
Data Systems 120
Davies, Richard Llewelyn 97
De Rosa, L.A. 152
decision theory 60
decision-making: algorithmic 104; design rationality 7, 60, 64, 65, 67, 72
decomposition 7, 58, 59, 64, 70, 71, 72, 151
Defense Advanced Research Projects Agency (DARPA) 88, 89
defense research 206
Department of Defense (DoD) funding 88, 89
design: art and 37, 49, 123; computer-aided 73, 80, 98, 189n1; computers and 1, 21, 23–24, 122, 123; discourse 1; and domestication 128; of the Elea 9003 computer 39–43; methods 1, 60; science and 7, 45; *see also* environmental design; graphic design; metadesign; parametric design; Ulm School of Design; urban design
Design with Nature 28
design rationality, quest for 7, 58–74; computer architecture 70–73; cooperative game 63–65; image of 68–70; logical structure 65–67; need for choice 61–63
designers: computing aesthetic 122; environmental 21, 27; exchange among 7; graphic 182, 183; machine tools 46; modernist 7, 15, 16; need for sensory involvement 87; role and responsibility 19–20, 21, 23
Development Index 66
diagrams 72, 149; computer architectures 6; *see also* graphs/graph theory; utility maps
dialogue: interface enhancement through 83–85, 91
digital architecture: as a field of practices 3–4; history writing 4–5; media perspective 2–3
digital cultures 1

Index

Digital Development Corporation (San Diego) 124
digital innovation 4
digital lineages 1
diode-transistor logic 38
dirt/dirtiness 116, 117, 120, 124, 125, 129
disappearing interface 8, 90
discourses: obsolescence of 4
discovery 202
disk: behaviours 125; cartridge cleaners 126; drive cleanliness 124; handling 125
disorder 144, 145, 146, 147, 148, 150, 151, 155
disposal of files 169
Doctor-Machine Symbiosis 95
Doesburg, Theo van 175, 184, 186
domestication 127, 128–129
domesticity 114, 121
Dourish, Paul 92
Dreyfuss, Henry 43
Dunican, Peter 98
dust-free environments 117, 118, 119–120

Eames, Ray and Charles 87, 88
Easterling, Keller 92
ecological equilibrium 22, 23, 28
effects (artistic) 184, 185
Einstein-Smoluchowski studies 148
Elaboratore Elettronico Automatico (Automatic Electronic Processor) 39
Eldred, Kenneth 125–126
Elea 9002 computer 38
Elea 9003 computer 7, 36, 37, 38, 39–43, 46
electronic brains 119, 186
Elias, Peter 154
embodied virtuality 90
embodiment 8, 52, 60, 87, 115, 117, 123, 136, 147, 163, 167, 169, 173
Emery Roth & Sons 119
emotion: in concrete poetry 177–178
Engelbart, Douglas 79–80, 80–83, 84, 91
engineering-related information theories 138, 141
English, Bill 79
English School of information theory 139
entropic universe 147–149

entropy: information and 143–145, 152, 156
environmental concerns 22
environmental contaminants 119–120
environmental design 6–7, 15–29
environmental intervention in poetry 179
epistemic culture 5, 60, 73
equilibrium (ecological) 22, 23, 28
ergonomics 8, 43, 46
ethical robots 85–86
ethics: of care 115; of design 19–20
Eugene Onegin 143
experimental aesthetics 187
eye-as-computer metaphor 71

FAC milling machine 55n7
Fafnir Bearing Company 118
failure(s): of man-computer symbiosis 8, 96, 104–107, 108; quest for design rationality 66–67
feedback loop (worker-machine) 52
Fermi, Enrico 37
Ferranti Mark 1 mainframe computer 37
Festive Permutational Poems 179
field 3–4
Files: Law and Media Technology 162
filing/filing systems 9, 161–169
Film as Pure Form 175
filtering theory 156
Finger Film 86
fingers 86
Finlay, Ian Hamilton 177, 179, 183, 184
First International Exhibition of Concrete and Kinetic Poetry 174, 179
Fisher, Howard 27–28
floppy disks 125, 126
Fordist assembly line 107
form(s): -determinants 63, 65; and management 9, 163; structuralist art and construction of 182
Form 10, 173; and algorithmic architecture 183–186; structuralist activity in 174–183
Fortini, Franco 39
Fowler, Glen 122
fragility (computer) 8, 114, 115, 117, 126
Francis, George 210
French mathematicians 199–200
French philosophers 173
Freud, Sigmund 117
Friedman, Bernard 204, 205

Friesen, Gordon A. 97, 107, 110n19
Fry, Donald 141
Fuller, Buckminster 195, 198
Fuller, Matthew 2
functional units 68–70, 182
furniture 127, 166

Gabor, Dennis 139–140, 141
Galison, Peter 197
Galloway, Alexander 92
game theory 62, 64, 65, 67
Games and Decisions 64
gender: computer care-taking 116, 119; and Hospital Computer Project 8, 108, 109n5
Geographical Information System (GIS) 28
gestural interaction 88, 89
Gibbs, Josiah Willard 147, 148
Ginsberg, Allen 174
Glimcher, Arnold B. 210n6
Goffey, Andrew 2
Goldberg, Adele 2
Gombrich, Ernst 177–178, 178, 182
Graduate School of Design (GSD) 20, 61
graphic design/designers 42, 179, 181, 182, 183
graphs/graph theory 7, 60, 64, 67, 68–70; *see also* trees
Gray, Jeremy 210n6
Graziosi, Roberto 48
Groisser, Leon 85
Gropius, Walter 16, 19, 20, 27, 61
Groups Network Laboratory (MIT) 141
Grudin, Jonathan 82, 91
Gumbrecht, H.U. 3

Haddon, L. 128
Haldane, J.B.S. 19
Hall, Jack 16
Halmos, Paul 202
hardware: cleanliness 128; structuralist art 185–186
Hardy, G.H. 148
Harness Hospital System 98
Harpold, T. 116, 119
Hartley, Ralph 150
Harvard: -MIT Joint Center for Urban Studies 62, 65; Graduate School of Design (GSD) 20, 61; Laboratory for Computer Graphics and Spatial Analysis 28; Medical School 100
Harwood, John 3

Haussmann, Raoul 174
Hayles, Katherine 90, 149, 156n2
Hecht, J.C. 121
Henderson, Andrea 210n6
Henderson, Linda 195, 210n6
Hidden, A.E. 120
HIDECS 2 program 7, 70–71, 72
highway route location 70–71
Hilbert, David 199, 201
Hill, Anthony 201
Hill, G. Angus 28
Hirschfield-Mach, Ludwig 185
histories of computers/computing 1, 3, 4–6, 15, 73, 82, 115, 116, 117
Hitchcock, Henry-Russell 183
Hoberman, Max 152
holography 140
home computing 126–127, 128
Honeywell Education and Computing Center 122–123
Horizon 3 NC machine 46
Hospital Computer Project 8, 94–110; epilogue 107–108; failure of man-computer symbiosis 104–107, 108; partners 98–100; technological development of man-computer symbiosis 100–104
hospital design 96–97
Houédard, Sylvester 183
housing research 63
housing/shelter (computer) 8, 114
human contaminants 119
Human Enhancement: Beyond the Machine Age 83, 84
Human Enhancement through Evolutionary Technology 83
The Human Use of Human Beings 147
human-architecture interaction 105, 106
human-computer interface 79–92; architecture machines 85–89, 90, 91; augmented human 80–83; Engelbart demo 79–80; enhancement through dialogue 83–85, 91; failure of man-computer symbiosis 104–105, 107; ubiquitous computing 90–91
human-machine: assembly line 51; coexistence 122; communication 45; interaction 83, 84, 86, 116, 128; relationship 43, 108, 117, 122; *see also* unclean human-machine interface
humanism 22, 23, 36, 39; *see also* scientific humanism
humanization 128

220 *Index*

Husserl, Edmund 148
Huxley, Julian 19
Hyannis Port 18
hygiene *see* cleanliness
Hypothetical Description of Computer-Based Augmentation System 81–82

IBM 66; 704 computer 21, 23; 709 computer 38, 59, 70; cleanliness 117, 118–119; MT/ST 80
ideal consumer/user 128
idealization of computers 116
ideas 136–137
identification: creativity as 194
Image 174–175, 177, 182, 183
industrial design 48
industrial information 149–151
information: -based collaborative work 63; complexity 27, 81, 145; computerized management 81; dematerialization 156n2; enmeshing of interface and 90; and entropy 143–145, 152, 156; environment 87; industrial 149–151; quantity 27, 144, 145, 154–155, 155; storage and retrieval 65, 66, 94
Information and an Organized Process of Design 68
Information Processing Techniques Office (IPTO) 88, 94
information theories 9, 44, 135–157; divergences 138–141; and their sources 137–138; *see also* Shannon, Claude Elwood; Wiener, Norbert
Infosystems 124
InfoWorld 125
Ingalls, Dan 2
inhuman computing environment 121–122
innovation 4, 50, 52, 194
input/output 6, 8–9; augmentation and interface 79–92; first failure of man-computer symbiosis 94–110; the unclean human-machine interface 114–129
Institute for Calculation Applications (Naples) 37
intelligence 150, 156n2; *see also* artificial intelligence; augmentation and interface
interaction(s) 66, 68; cognitive 106; human-architecture *105*, 106;

human-machine 83, 84, 86, 116, 128; social 85
interdisciplinarity 20, 60, 61, 65, 136, 155, 195
interface(s) 8; Oxford definition 82; *see also* human-computer interface
Interface Age 126, 127
The Interface Effect 92
interface-as-architecture 8
"interfacing in depth" 84
International Congresses of Modern Architecture (CIAM) 61
interpretive communication system 95, 103–104
intuition 59, 60, 61, 71, 72, 202
Inventing Abstractions 210n6
invisibility: of art and science, structure and the 198
inward vision 97, 100, 107
isomorphism 68, 72, 146, 199
Italian Economic Miracle 50
Italian Marxists 50
Italy 7; *see also* Olivetti
Ivrea 35, 48, 51, 52, 54

Jameson, Fredric 211n15
Johnson, Mina 160, 162, 166, 167
Joint Center for Urban Studies (Harvard-MIT) 62, 65

Kafka, Ben 169
Kallaus, Norman 160, 162, 166, 167
Kant, Immanuel 140
Kay, Alan 2
Kennedy family 15, 18
Kennedy, John F. 17, 18
Kepes, Gyorgy 194, 195, 196, 197, 198, 199, 200, 201, 208, 210n5
Keynesianism 50
kinetic art 174, 175, 179, 182, 186
Klier, Hans von 43, 55n5
Kline, Ron 138, 139, 145
knowledge: cryptography and 151; mathematical 194, 195, 198, 200, 205; scientific 197, 206; structural 200; technical 36–37, 53, 108
Kuhn, Thomas 178
Kurzweil, Ray 142

La Disparition 182
labor: advanced machines and reform of 51; capitalist profit and control of 50, 52; and cleanliness 116; immaterial

53; NC machines and design/reorganization of 7, 46; *see also* women's labor; workers
Laboratory for Computer Graphics (Harvard) 28
Landscape 58
landscape architecture 28
language(s) 8, 79; about contamination 125; and augmented intellect 81; computer graphics and pictorial 209; and pattern 28, 143, 150, 151; set of possibilities within 149; structuralism and architecture 187–188; symbolic 45; *see also* linguistics
Larson, Theodore 66
late modernism 211n15
Lax, Peter 204–205
Lefschetz, Solomon 208
Léger, Fernand 175
Leitz company 167
Lejeune, Augustin 169
letters: in poetry 177
Lévi-Strauss, Claude 136, 177
Lewis, Philip 28
Licklider, J.C.R. 8, 86, 94, 95, 96, 98, 102, 107, 108, 140
light pens 186
Light-Space Modulator 184
Lindgren, Nilo 83–84, 85, 91
linear graph 67
linear programming 60
linguistics 152, 154, 181, 197; *see also* language(s)
linkages: between failures 66, 67
Loeb, Arthur 207–208
logic 62–63, 66, 199, 202
Logically Consistent Poetry 177
logico-mathematical methods 7, 58, 59, 60, 61–62, 72
Lönberg-Holm, Knud 66
London Symposium on Information Theory (1950) 141
Longmore, Donald 107, 110n18
Lowe, E.I. 120
Luce, R. Duncan 62, 64
Lumia 185
Lystra, Margot 21

McBee Key-Sort 163
McCarthy, John 102
McCulloch, Warren S. 85–86, 137, 139
McHarg, Ian 28

machine(s): -aided administration 105; correlation between workers and 51; metaphors 190n29; tool automation *see* numerically-controlled (NC) machines; unreliability and failure of man-computer symbiosis 106–107; *see also* abstract machines; architecture machines; human-machine
Machine Zero computer 38
Machines in Medicine 107
machining centers (Olivetti) 46, 48
MacKay, Donald 137, 139, 141
McMahon, Peter 16
Macy Conferences 137, 139, 140
magnetic core (Elea 9003) 38
magnetic tape: handling and cleanliness 120, 124
mainframe computers 37, 38, 43, 114; *see also* Elea 9002 computer; Elea 9003 computer
maintenance *see* repair/maintenance
Maldonado, Tomás 7, 45
Malina, Frank 175
Mallarmé, Stéphane 176
"man-artifact interface" 81
man-computer symbiosis 8, 86; *see also* Hospital Computer Project
management: form and 9; *see also* records management; scientific management
managerial culture 18
Manheim, Marvin L. 70, 71
manufacturing: cleanliness in 118–119, 126; machine tools in 48
Markov, Andrei 143
Markov series 143
Martin, Leslie 173, 183
Marx, Karl 52
Marxists (Italian) 50
Massachusetts General Hospital (MGH) 8, 94, 98–100, 104
Massachusetts Institute of Technology (MIT) 102, 139, 186; Architecture Machine Group 83, 85, 86, 87, 88, 89; Artificial Intelligence Laboratory 85; Groups Network Laboratory 141; and Harvard Joint Center for Urban Studies 62, 65; Media Lab 85, 88
"materialities of communication" 3
mathematical knowledge 194, 195, 198, 200, 205
A Mathematical Theory of Communication 136, 142, 149, 150

A Mathematical Theory of
Cryptography 146
*The Mathematical Theory of
Communication* 142
mathematics 148; aesthetic quality
204–208; and art/creativity 10,
202–204, 210n6, 211n15; claimed as
an art and a science 196–197;
computer graphics 208–210;
information theory 9, 141; modernist
10, 194, 197, 198, 204; postwar
research 204–205; structuralist 10,
195, 198, 199–200, 201, 203, 204,
208; *see also* applied mathematics;
game theory; graphs/graph theory;
logico-mathematical methods; pure
mathematics; statistics; topology
Mathematics and the Arts 202
Mead, Margaret 140
meanings: function and fabrication of
182; media perspective of digital
architecture and 3; obsolescence of 4
The Measure of Man 43
Media Lab (MIT) 85, 88
Media Room 87–88
medium 2–3
Memorex 120
memory *see* storage
memory devices: storing and cleaning
125–126
men's cognition: miscasting women's
labor as 8, 108
message transmission 139, 144,
145, 146
meta-media 2, 190n32
metadesign 48–49
metaphor(s) 5, 7, 8, 58, 71, 87, 116,
117, 123, 190n29
method 7
methodology 81, 86
Meyerson, Martin 62, 65
micro-computers 114, 123, 126, 127
Milanese design scene 7, 44–45
military research 88, 89, 142; *see also*
artillery fire control
milling machines (Olivetti) 51, 55n7
Mills, R.G. 119
Minsky, Marvin 85, 142
mobile technologies 129
modernist(s): architects/architecture 7,
19, 21, 23, 61, 173; designers 6, 15,
16; mathematics 10, 194, 197, 204
modular-based mainframe computer 40

Mohl, Bob 88
Moholy-Nagy, László 15–16, 19, 20,
184, 190n28
Mondrian, Piet 201
Monteiro, E. 128
Montgomery, Roger 60
Moore, Henry 207
Moravec, Hans 142
Morgan, Edwin 179
Morse, Marston 202–203, 206, 211n12
Mother of All Demos 79–80
MT/ST (IBM) 80
A Much Asked Question About
Computers in Design 73
multilingual inquiry 5
Mumford, Lewis 22
MUMPS 110n15

National Defense Research Council
(NDRC) 142
National Institutes of Health (NIH)
94–95, 100
natural language 146, 151
natural sciences 148, 202
navigation 87, 88, 89
negative entropy 144, 147, 149, 155
Negri, Antonio 50
Negroponte, Nicholas 83, 85, 86, 87,
89, 91, 123
Nervi, Pier Luigi 195
nested subsets 70
Neumann, John von 6, 137, 205,
211n14
neuroscience 85
New Building Research Conference
(1961) 68
Newtonian mechanics 147
NLS (oNLine system) console 79, 80
noise: in communications 146, 147
Northwick Park Hospital 98
Notes on Computer Architecture 58,
60, 73
Notes on the Synthesis of Form 7, 58,
59, 59–60, 61–62, 64, 65, 66, 71, 72
Noyes, Eliot 43
numerically-controlled (NC) machines
37, 45, 46–50, 51, 52, 55n6, 55n7
Nyquist, Harry 150

object-orientation 2
objectivity 15, 197, 199
obsolescence 4–5, 96–97
office environments 124

Office of Naval Research 88
office workers 53, 114, 120, 121, 124, 126
Olivetti 7, 35–55; and computing 37–38; economic success 36–37; Elea 9003 computer 7, 36, 37, 38, 39–43, 46; management approach 35–36; metadesign and machine tools 45–50; new economic and technological forces 50–52; the potentially subversive "technician" 53; Ulm School of design 43–45
Olivetti, Adriano 38, 51, 54
Olivetti, Roberto 38, 39
Onck, Andries Van 43, 45, 48, 49–50
Online Man-Computer Communication 98
operational bond: art and mathematics 202
operations research 97, 109n11, 206
order: computers and the myth of 116; in concrete works 184; filing systems 167, 168; information theory 9, 139, 144, 145, 146, 147, 148, 149, 155; logical structure and 60; need for a new environmental 22; program as a vehicle for 7; structural vision and 197
organization: and information theory 9, 139, 148; *see also* records management
Oulipo Group 181
outcome (design): abstraction 60
OXSYS 98

the page: as a visual space 175
Palais, Richard 208–209
Pangaro, Paul 86
Panzieri, Raniero 50, 52, 54
parametric design 37, 45, 48, 49, 98
Pasmore, Victor 174
pattern(s) 60, 84, 143, 146, 147, 150, 151, 198, 202, 207–208
Pavlov, Ivan 141
PDP-1 DEC computer 94, 95, 102, 107
perception(s): in art and science 210n6; of computers 118; in poetry 10, 177, 178, 179; structuralist vision as new form of 208
Perec, Georges 181–182
perforated band reading unit (Elea 9003) 40, *41*

"personal computer with the person inside" 87
Pfeiffer, K.L. 3
Philip, K. 116, 119
philosophy 148
physical closeness (user-computer) 102
physical computerization 96
physical environment 20, 28, 85, 87
Pierce, Charles 148
Pignatari, Décio 179
Pirelli 37
Pitts, Walter 137, 140
planning (environmental) 15
Plexiglas boxes 175
Politecnico di Milano 37
polyglot space 2, 5–6
polyphonic inquiry 5
Poor. Old. Tired. Horse. 183
post-Fordism 53
post-organic universe 9, 149
posthuman communication theory 149, 150
postwar architectural research 63
postwar research hospital 96–98
premises: in logical inference 62
Principia Mathematica 199
privacy (environmental) 21–26
problem-solving 82, 91, 139
problems (design) 27, 58, 59, 60, 66, 68, 70, 72
problems (interface) 104–107
procedural aspects: of programs 67
process (design) 3, 58, 60, 62, 64, 66, 67, 68, 69, 70, 71, 72
production: automated 46, 54
productive failure 108
professional identity 7
profit (capitalist) 50
program 6–7; computer architecture and the quest for design rationality 58–74; environmental design 15–29; Olivetti and the political economy of its early computers 35–55
Programma 101 desktop computer 54
programmers 47, 82, 101, 104
programming 2, 60
"proof-of-concept of general-purpose human-computer activity" 186
protean inquiry 6
protection *see* conservation/protection
Prynne, Jeremy 178
psychology 71, 136, 140, 141, 143, 150, 152, 153, 194, 197

224 *Index*

pure mathematics 197, 202, 204, 205, 206
purpose: information and 142–143
Pushkin, Alexander 143
Put That There 88, 89

Quaderni Rossi 7, 50, 51, 52, 54

Rabinbach, Anson 110n20
"randomness of effect" 185
rationality *see* design rationality
re-structuring (capital) 50
reactive repair 126
Read, John 124
records management 9, 160–169
redundancy (informational) 137, 140, 144, 146, 147, 150, 152
reflected light compositions 184, *185*, 186
reform: of hospital design 96–97
reform capitalism 7, 36
remote sensing 89
repair/maintenance 114, 115, 126, 128, 129
research agenda: artistic agenda as 187
A Research Center for Augmenting Human Intellect 79–80
Resistance and Difficulty 178
Rexroth, Kenneth 22
Reynolds, C.F. 127
rhythm: in poetry 177
Richardson, John Adkins 210n6
Richter, Hans 174
Rodchenko, Alexandr 180
Rodwin, Lloyd 65
Rosa, Alberto Asor 50
Rosenberg, Charles 97
Rosenblueth, Arturo 143
Rowe, Colin 183
Royce, Josiah 148
Rubin, James 86
rule-based rationality *see* calculative rationality
rules (communication) 138
Russell, Bertrand 148, 199

Saarinen, Eero 16
Sacerdoti, Giorgio 55n3
Sachs, Avigail 63
SAGE 94, 109n2
Saussure, Ferdinand de 141
scalarity 6, 9, 104
Schmandt, Chris 88

School of Design (Chicago) 19
Schwittzers, Kurt 168, 177
science: and art 7, 23, 194, 195–198, 203, 210n6; and design 7, 45; emancipation of mathematics from 204; and information theories 138; innovation in 194; mechanistic vision of 206; need for public support 135; supra-disciplinary 148
Science of Environmental Design 26
Scientific American 2, 90, 194
scientific humanism 10, 45, 194, 195, 197, 198, 206, 209
scientific knowledge 197, 206
scientific management 51–52
scientific rationality 36, 208
Segal, Jérôme 138
Sekler, Eduard 62
"selection from a set" of possibilities: communication as a 149
self-organized cooperation 53
self-organizing systems 86, 91
semantic space 178
semantic theory of information 141
senses (human) 10, 80, 81, 91, 197, 206, 208
sensitivity (computer) 117, 119, 121
sensory involvement: in design 87
Sert, Josep Lluís 20, 61
"set of Mondrian axioms" 201
Shannon, Claude Elwood 9, 135, 136, 137; definitions of information 139, 140–141; epistemological architectures of information 145–147; industrial information 149–151; information and entropy 144, 145; information and purpose 142–143; information theory and meaning for the profession 151–154; socialization of information 154–156
shape 72, 207
Shape of Community 28
ship fleet navigation 88
Shugart floppy disks 126
signals (communication) 138, 140, 142, 144, 146, 147, 151, 152, 154, 156n1
SIGSALY telephone system 146
Silent Spring 18, 22
Silverstone, R. 128
SKETCHPAD 2, 80, 186, *187*
skilled workers 46–47
SMALLTALK 2
Smith, Cyril Stanley 194, 211n12

Snow, C.P. 194
social computerization 96
social interaction 85
social responsibility (designer) 19–20
social therapy 19
Socialism/Socialists 19, 36, 46, 50, 51
socialization of information 154–156
socio-technical systems 115
sociology 138, 197
Soft Architecture Machines 83
The Software Works 125
Sottsass Jr., Ettore 7, 39–40, 43, 45
space: in structuralist art 175–176, 178
Space and Place 58
Space Structure 207
spaceship models: ecological
    equilibrium 23
spatial metaphors 8
spatial representation 88
speech 143, 149, 151, 156n2
Speed Index 165–166
Star Wars 89
statistics 27, 28, 109n11, 138, 139,
    142, 143, 144, 145, 147–148, 149,
    150, 151
Steadman, Philip 174, 179, 182,
    183–184, 185–186
Stevens, Hallam 108, 110n22
Stockhausen, Karlheiz 174
Stoler, Ann 168
storage 6, 9; information theories
    135–157; of memory devices
    125–126; records management 9,
    160–169
STRESS software 27
Strickland, Rachel 86
structural knowledge 200
structuralism 173; in art and science 10,
    174–183, 195–198
structure: axiomatic aesthetic 10,
    198–201; for building knowledge/data
    68; double meaning of 207; of
    programs 67; sense of 200
Structure (journal) 201
Structure in Art and in Science 195,
    196, 198
Structure and Patterns in Science and
    Art 207
subsystems *see* functional units
Suchman, L.A. 115
Summerson, John 187
suspended busways (Elea 9003) 42–43
Sutherland, Ivan 2, 80, 186

SYMAP program 27, 28
symbiosis *see* man-computer symbiosis
symbolic alphabet 45
symbolic communication 43
synthesis (design problems) 72
System/360 mainframe computer 43

Talcott 123
Taylor, Walter 63
Taylorism 51
Tchou, Mario 38, 39, 54, 55n2
technical knowledge 36–37, 53, 108
technicians 37, 53, 115, 182, 184, 187
techniques (artistic) 180–181, 184, 185
Technocracy Digest 121
technological development:
    man-computer symbiosis 100–104
technological innovation 50, 52
Tecnica ed Organizzazione 51
telecommunications 138, 146
teleology 143
Teletype terminals 99, 102, 104, 106
Testore, Ezio 46–47, 48
Theodore, David 3, 8
theory construction 203
thermodynamics 147–148
Thoreau, Henry David 18
time-shared computing 100–102, 104
"topological 1-complex" 67
Topological Picturebook 210
topology 10, 49, 68, 195, 197, 207–208
"total architecture" approach 19, 20
"total information system" *see* Hospital
    Computer Project
touch screens 86
Toward Some Circuitry of Ethical
    Robots 85–86
Toward a Theory of Architecture
    Machines 86
training: and augmented intellect 81; NC
    machine operation 48
Transactions on Information Theory
    152–153
transistor architecture 38, 39
translation of architectural concepts
    60, 73
transmission of intelligence 150
trees (graph) 58, *59*, 60, 64, 69, 70, 71,
    72, 73
Tronti, Mario 50
truth: of an axiomatic system 199
Tuan, Yi-Fu 58, 59, 60, 73
Tukey, John 205

226 *Index*

Turing, Alan 137, 156n2
Turkle, Sherry 136

ubiquitous computing 8, 83, 90–91
Ulm School of Design 7, 43–45
unclean human-machine interface 8–9,
 114–129
uninformed audiences: of poetry 178
Univac computers 120, 122
University of Cambridge 173,
 174, 178
University of Pisa 37
unreliability: of machines 106–107
Upitis, Alise 73
urban design 61, 65, 72
The Urban House project 65–66
usability 89, 92
user interfaces *see* human-computer
 interface
utility 62, 70
utility maps 71, 72

Variadex system 163, *164*
Vienna Circle 148
"virus" metaphor 116
visibility: of art and science, structure
 and the 198; of problems through
 logico-mathematical methods 58, 68
vision: structuralist 195, 197, 198, 200,
 201, 204, 206–207, 208, 211n10
Vision + Value 195
Vismann, Cornelia 162, 163, 166,
 167, 168
visual grammar 210
Vitz, Paul C. 210n6
Vogue 135, 136
voice recognition 88, 89
vulnerabilities (computer) 114–115,
 115, 117, 124, 128, 129n1

Waddington, Conrad H. 194
Wallach, Hans 62
Weaver, Mike 174, 175, 177, 178, 184
Wedemeyer, Dee 114, 123

Weeks, John 98
Weidlinger, Paul 16
Weil, André 203
Weil, Simone 203
Weiser, Mark 83, 90, 91
Weissinger, J. 203
Welfleet Study Group 17
Wellfleet 15, 16, 21
Weyl, Hermann 201, 202, 204, 211n11
Whitehead, Alfred 199
Whyte, Lancelot 199
Wiener, Norbert 9, 135, 136, 137;
 definition of information 139;
 entropic universe 147–149;
 epistemological architectures of
 information 145–147; information
 and entropy 144–145; information
 and purpose 142–143; information
 theory and meaning for the profession
 151–154; socialization of information
 154–156
Wienerwegs 139
Wiesner, Jerome 137, 141
Wilkinson, Jack 160
Williams, William Carlos 175
Willis, Jackson 141
Winston, Patrick 88
women's labor: cleaning and caretaking
 associated with 116, 119; miscasting
 as man's cognition 8, 108
worker antagonism 50, 52, 54
Workerism/Workerists 7, 37, 50–51,
 52, 53
workers: correlation between machines
 and 51; *see also* computer workers;
 labor; office workers; skilled workers;
 technicians
worker's inquiry 50–51, 52
World Health Organization 97

Xisto, Pedro 176

Yale Computer Graphics Conference
 (1968) 83